Understanding Your Dog

UNDERSTANDING YOUR DOG

by
Eberhard Trumler

Translated from the German
by
Richard Barry

With a Foreword by Konrad Lorenz

Faber & Faber
3 Queen Square London

*First published in England in 1973
by Faber and Faber Limited
3 Queen Square London W.C.1
Printed in Great Britain at
The Pitman Press, Bath
All rights reserved*

ISBN: 0 571 10373 1

*Originally published as Mit dem Hund auf du
© R. Piper & Co. Verlag, München 1971
© This translation Faber and Faber 1973*

The Author

Eberhard Trumler was born in Vienna in 1923. He studied under Konrad Lorenz and Wilhelm von Marinelli. From 1955 to 1964 he was unpaid assistant working in the Bavarian State Zoological Collection in Munich. Since 1964 he has been conducting experiments with dingoes (the Australian wild dogs) and elkhounds in his research establishment near Weilheim.

Foreword
by Konrad Lorenz

Unprejudiced observation of nature is the starting point and the foundation for all research, and the more complex the subject of research, the more essential this is. Next to the human, the more highly developed animals are the most complex beings on this planet; today we know a great deal about the most abstruse problems of physics and chemistry but lamentably little about ourselves, and the reason largely is that observation has become outdated and only the quantifiable is regarded as a legitimate object of scientific effort. In the great world of science today anyone who carries on research merely for the pleasure of observing carries very little weight.

Acquisition of some insight into the character of one of the more highly developed animals demands not only very prolonged observation but also a very 'good eye'. A long period of observation is required to distinguish the main behavioural traits of a single animal or a single breed of animals; unless the observer observes for pleasure, not even the patience of an Asiatic monk would be enough. The greatest and most successful students of behaviour, therefore, have invariably been both dilettantes in the true sense of the word (it comes from the Italian verb 'dilettarsi' meaning to enjoy oneself) and also amateurs (again in the true sense of the word), devotees of certain animals or classes of animals. Charles Otis Whitman, one of the great pioneers of comparative behavioural research, was totally preoccupied with the regimen of the pigeon and another, Oskar Heinroth, with that of the duck. These are the qualities essential to any successful behavioural research but to the mass of modern civilised mankind, whose only value is that of money, anyone possessing them must appear doubly crazy.

Such a doubly crazy man—in other words a real genuine student of behaviour—is Eberhard Trumler. He has the 'good eye' necessary for observation and discernment of the essentials; this is clear from his great gift for drawing animals and their expressive movements. The slight over-emphasis, bordering on the caricature, is characteristic of the work of an artist who—like Lynkeus the watchman—was born to see and destined to look. A really good caricature is proof that the artist has fathomed the character of his subject and anyone who has seen the drawings in Trumler's book on horses will have some inkling of his capacity.

Horses are the great love of Trumler's life; dogs come second. At present he lives in an old mill in Upper Bavaria and spends the money which he earns from his excellent animal books on maintenance of a mob of dogs of 'unknown breed' whose breeding earns him nothing and whose feeding is certainly not cheap.

I think I know dogs fairly well and I have even had the temerity to write a popular book about them. Trumler, however, knows them far far better; when I read his book I was both astounded and ashamed to note how many details he had observed and evaluated, details of which I knew, which I had seen but not observed. Trumler's strength lies in the fact that, by close personal contact, he has come to know so many and such different canine personalities. I use the word 'personality' advisedly. The original meaning of the word 'persona' is a mask and it came to be applied to the part in a drama played by the actor who wore it. The concept of the 'person' in human terms is governed by the role which the individual concerned plays in the system of relationships obtaining within his family and his society. If one refuses to admit that 'an animal' has the capacity to assume a comparable social 'role', then one is vastly underestimating the differences between individuals in a highly developed breed of animals. As any knowledgeable person will tell you, in the case of the superior animals such as elephants, horses and dogs, individual differences are so marked that no proper idea of the structure of their society can be gained unless these differences and the consequent capacity to assume defined roles are taken into account.

Eberhard Trumler gives us a picture of a variety of canine personalities. He describes them to us from the cradle to the grave, including all aspects of their physical and behavioural development, the specific features common to all individuals of the same species and, in contrast, the differences characterising individual personalities. He deals with the questions of ancestral origin, the development of the domestic dog from its wild forbears, whom he knows as well as he does our *Canis 'familiaris'*. He is particularly interested in the savage but domesticated dog, the dingo.

The compendium of knowledge contained in this book will not only entrance the animal lover but also be of use to the expert. I am especially happy that Trumler's book should once again be illustrated by his wonderful drawings.

May this new book about dogs attract the interest which it deserves. May it make numerous dog-lovers aware of an author who possesses a sense of the beauty of nature combined with genuine enthusiasm for research.

Contents

	page
Forward by Konrad Lorenz	7
1 My 'Dog's Life', *in lieu of introduction*	17
2 Uniformity in Diversity	20

Troubles with Stina – My 'Basic Dogs' – Elkhounds and Dingoes – Wolves and Jackals – My Half-breeds

3 Roads to Diversity 41

Marks of Inbreeding, Different Mutations – White Coat and Red Eyes – Individuality of our Dogs

4 The Puppy's First Weeks 54

A half-formed little Dog? – The first few Minutes – Birth Weight – The Vegetation Phase – Methods of Locomotion – The Senses – Sucking – The Puppies together – The Transitional Phase – The Nose – Hereditary Reflexes and Power of Learning

5 Imprint for Life 90

The Imprint Phase – Imprint of Man as a member of the Breed – Buying a Puppy – Paw-giving – Nose-nudging – Sleeping – Childhood Image and induced Juvenility – The Socialisation Phase – Introduction into the human Community – Play – Discipline

6 School-time and Lessons 154

The Seniority-Classification Phase – Gestural and Facial Expressions – The Body as an Instrument of Expression:

Aggression and Demonstration of Superiority and Inferiority – Acoustic Expression – The Pack-Formation Phase – Man as Pack-Leader

7 Puberty and Maturity 204
Scent Controls – Individual Scent as a Visiting Card – The Time of Maturity – Mating and Pregnancy – Puppies are born – Björn's family

Bibliography 257

Index 259

Line Illustrations and Photographs

Stina. The shy cross-bred bitch. *p. 21*
Binna. Grey elkhound bitch from Norway. *p. 25*
Aboriginal. My first dingo dog. *p. 28*
The 'ancestral' Wolf. *p. 31*
Potrait of a jackal. *p. 33*
Björn, the first cross-bred dog. *p. 35*
Strixi, a village mongrel. *p. 39*
Forepaws of a normal dingo (left) and of Arta, the inbred dingo bitch (right). As with my jackals the central forward pads are joined. *p. 42*
Two views of a new-born dingo puppy. *p. 55*
Head of a new-born alsatian puppy. *p. 58*
The different sexes (Björn and Bente aged two days). *p. 67*
The lateral searching movements of a new-born dingo puppy (not yet licked dry). *p. 72*
His muzzle pushes upwards from below into the fold of skin between forefinger and thumb. *p. 74*
Head of a two-day-old puppy with mouth open and tongue in the 'sucking position'. *p. 75*
Head of a new-born dingo puppy. Eyes and ear orifices still closed. *p. 76*
Puppies aged twenty-three days biting at each other. *p. 83*
A four-week-old dingo: Tanila trying to jump down from the table. *p. 92*
A puppy feeding in the sitting position using one paw for kneading. *p. 101*
She-wolves lying huddled together—an exceptional position showing great attachment. *p. 106*
Rana, the alsatian bitch, lying curled up. *p. 107*

Illustrations

Binna in the 'hearthrug' posture. *p. 108*

Infantile face of a two-day-old dingo puppy. Note the vertical searching motion of the head. *p. 111*

The rounded head of an Italian greyhound. The infantile expression is the result of miniaturisation and is emphasised by the comparatively large eyes. *p. 114*

Twelve-week-old dingo puppies playing the biting game. *p. 120*

The English Pointer, bred 'for nose'. *p. 130*

Young alsatian playing at retrieving with a rag. *p. 135*

How to carry a four-week-old dingo puppy. *p. 139*

Photographs between pp. 144 and 145:

Top: Knud and Kala, children of the cross-breeds Björn and Bente, aged 30 days. Their 'submissive' attitude shows that they have still had little contact with human beings.

Bottom: Peer, cross-bred dog aged 40 days. He had long been in contact with human beings and was not in the least perturbed at being photographed.

Sascha, the alsatian dog, is very good with children and beloved of all puppies. As soon as they hear him at the door they wait eagerly for him. At once they begin to play happily with the indulgent great dog.

Top: Dingo puppies like to push their little muzzles between Sascha's great jaws, as they would do to their mother in order to get at the regurgitated food.

Bottom: Nose-nudging derives from the request for food and is a gesture of affection. Similarly 'paw-giving' derives from the teat-kneading motion. Both gestures demonstrated by Aboriginal, the dingo.

Two half-grown dingoes look suspiciously at the photographer—a new experience for them. The tucked-in tail betrays uncertainty.

Top left: Rana, the alsatian bitch, on the watch. Her expression and the position of the ears indicate excitement.

Illustrations

Top right: Paroo, the dingo dog, 'giving tongue'
Bottom: Luxl, the New Guinea dingo, at his first encounter with Aboriginal. Being older, though smaller, he is quite self-assured and 'inspects' the younger dog, whose attitude and raised hackles indicate uncertainty and an 'on-guard' position.

Top: Aboriginal meets an alsatian for the first time. Although he is the smaller dog, he approaches stiffly and menacingly with hackles raised and a low growl. The friendly alsatian is uncertain in face of his threats.
Bottom: During a game Rana and Peik have overpowered Pira, Peik's sister. She turns on her back in a gesture of submission.

Binna, the elkhound bitch, and Suki, the dingo bitch, both in season at the same time and therefore aggressive towards each other. They clasp each other's shoulders and show their teeth with muzzles wrinkled.

Two half-grown ridgebacks (South African lion dogs) want to play with this small girl, who runs away screaming. Children who are afraid of dogs have been badly brought up.

Top: Having retrieved his stick, an alsatian jumps a burning pole. Such a high degree of training can only be reached through the closest co-operation with the handler.
Bottom: The alsatian Schlapp must have had a difficult upbringing for he shows every sign of fear when placed against a wall to be photographed.

Binna giving birth.
Top: The membrane containing the foetus as it emerges, the bitch looking back at it.
Bottom: The puppy out of the membrane. Binna sniffs it over.

Top: The puppy puts out his tongue and takes his first deep breath.
Bottom: While being licked dry the puppy tries to avoid

his mother's tongue, squeaking in protest. As soon as released he makes his way to a teat.

Character test with Leonbergers (see p. 228)
Top: Sascha, always friendly, is on a lead beyond the hedge. After a preliminary sniff Asko invites him to play.
Bottom: His brother Arras, on the other hand, charges at the hedge barking loudly. He dislikes other dogs on principle, thus showing considerable deficiency of instinct.

Little Binna affectionately nose-nudging her aunt. *p. 145*

All dogs like digging in soft ground (a young pug). *p. 163*

Sketch of a wolf's face. This emphasises capacity for expression particularly when combined with the winter coat. *p. 166*

Nine possible differing expression of a dingo's face showing the frame of mind (lay-out based on Lorenz). *p. 169*

Sascha and Susi jumping up against one another (play preliminary to mating). *p. 174*

Aboriginal as a young dog instinctively plucking his first pigeon. *p. 202*

A dingo muzzle. *p. 205*

Bente, the cross-bred bitch, rubbing the side of her neck. *p. 207*

Schlapp, the alsatian dog, giving a demonstration of leg-lifting. *p. 217*

A spasm of scratching before childbirth. *p. 245*

Binna is always busy with her puppies. Her body, forelegs and hind legs form a rectangle enclosing the puppies. *p. 247*

Binna dragging a puppy into the whelping box. She seizes it by the first part of the body within reach. *p. 251*

1 My 'Dog's Life'
in lieu of introduction

The foundations of my mill are two hundred years old; it, or rather what remains of it after a big fire, stands in a little hollow surrounded by woods and fields. A stream curls round the property; there is a reed-covered pond, meadows and a marshy little wood of poplars, elms and willows. We can also see beeches, oaks, pines, maples and birches interspersed with hazel bushes, privet and elder. It is a charming little piece of countryside, far from the noise and bustle of the great cities.

My study is on the first floor of the mill. A pair of field-glasses lies permanently on my desk. Sometimes I use them to watch a water-wagtail savagely ejecting from her domain a pair of neighbouring grey wagtails or perhaps I spot a pair of buzzards carrying food to their nest. Usually, however, this most essential piece of equipment is directed on my 'family'. I can see almost all my dogs from this vantage point. If I have more time, I climb up another floor and sit on the balcony; from there I have an even better view into the pens. For years now I have been surrounded morning, noon and night by thirty to sixty dogs. I breed dogs. That must be good business, you may say—to which I should reply: it is a wonderful occupation. If I were breeding some valuable pedigree type of dog, then perhaps it would be good business as well. The trouble is, however, that I cannot sell my dogs; I cannot even give them away. What sort of dogs are they then, if they cannot even be given away? They are dingoes, the wild Australian dogs sometimes to be seen in zoos. My original pair of dingoes came from a zoo; I owe them to Alfred Seitz, director of Nuremberg Zoo until 1970. Dingoes are not suitable as house-dogs in the normal sense of the word; they create too many difficulties. But that is not the end of the story. I have crossed my dingoes with domestic dogs and have gone on to raise several generations of these half-breeds. This too produces dogs intolerable to anyone who sets store by a clean house. Then I have jackals—not strictly dogs at all. A pair of elkhounds live here too. They have a vast 'pedigree' and possibly

I might actually be able to sell their offspring; but that is still some way off since the male is only a youngster and who can tell whether the first litter would prove to be what one wanted? I must not forget my two alsatians—lovely dogs, beautiful dogs. But they are father and daughter and experience proves that you do not get very far that way; moreover they have no pedigree. So I cannot sell alsatians.

Here I am, therefore, sitting tight, as the saying goes, on my dogs. But that is precisely what I want, for they are all intended to help me unravel the problems of domestication and its associated behavioural changes. This was my reason for choosing the dog.

I carry out planned breeding experiments in order to see how wild animals have become domestic animals, how so many things have been changed—anatomy, colouring, coat but primarily behaviour, which is the special subject of this book. I shall show that research into the behaviour of the domestic dog cannot be carried out with dachshunds, alsatians or terriers; they can only show us certain aspects of behaviour and so much has been changed in one way or another and differs from individual to individual. Konrad Lorenz, the pioneer of behavioural research, who has himself contributed so largely to comprehension of canine behaviour, has given us the following key to the problem: only the wild animal possesses, complete and unaltered, the range of behavioural habits peculiar to his breed; in the case of the domestic animal, on the other hand, the process of hereditary mutation has introduced numerous unknown ingredients resulting in inexplicable and often highly complex changes; it is therefore no longer possible, with so much multiplicity, to discover the fundamental constants. It can only be done if we are familiar with the behaviour of the primitive untrained prototype and if, furthermore, we can establish how and by what means that which we call domestication has changed the basic habits of behaviour. The more we know about this and the more we learn about it in future, the better shall we be able to understand each individual member of our present-day multifarious breeds of dog.

This is the reason why the reader will find in this book a great deal about wolves, jackals and dingoes but only comparatively little about the domestic dog with which he is familiar. I can promise him, however, that my descriptions, observations and experiences will teach him more about his dachshund, boxer, terrier, alsatian, miniature poodle, greyhound or whatever breed he possesses than if I were to write about these types of dog. I can say quite honestly that my years spent among these animals, apparently so different from our canine friends, these fox-masked and ostensibly exotic dingoes, has taught me more about the canine nature than I could ever have learnt from any of our domesticated dogs.

The dog world is richer than one thinks when one goes for a walk with 'Fido' or 'Rex' on the lead. Anyone who takes the trouble to penetrate a little way into this world will find himself looking at his dog through different spectacles. Most important, he will cease to regard the dog as a creature characterised primarily by house-training, obedience and requirements for nourishment, brushing and combing. He will also realise that everything which love of animals had led us to inculcate into our dog is only a pale shadow of that which in reality is latent in the dog, of what the dog can become, of what he really is—in short a dog.

I have written this book in the hope that it will contribute somewhat to an alleviation of the slavery to which traditional ignorance and habitual thoughtlessness have condemned so many dogs. It would be good if these pages caused the reader to reflect whether we really do all we can to do justice to our dog and to prevent his existence becoming an unworthy 'dog's life'.

2 Uniformity in Diversity

One can only write about dogs one knows. Since, however, one cannot know all the millions of present and future dogs, there will always be some which are different in one respect or another. We would be wise, therefore, before enquiring into general patterns of behaviour, to deal first with the question of this marked individuality among our dogs. Only in this way can I avoid the risk that in future all dogs will approach me snarling and with hackles up and call me a 'standardiser', someone who disregards their pronounced personality and their individual peculiarities, who is trying to tell their beloved master and mistress that there is a uniform pattern of canine behaviour.

All the industry and energy expended on research are useless if study is based on inadequate foundations and still more so if it starts from unsuitable 'material', as the dogs into whose behaviour we propose to enquire must be called in scientific jargon. It is obvious to anyone that I cannot use cats to examine the behaviour of dogs; it should be equally obvious that an enquiry into canine behaviour cannot be based on highly bred pedigree dogs—they are the most unsuitable material conceivable for this purpose. All we can study in their case are the behavioural changes which have occurred throughout history as compared to a former pattern of behaviour, of which for this purpose we must also have precise knowledge. What we need to know, therefore, is the original or 'primitive' pattern of behaviour, that which nature, uninfluenced by man, implanted in the wild dog before man, with his art of breeding, 'improved' nature and produced breeds of dog according to his own ideas.

TROUBLES WITH STINA

My bitch Stina taught me how pronounced is a dog's individuality and what problems the behaviour of an individual dog can raise. Here is the story of my troubles with Stina.

Stina is one of three from the same litter, all of whom are very different; I bred them by devious ways from my elkhound bitch Binna and a dog with a dingo cross further back in his ancestry. At the age of eight months two of them stood about $17\frac{1}{2}$ inches at the shoulder but the third was a proper little runt measuring barely 12 inches. The little dwarf, however, was the one who invariably

Stina. The shy cross-bred bitch

welcomed me at the fence of the pen with overwhelming affection. One day I said to myself: No—this enchanting little dog is not for the kennel; she shall be the first dog allowed to share my study with me; I will spoil her; she shall be with me always and lie on my lap while I am writing my book about canine behaviour.

Naturally a dog reared in a kennel cannot know that in its master's study it is not allowed to obey the calls of nature on the floor or an armchair. For an experienced keeper of dogs, however, rapid eradication of the habit is a trifle.

This was what I thought as I collected the first little sausage in the shovel.

Yet three weeks later, as far as this was concerned, nothing had changed. My alluring Stina was extremely nervous if she spent any length of time outside; she could hardly wait to get back into my study. Here, and nowhere else, was it good to satisfy one's internal urges. This was clear from the pleased and relieved expression on her little black face after inspection of the results! Moreover every day my Stina discovered a new and original spot on which to do her businesses, both large and small.

Stina was by no means stupid. Within twenty-four hours she had realised that cleanliness in the house was of importance to me. But she just did not agree with my odd eccentric ways. Accordingly, as time went on, she became increasingly concerned with the problem of outwitting me. In ninety-nine cases out of a hundred she had the answer. She must have thought a lot about ways to avoid becoming a lapdog. Basically I do not believe that a dog can think, at least not in terms as abstract as a man. But in Stina's case it must somehow have been different.

Almost everything is different with Stina, and when she looks up at me sideways from a safe distance I have a feeling that she is not taking me seriously—at least not my ideas on canine behaviour. These she seems to regard as a definite joke.

At first I thought that I merely had to be patient—after all Stina had been brought up in the kennel and was used to conditions there. I had often been with her there and each time she had been affection itself—or to be more precise, she had been bold and importunate, like the two others of her litter. The reason must therefore be her surroundings, I thought, which were still strange and to which she must become accustomed. But my conclusion was wrong.

So I was totally disconcerted by this little dog and she led me a dance lasting more than three weeks. It is just not possible to retain the feeling of elation resulting from the first few lines of a book if someone like Stina is closely observing your every movement in order to trot off to some other corner of the room if she thinks that that might serve her purpose.

Finally I became more and more unsure of myself and began to doubt my own ability because I could not get the better of so small a dog. If, for instance, after two years in the kennel I take into my room a dingo, who can be as fierce and dangerous as a wolf, he will, in the space of a few hours, reduce the place to an inextricable jumble of splinters of wood, pieces of glass and shreds of paper; meanwhile, however, he will spend every spare moment in licking my face, jumping on my lap, climbing on my head or otherwise giving me to understand how wonderful such contacts between dog and man are. A farmer once wanted to shoot his notoriously alert guard dog because it had not torn me to pieces but had made friends with me. The father of one of my friends once sent me one of his best cigars because, as soon as she had made my acquaintance, his extremely shy dachshund bitch clambered on to my lap and happily burrowed her slim head between my shirt and my coat.

Until this very day, however, I have been unable to succeed with Stina. If I am sitting in my usual place when she comes in at the door, she shows every sign of friendship. She greets me most affectionately, puts her forepaws on the seat of the chair, wags her tail and licks my hand; she allows me to fondle her and quite clearly likes it. As soon as she feels, however, that my welcome has been sufficiently long and affectionate, she disappears under the sofa in a flash and only emerges when I open the door wide and call 'Out, Stina'. She then whizzes through the open door into the passage and, if I pass her, cringes with her tail down. Outside she plays with the big alsatians but will only come to my call occasionally or exceptionally and finally has to be lured back into the house.

This is the way it is with Stina, the little dog whom I have known from birth, whom as a puppy I weighed every other day and whose brothers and sisters are friendliness itself without a trace of shyness.

Any reader of this book may have an experience similar to mine with Stina. He will then look at his dog, shake his head, resignedly throw away all books about dogs—including mine—and say: not a word of truth in them! And I shall not be able to contradict him in so far as his—and I mean his—dog is concerned.

MY 'BASIC DOGS'—ELKHOUNDS AND DINGOES

I am always amused when I see a car drive fast along the road some two hundred yards away, come to a sudden halt, reverse and then, somewhat hesitantly, take the track leading to the pens. I know then that these are strangers who have lost their way on this new little-known road. Most of them stop at the first pen, get out and then stand looking at the dogs in obvious puzzlement. They are even more puzzled when they turn and see the other pens. Many get back into their car, shaking their heads; others want to know all about it; they come and ask: 'What sort of dogs are these, please?' or 'Are they foxes?'

When I have explained, the next question invariably is: 'Can one buy an animal like this?' To my sorrow my answer is always 'No'—I have already given the reason. The enquirers thank me amicably and then, once back in their car, they too scratch their heads; they do so not because there is no dog for them; they just wonder about the madman who breeds dogs with which he can do nothing.

In fact, however, one can do a great deal with them, so much that this book by no means contains all that there is to say. The reader is expecting me to tell him about canine behaviour and so I shall have to leave out many other equally interesting matters. I shall touch on a number of other things, however, in so far as they are connected with behaviour. But I must first introduce my 'basic dogs'.

I decided to acquire Binna, my elkhound bitch, after learning something of the history of these animals. According to Scandinavian cynologists they had been bred in their present form several thousand years ago. Initially they resembled the northern moorland spitz, the remains of which have been found on Lake Ladoga in settlements at least 6,000 years old. This type of dog was already widespread at this period; they were the guard dogs too in the lake-dweller settlements in Switzerland.

My Binna, therefore, comes of a very ancient strain of dog; to some extent she is an incarnation of the stone-age type of dog. This was precisely the reason why I wished to study this breed of dog more closely; it was a breed which had been subjected to no 'changes of fashion' like so many of our present-day strains. So I

My 'Basic Dogs'—Elkhounds and Dingoes

now had a domestic animal, the hereditary traits of which had remained unchanged and uniform from ages ago. Naturally the expert can detect differences between individual elkhounds, but

Binna. Grey elkhound bitch from Norway

they are minor; I like to think that they are no greater than the differences within a pack of related wolves.

Elkhounds are, of course, domesticated dogs in the full sense of the word. They are even pedigree dogs, carefully and selectively bred by man over thousands of years. At dog shows, for instance, it matters a great deal whether the long bushy tail curls precisely over the backbone. Can I, therefore, expect primitive traits of behaviour to manifest themselves in such dogs?

An answer to this question is perhaps to be found by considering why and in what way the elkhound was bred. It must first be remembered that all Scandinavians are marked dog-lovers with a great understanding of nature. In the few big cities hardly anyone keeps an elkhound—why should they? The northerners' understanding of the dog guarantees the elkhound the home which suits him: he lives on the farms, whether large or small, out in the country. In Oslo or Stockholm people are obviously dog-lovers because every breed in the world is to be seen, frequently outstanding specimens. But to see elkhounds one must go out to the fjords and the mountains, to the endless pine forests interspersed with birch-ringed marshes—in short to the homeland of the elk.

The elkhound has been bred and kept from time immemorial to hunt these giant stags with their massive heads and spreading multipurpose antlers. The stately elk is an extraordinarily difficult animal to track, adept at evading his pursuers. Without the elkhound an elk-hunt would have small prospect of success. The hound follows the scent indefatigably, nose to the ground; he can distinguish between an old or a fresh 'hot' trail and he will eventually find his elk even if he must stay on the trail for three days at a stretch. The scent leads up hill and down dale, sometimes climbing steep rocky hills and then descending into the swamps; it is a considerable effort for the hunter to keep up with his dog. The dog pulls with all his might at the long lead, nose to the ground. As soon as the elkhound is obviously becoming more eager, the lead is slipped and the dog charges off to bring his quarry to bay. It is almost incredible how a dog, standing less than two feet high, contrives to keep the seven-foot giant, who is still full of fight, at bay until his master arrives and can bring his gun into action. The hound circles round, baying loudly, but dexterous though he is, the elk never manages a strike with his antlers.

This is what the elkhound does and it constitutes the foremost principle of selection in elkhound breeding. The more elks a dog has brought to bay, the better known he will be and the more he will be used for breeding. This whole business of hunting the elk, however, is one of the basic habits or attributes of this breed of dog; wolves similarly hunt elks but they bring them to bay and kill them as a pack. In the wild state a wolf who has not a good enough nose or cannot stand up to the exertion of a long chase, will be debarred from breeding, just like the elkhound. Later we shall see that young wolves learn the refinements of the chase from their elders. It is the same with elkhounds: the inexperienced are taught by the older experienced members of their race. A young dog too stupid or too sluggish to learn is placed on one side, just as a wolf who is a failure is thrown out.

So from time immemorial the elkhound strain has ensured that only those animals which are healthy, intelligent, tough and with the right instincts propagate their species. The process has also guaranteed that at least a large part of the primitive behavioural pattern has remained unchanged.

When she is on a scent my Binna is blind and deaf—I can bawl my lungs out but she does not react. Why should she?—it would be nonsensical, she thinks, to abandon her chase. But when she has brought her animal to bay, that is the end of the matter as far as she is concerned. There is no pack leader to tear the animal down and no hunter to shoot it; so she turns back and goes home; she cannot kill it. I believe that when wolves bring a large animal down they are not acting from innate instinct, but that this is something which has to be learnt. In the case of the elkhound, therefore, this is not a failure of instinct but a 'gap in education'. Something which certainly is innate in the elkhound is hunting small animals such as mice. Binna is very good at this; she loves digging for mice.

I made my first beginnings in the observation of canine behaviour with my elkhound bitch Binna. Then, when Alfred Seitz offered me two dingo puppies, I did not stop to think but seized my opportunity. So 'Aboriginal', the dog, and his sister 'Suki' arrived.

Dingoes, the wild dogs of Australia, are undoubtedly a very ancient breed. It is supposed that these yellow dogs arrived 8,000–10,000 years ago with the original inhabitants of the continent, the aborigines as the white Australians call them. Southeast Asia was probably the original homeland of this stone-age dog and he reached Australia via New Guinea.

In certain areas of New Guinea there are still 'Papua dogs' which at first sight could be taken for genuine dingoes. Thomas

Schultze-Westrum, who has done much research in these parts, showed me a series of coloured photographs of these dingo-type domestic dogs. I doubt whether they will exist much longer, for the Papuans find European dogs much more attractive than their

*Aboriginal.
My first dingo dog*

normal pie-dogs which are mostly hopeless mongrels. In addition to these 'Papua dogs' which are very tame, however, there still exist in New Guinea 'wild dogs' living off the country. In 1955 an Australian government official named Hallstrom presented a pair of such dogs to Sydney Zoo. Troughton, the Australian zoologist, thought that they were genuine wild dogs somewhat like wolves

My 'Basic Dogs'—Elkhounds and Dingoes

or jackals and gave them the scientific name *Canis hallstromi*. It was soon proved, however, that they were no more than a special type of dingo.

In Sydney Zoo these two animals bred industriously. Some of their progeny arrived in San Diego Zoo. In 1962 these had puppies, a pair of which reached the private zoo of the Institute of Domestic Animal Science of Kiel University and there, in 1964, they produced a litter of four dogs and three bitches. Luxl, one of the dogs, is the ancestor of my dingoes.

So far as I can judge from Luxl's appearance and one or two photographs of others of this breed, the New Guinea wild dingo differs from the Australian dingo in that he is somewhat smaller. Luxl stands 16 inches at the shoulder and is therefore about the size of a beagle, Bedlington terrier or well-grown larger spitz. He was therefore a comparatively small dog. When we once tried to mate him with Binna, the elkhound, he had a most unhappy time and achieved nothing—he was simply too small for Binna, who stands nearly 19 inches. I suspect that the New Guinea dingo is the mountain forest form of dingo; this would account for the fairly short legs, broad foxy head and long coat. Australian dingoes are slim, long-legged, narrow-faced and somewhat like a greyhound. Another notable difference is the bushy curly tail of the Hallstrom dingo compared to the thin curving tail of his Australian counterpart. We know nothing about the life of the New Guinea dingo. As far as the Australian dingo is concerned, however, it can be said with certainty that, ever since he arrived in the continent, he has led a free uninhibited existence similar to that of wolves. To this day dingoes are subject to the natural laws of selection and no human being decides which dog and which bitch shall reproduce.

They possess, however, a whole series of other features normally to be found only in genuine domestic animals. There is no single typical representative of the canine race—of the *canis* branch, any more than of the other varieties of the family—with the curved tail, in other words a tail normally held bolt upright with the end bending over towards the animal's head. This appears only in the domesticated dog and in the dingo. The Hallstrom dingo from New Guinea in fact has a curly tail like a spitz. Moreover, dingoes all have white 'markings', principally white paws, a white patch on the breast—which may extend to the stomach—and a white tip to the tail. There are also frequently white patches on the throat, the chin and towards the end of the muzzle. These are also features of the domestic dog; I shall be reverting, however, to the fact that such 'domesticated features' sometimes appear on animals in the wild state.

In any case, for a very long time the dingo has lived wild, totally uninfluenced by man; he has been subject to the laws of natural selection and so we are fully justified in assuming that his hereditary pattern of behaviour is purer than that of any domestic dog. This leaves the question: what has the dingo to do with our domesticated animals?

If the scientists who have dealt with the subject are right, the dingo has a great deal to do with our domestic dogs. Many in fact maintain that all our breeds of domestic dog originate from the dingo or at least have many dingo traits. To quote one interesting example, in the Senckenberg marsh near Frankfurt on Main the bones, including the skull, of a dog were discovered near the skeleton of a bison and the dog was held to be a domestic animal. The age of the settlement was given as about 11,000 years! Robert Mertens, who made the discovery, pointed out the astounding similarity of the bones and skull to those of a dingo; he was convinced that the animal could not be a wolf. This was in 1936; meanwhile doubts have been voiced about the age of the discovery but not about the similarity to the dingo; the find is now said to be 'only' about 9–10,000 years old but I hardly think that we need worry about one or two thousand years! In any case we have here one of the oldest known domestic dogs and it is similar to the dingo; it can hardly be supposed that dingoes migrated on their own from their Asiatic homeland to Germany and so man must somehow have brought them there—just as the Australian aborigines, at about the same time, were taking them to Australia.

WOLVES AND JACKALS

Many readers have undoubtedly already said to themselves: why so much bother? Why not say straight away that the wolf is the ancestor of all dogs? There, surely, the primitive behaviour which you are looking for would be found in its purest form.

Wolves and Jackals

Agreed—but perhaps we should first think a little more about the wolf. To start with a flat statement—*the* wolf as such does not exist; there are numerous types of wolf described by zoologists as varieties of the wolf family. Experts can enumerate twenty-one such varieties. They exist because the wolf is, or until last century was, to be found all over Europe, in Asia and in North America. Obviously the area in which a Siberian wolf lives is quite different from that inhabited by the southern Indian or Spanish wolf. All animals adapt themselves, both structurally and in their habits, to the area in which they live. Accordingly an arctic wolf not only looks quite different from an Indian wolf but behaves differently.

The 'ancestral' Wolf

Unfortunately I can only make this statement based on knowledge of other animals. I can only say: it seems improbable that the wolf will be different from all other animals on earth. In fact we know least about the southern wolf. For certain reasons he would be particularly interesting.

In this connection it should be remembered that the domestic dog is supposed to have originated between 10,000 and 12,000 years ago. At this time the European ice-cap had already retreated a long way northwards but civilisation had hardly developed to the stage of genuine animal breeding. It is therefore far more likely that the first varieties of domestic animal reached our area from the Middle East, where highly developed cultures already existed

So it is conceivable that the domestic dog is even older than I have already indicated.

In any case I am convinced that the area in which the dog was first domesticated may be assumed to be that lying between the Middle East and India. Here, however, there are indigenous varieties of wolf, primarily the Indian wolf (*Canis lupus pallipes*), and we know far less about its behaviour than that of the north European, north Asian and north American wolf.

Nevertheless I think it important to examine in full detail the life and behaviour of the northern wolf; quite apart from the part he has played, as already mentioned, in production of many of our present-day breeds of dog, he can definitely provide us with a highly developed example of communal living transcending the bounds of the immediate family. The severe conditions under which he lives necessitate the formation in winter of packs providing a reasonable prospect of success in hunting. The result is a pronounced form of social behaviour such as is to be seen in our best breeds of domestic dog. I am prevented from studying the basic habits of these wolves by the fact that I cannot provide them with the conditions essential to enable them freely to develop their natural habits of life. During the mating season in February and March these wolves live in pairs and they rear their young as a pair in April and May; in the autumn they form, with these young and probably with the previous year's offspring, a sizeable pack. I should have to possess an area of at least 250 acres, variously constituted but primarily wooded, surrounded by a six-foot fence. It is to be hoped that Erik Zimen, a young man from Sweden who is carrying out research into the habits of wolves, will soon be able to launch a scientific project of this sort in the great German nature reserve in the Bayerischer Wald. This would be a major step forward in the science of research into domestic animals.

It is frequently said that one, if not the sole, ancestor of the dog must be the jackal. This is a very vexed question, but since so far there is no proof to the contrary, we must deal with it. One argument, for instance, is that the yellow or Asiatic jackal referred to here (*Canis aureus*) is a follower of the lion. He lives near a pride of lions and waits until they have taken their fill of their prey. As soon as the lions have left the remains of the zebra or gnu and returned to their usual resting place, the jackals fall upon the remnants.

Therefore, so it is argued, it is in the jackal's nature to follow successful hunters and so when man, the greatest of all animal-hunters, appeared, the jackal may have transferred his allegiance. This again could have given man the idea of taming the jackal and turning him into a domestic animal.

This all sounds very fine and there are other arguments such as the conclusions about behaviour drawn by Konrad Lorenz. Moreover, jackals are basically beautiful-looking dogs and so I

Portrait of a jackal

was not content until I had given my dogs a couple of jackals as companions.

They were just six weeks old when they arrived at the mill, tiny, terribly timid creatures, far more graceful than all the dog puppies which I had seen. They were already much further developed, however, than dog puppies of similar age. Despite all my hopes of seeing jackals give evidence of canine behaviour, after only three days I was forced to admit that, even if jackals bear some relation to our dogs, these two certainly bore no relation to my Ben and my Ali. In fact they showed certain patterns of behaviour which I have never seen either in a dingo or in any of our domestic dogs. Moreover they have a certain physical feature which I have never seen either in a dog, a wolf or a dingo; the two centre pads of the paws are not completely separate but are joined together at the rear end to produce a horseshoe-shaped double pad; this was so in the case of both animals both in the forepaws and hind paws. This quite shook me at the time; today I think somewhat differently since, by complicated methods of inbreeding, I have meanwhile produced a dingo bitch of a different colour with similarly joined pads. Precipitately drawn conclusions are therefore very dangerous and so I propose to wait until further comparison between my jackals and my other dogs can indicate whether my first impressions and observations are really valid. (See p. 42.)

It is, of course, true that, like the wolf, the yellow jackal appears in numerous—nineteen to be exact—different varieties with considerable differences in colour and size. Moreover the yellow jackal is to be found over a very wide area, from Sumatra across the whole of southern Asia to the Mediterranean. I cannot yet say to which of these varieties, many of them little known, my two little jackals belong, since they are not yet fully grown. I introduce them here, however, as genuine wild dogs forming part of my stock.

MY HALF-BREEDS

The words 'bastard' or 'mongrel' carry a sense of opprobrium. There are many owners of such dogs, however, who swear that the finest, most aristocratic pedigree dog cannot hold a candle to their 'Fido'. There is much in this because one of the more important discoveries of modern animal breeding is the fact that, by mixing different hereditary qualities, outstanding animals can often be produced. People talk of 'revelling in mongrel qualities', by which they mean that these half-breeds are frequently better than their pure-bred parents. In the case of hens, for instance, people experiment with 'hybrids', as they are also called, in order to beat the egg production record; modern pig and cattle breeders do the same. One disadvantage must be accepted: these hybrids cannot be used for further breeding; they are only of value as high-performance animals. To produce such hybrids the two parents, with their differing hereditary qualities, must be pure-bred themselves.

My Half-breeds

Hybrids are bred to raise the production of eggs in the case of hens, meat in that of pigs, and milk in that of cows. In the case of dogs mongrels are said to be particularly intelligent and to possess other favourable qualities which cannot fail to arouse the interest of someone conducting research into canine behaviour. I therefore wondered whether I could not produce 'mongrel qualities' in so far as behaviour was concerned. Dogs with a marked behaviour

Björn, the first cross-bred dog

potential, I thought, might really be interesting. One day, therefore, I mated Binna, my elkhound bitch, with Aboriginal (called Abo for short), the dingo dog.

The result was all I had hoped. Binna had a litter of seven, of which I kept one dog and two bitches. All developed into quite magnificent dogs, a pleasure to see. Björn, the dog, is strong and beautifully built, full of self-confidence and energy. Bente, his sister, is as good—she is stronger than either an elkhound or dingo bitch. Fella, the other sister, was the same but she was unfortunately mistaken for a 'wild dog' by a hunter and shot—an understandable error in view of the markedly primitive behaviour of these dogs. We had constructed a new pen. Within hours the three half-breeds, who were far more intelligent than either an elkhound or a dingo, had found the weak spot which every new pen has. They dug their way under the fence; Fella and Bente departed into the neighbouring wood. This was at 8.0 a.m. At midday Bente returned alone. She dragged herself laboriously up to the house and then collapsed. Her yellow coat was streaming with blood and we discovered that her entire right side was literally riddled with shot from the tip of her muzzle to the root of her tail. But it must have been a long shot for the pellets had not penetrated very far. We therefore had reason to hope that we could save Bente; Fella never reappeared. Bente recovered quickly from her 'lead-poisoning' and then came in season—they are tough resilient dogs, these dingo-elkhound mongrels.

I had therefore bred some mongrels which were particularly well developed physically and which in some respects could be called model dogs.

But I was still not satisfied. I was not merely wrestling with the question of the basic primitive behaviour of dogs; I wanted to use this knowledge to discover how and from what cause the behavioural habits of our dogs had become so different in many respects. I therefore did exactly that which one should not do with half-breeds: I mated Björn with his sister Bente. From the point of view of breeding for performance this was a doubly serious crime. In the first place I was continuing to breed with hybrids; secondly I was mating brother and sister—surely this could not go right.

It was not destined to go right. I wanted to observe changes in behaviour, or at least certain deviations. The first puppies from this pair will soon be two years old and so far I have hardly observed any changes in behaviour, though this is not to say that there may not have been minor differences. Knud and Kala, as Björn's and Bente's puppies are called, are perfectly strong healthy dogs, well built though a little smaller than their parents. The two of them then produced puppies, strong healthy good-looking children, though again smaller than their parents. They are still too young for conclusions to be drawn on their behavioural habits, but as puppies and young dogs they seem to be perfectly normal.

If one wants to probe something in detail, one will shrink from nothing. Accordingly I mated Binna, my elkhound bitch, with her son Björn once more and then a second time with her grandson

My Half-breeds

Knud. Here there was, in fact, something to see. In each case she had a litter of seven but not all the puppies were perfect. In one case, in fact, a puppy continually lost weight and had to be put to sleep before it starved—such a thing had never happened in my kennel before. The pups which developed normally, however, were all good-looking dogs, though small.

But there was one exception—Stina, my 'problem dog'. As I have already said, she is smaller than the others of her litter and is also unusually shy. Sometimes I think that she might be a sort of miniature wolf. In this connection the following is of interest: Lutz and Heinz Heck, who are well known as zoo-keepers and zoologists, one formerly in Berlin and the other in Munich, have carried out numerous breeding experiments with a wide variety of animals. In the process they uncovered a most interesting fact: when they crossed a domestic animal with its wild counterpart, they did not simply produce half-breeds showing the characteristics of the two parents. Qualities came to light possessed neither by the one breed nor the other but which were those of the prototype of the domestic animal. This 'Heck Law' has been confirmed, though in a different sense, by behavioural research. If certain different types of duck are crossed, for instance, the progeny show certain behavioural characteristics proper to neither breed of parent; they are those of another unconnected breed of duck which in some respects may be regarded as the basic type. In other words, in these half-breeds there have been 'reactivated' certain ancient habits of behaviour, which the parent breeds must have possessed in the early stages of development of the race and which are perpetuated in this present-day half-breed.

To go back to Stina, whose story we already know and who is also a half-breed. It may be thought that, as a result of her peculiar parentage, certain ancient characteristics have come out in her. Remarkably enough she shows (as do also her offspring) certain distinctive colour markings which I have otherwise seen only in jackals, not in wolves. Her extremely small size should not simply be written off as 'regressive'. In other respects Stina shows no signs of regression whatsoever; she is completely viable. It may be that in her case a size is being 'reactivated' which was the normal size for a dog in the early periods of the world's history. After all, the primitive ancestors of our larger canine-type beasts of prey were no larger than a weasel. Many of the present-day types of fox, for instance, stand no more than 10–12 inches high; the Bengal fox in India is one example and the north American kit-fox another. The smallest present-day type of dog alive is the raccoon Dog (*Nyctereutes*) originally indigenous to eastern Asia; some of these were recently exhibited in Russia and Poland and are now said to have reached this country (Germany); they stand only some 7–8 inches high. Stina's shyness with human beings may also perhaps be ascribed to some such 'reactivation'—she is on perfectly good terms with the larger dogs and with the young jackals and in this case shows not the slightest timidity.

Research into behavioural changes resulting from the process of domestication is one aspect of the science of domestication ethology; it is still in its infancy and must first be properly developed before it can bark with the rest.

Lest the reader think, however, that I cannot offer him much of interest, I must mention yet another dog. This is Strixi, the village mongrel who arrived from Rott. He is a sweet dog, an intelligent dog, of totally unknown breed, though of a type often to be seen in these parts; I suspect that they originate from very ancient breeds of farm dog. With so much breeding going on, the good Strixi could not be left out and, being a bright young man, he was given a beautiful dingo bitch as his wife; being also highly intelligent, he betook himself a second wife on the sly and this too was no childless marriage. Naturally I could only keep one of these half-breeds, a bitch as coal-black as her father, and thereafter he and she lived together. The result was a litter of illegitimate children. They were distinguished by heads of a remarkable size and looked out upon the world so timidly that I found them extremely alluring. Unfortunately I did not have them long. They died when something over two months old. The post-mortem showed signs of degeneration in the liver, the kidneys and even the heart muscles.

At this point I realised, unfortunately too late, that I had made a false move with my mongrels. All my dogs grow up lively and healthy in the pens without supplementary nourishment produced by man. I ought to have done what (unfortunately) the people in our breeding establishments like to do; I ought to have taken these puppies into the house, given them vitamins and broth, kept them warm and coddled them with all that mistaken solicitude which is responsible for the fact that many of our most attractive breeds of dog are practically unable to survive without human assistance.

To prove the point I waited for a second litter from these two dogs; it duly arrived and I acted as indicated above. The three puppies are now 'in the best of health' (at one point they were at

Strixi, a village mongrel

death's door but I wanted to know whether they were basically as weak as the previous litter); they are lively, happy, playful and undoubtedly the most 'enchanting' of all the thirty-eight dogs I possess. At the age of ten weeks they behaved exactly like a somewhat stupid four-week-old puppy; then, however, they made up ground quickly and today, at over three months, they give an astonishingly intelligent impression—comparatively I should add.

Nevertheless they still look like small puppies: they have large round heads and are frequently clumsy in their movements. They have not grown since the age of six weeks; so far as one can see at present, they will remain little miniature dogs about 10 inches high.

In many respects Strixi, the village mongrel, does not behave like a dog in possession of all the normal instincts, particularly in company with other dogs. I do not, however, know his background when young, though I suspect the worst. It is therefore possible that he suffers from behavioural disturbances developed during his lifetime—a subject which we shall be discussing on several occasions in this book.

As far as his offspring are concerned, however, they are living proof of the way in which a breed of dog can be sent 'to the dogs' if puppies which do not develop normally are artificially assisted to grow by all sorts of external aids. My example is, of course, extreme. One has only to reflect, however, what is likely to happen if, over many generations, our so-called love of animals leads us to compensate for certain small and apparently entirely unimportant weaknesses in development; their sum total will lead inevitably to the complete ruin of the breed and ultimately to dogs unable to give birth normally who would have to be delivered by caesarian. Such things do in fact happen today, and if this type of 'breeding' is synonymous with love of animals then prospects are poor for man's sense of responsibility towards animals. It should lead him not to rear freaks but to prevent the appearance of freaks.

3 Roads to Diversity

Our hunter ancestors of the stone age certainly did not begin breeding dogs by capturing several hundred wolves or other form of wild dog; they started by finding a litter of very young cubs somewhere and rearing them. These animals became tame and remained with their human tribe. They then became capable of reproduction and no doubt mating took place between brother and sister. Their offspring in turn became capable of reproducing and mated not only with each other but with their parents, uncles and aunts. So here we have a fine example of inbreeding. All grew up with the kind human beings who took care of them; they were faithful and friendly. On their side, like all dog-breeders, the good human beings took care that no wild wolf intervened to spoil the docility of the inbred wolves.

What was the result? The 'domestic wolf' became smaller and smaller and a number of distinctive mutations developed. This is the lesson of archaeological discoveries, not only of canine remains but those of other animals of the early domestication period.

MARKS OF INBREEDING—DIFFERENT MUTATIONS

This was precisely the direction in which my breeding experiments tended and numerous examples provided by different breeds showed how, within a very short time, reduction in size and changes in other distinctive characteristics took place. To pursue the picture given above of the initial domestication of the dog, I will confine myself to a simple case of brother-and-sister mating between dingoes. Their offspring already showed a general reduction in size, though there were exceptions—caused by the fact that the experiment started with the pair already mentioned who came from different branches of the dingo family. We shall be reverting to this later. A clearer example of reduction in size, to which there were no exceptions, is the following: Buna, my dingo bitch, was born in Nuremberg and, as is usual there, was mated with her brother Dingo (this is his name—he is privately owned). The result was a bitch with the attractive name Tanila. Later I obtained from Alfred Seitz one of Buna's brothers, a dog from the same parents though not from the same litter. He was christened Motu and developed into an extremely well-grown dog. When he grew up he was mated with Tanila. She might be called his niece, but this is not quite right since—in Central Europe at least—

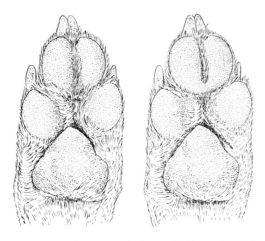

Forepaws of a normal dingo (left) *and of Arta, the inbred dingo bitch* (right). *As with my jackals the central forward pads are joined*

nieces do not have brothers and sisters as parents. Tanila and Motu have so far had two litters.

The first litter consisted of two puppies only and they were comparatively small. They produced a major surprise, however. They were not dark brown at birth, as dingo pups usually are, but light silver-grey. The dog had a tinge of blue and the bitch a tinge of yellow. Unfortunately Tanila was in such a hurry to bite off the dog's umbilical cord that she seriously damaged his stomach. I therefore had to put this interesting puppy to sleep. The bitch pup, however, developed well, though she remained somewhat smaller than her mother Tanila who herself is a daintier animal than

Marks of Inbreeding—Different Mutations

other dingo bitches. In Arta, therefore, as this strange-coloured dingo bitch is called, I now had a sort of miniature dingo, whose behaviour in other respects, however, showed not the smallest sign of degeneration. On the contrary, this little dog is a bundle of energy, remarkably agile and intelligent, and anyone who knows anything about the points of a dog admires her elegant figure. Moreover Arta is extraordinarily friendly to everyone, in contrast to other dingoes who are noticeably shy of strangers, at least initially. Arta, who has meanwhile grown up, has lost her light silver-grey coat but her colouring is still quite different from the normal dingo's. In fact it largely resembles the 'apricot' of the poodle, which itself is a special hereditary colour mutation. Arta also has certain colour markings of her own, into which I need not go here. An important point is that the centre pads of her paws are joined together as already described.

Tanila's second litter consisted of four puppies, one dog and three bitches. All three bitches, again unusually small, were of the normal dingo puppy colouring; the dog, however, was once more silver-grey.

This example, therefore, shows that, by certain definite methods of inbreeding, mutations can be produced in size, physical features, colour and character.

It may be thought, of course, that the appearance of these changes within the space of so few generations was caused by the fact that the strain started with two dogs from different branches of the dingo family. The idea occurs to me because, in previous experiments, I have seen how quickly mutations can be produced by combining artificially reared mice with the natural strain.

This is the reason for my cross-breeding between dingo and elkhound, as already mentioned, and between dingo and the village mongrel Strixi; for the same reason I now propose to do similar cross-breeding with my jackals. There is another thought behind this: the prehistoric hunters who lit upon the idea of rearing a litter of cubs no doubt found this highly advantageous— puppies played with the children while grown dogs, with their sensitive noses, could give warning of the approach of strangers or dangerous animals far sooner than could their human companions; neighbouring hunter tribes no doubt soon followed this example and soon even more distant tribes would by this time be obtaining their own puppies and starting their own dog-breeding. Modern archaeology has produced numerous examples to show that, even in the early days of human civilisation, goods of all sorts were exchanged over astounding distances. It is therefore quite conceivable that 'domestic wolves' from one area arrived in another and eventually reached a race of men living in an area inhabited by quite a different branch of the wolf species. Differing blood-strains may therefore have been combined in the very early days of domestication and in this way development of the various differing breeds of dog might have begun.

Considering only the direct line of brother-and-sister matings, my dingo-elkhound cross-breeds show a reduction in size with each generation. Stina, again, is an example of the rapidity of this process when the mother is mated with her half-breed son.

No less striking are the marked differences in colouring shown by these various offspring—from almost white to almost black. Definite indications of wolf- and jackal-markings are to be seen and much else besides. I could write a separate book on the subject. Assuming, however, that the reader is primarily interested in the behaviour of these animals, I must now deal with that aspect.

Stina I have already described. Sven and Dove, both from the same litter as Stina, are very nice dogs, though they are sometimes shy with strangers in a way rather reminiscent of Stina. I thought, however, that Sven would make a most affectionate house-dog and one of my friends thought the same. He was most attracted by Sven, who was almost black with silver-grey markings, and was most anxious to take him. I brought Sven, then seventeen months old, into the house and he was soon on very good terms with my friend, who accordingly put Sven into his car and drove home.

A week later he brought Sven back. In strange surroundings he had been just as shy as his sister Stina. Once back in his old kennel he jumped around for joy, licked our hands and turned once more into the most affectionate dog.

Sven's sister Dove too on occasions showed that she could be as shy as a wild animal. Once she succeeded in reaching the loft. There, between piles of junk and the great forest of rafters, shyness overcame her. She had found a spot which I could not reach and into it she withdrew. For hours I stood a yard or two from her and tried to entice her out of her lair. It was all in vain; she merely

Marks of Inbreeding—Different Mutations

withdrew further. This game went on for three weeks. Dove had found a way on to the outside of the roof and so my visitors were greeted with the curious spectacle of a silvery, black-faced bitch resembling a spitz lying comfortably stretched out in the sun on the dizzy height of the roof-ridge.

I did not like this at all. I could think of nothing to do but starve Dove out. She looked down most attentively from her breezy height when I fed the other dogs, but even that did not lure her down. Of course there were a lot of mice up in the roof but I did not think that they would provide enough food. Moreover I was afraid that one day she would slip on the smooth surface of the roof and come tumbling down, in which case she could hardly have survived. A dog's paws are as efficient as a pair of climbing boots, however, and Dove contrived to clamber all over the roof. Even the other dogs gazed at her in astonishment.

Precisely three weeks later I climbed the stairs to the attic yet again—and my Dove came rushing to me, jumped up all over me and wagged her tail as only a dog can which has been missing its master for ages. I was speechless. As if nothing had happened, she allowed me to carry her down and place her back with Sven who equally greeted her uproariously. Dove had in fact lost a lot of weight but there was nothing to indicate that she was physically weak. At first I fed her sparingly to accustom her to normal feeding once more and now she is as friendly as ever she was.

Such experiences show, first how difficult it is to make definite pronouncements about the character of this sort of dog, and secondly that a half-breed strain can produce very different characteristics—compare this incident with the behaviour of the affectionate dingo bitch Arta. To complete the picture of the diversity shown by these dogs in their attitude to men, let me tell the story of the last bitch I have bred. She was Stina's daughter and her father was Sven. The mother, as we know, is very shy and the father, as we equally know, can be shy in certain situations, but as a house-dog the daughter is totally uncomplicated. The friend who had brought back Sven took her in his place and is overjoyed with this lively faithful little dog (she is slightly larger than her mother Stina); she is a splendid playmate for my friend's three-year-old son.

If we use the word character to mean the innate qualities which turn a dog into a good or bad companion for man, we are drawing a dividing line between character and innate habits of behaviour. The latter, however, include all those methods of expression used by dogs in contact with each other and much else which has a bearing on judgement of character; there is no distinct dividing line. I am not concerned with this here, however, but with the question whether my inbreeding and my cross-breeding can produce other changes in behaviour.

To confirm that the answer to this question is in the affirmative I would merely cite one example which again concerns Tanila, whom we already know. The dingo bitch Sydney brings her puppies into the world and looks after them with such calm self-confidence that on one occasion I was not even present at the ceremony although I had waited up for it. Tanila, on the other hand, gets into a vast state of agitation. As soon as the puppies are born she begins to howl, whines now and then, jumps excitedly out of her kennel and then hurries back at once when the puppies squeak; she then assaults the unhappy Motu with such violence that he is completely discomfited and I have to take him out of the pen; finally she goes half mad if I want to examine the puppies. She was even worse with her second litter than with the first. Meanwhile she is so busy with her puppies and fusses over them so much that she is in danger of achieving the exact opposite of what she intends. Some human beings suffer from the same malady!

We now have a good idea how this individual diversity both in colouring and behaviour has arisen within the great canine race. So far, however, we have referred only to reductions in size. This raises the question: how do we account for the large breeds of dog, the St Bernards or Irish wolfhounds which may stand 30 inches or more at the shoulder?

I have already said that in my dingo strain there are exceptions. One such exception is the dog Paroo who is considerably larger than either his parents or grandparents. He is my most handsome dingo, an impressive powerful animal with a serious expression heightened by the wrinkles on his face. His parents were Aboriginal and Suki, in other words the brother and sister with whom I originally began my breeding. They themselves were larger than their mother Gina, the slim Australian dingo, and of course much larger than their short-legged father Luxl from New Guinea (the New Guinea strain, it will be remembered, is shorter-legged than other dingoes). Paroo, therefore, is a clear illustration that, in the case of such half-breeds with subsequent inbreeding, an increase in size may occur and I am anxious to see whether I shall succeed in perpetuating this increase in later generations.

In all these observations and considerations we must not forget that we have so far concentrated upon only a few, strictly limited cases. If one thinks how many sub-species of wolf have contributed to the domestication of our dogs over the course of the years and if, in addition, one remembers that there is certainly an occasional jackal cross somewhere, then, with the little we now know, we have some inkling of the manifold possibilities of fresh combinations and reciprocal hereditary influences which may lead to more far-reaching mutations.

With all these possibilities in mind it is easy to see why our dogs are so different. It is in fact astounding that there are 'only' four hundred breeds! In view of this and of the fact that almost anything can be bred into or out of a strain, we can only be astounded that our dogs retain so many of their original habits of behaviour. Apart from certain highly exotic breeds it is a fact that expert breeding and a little luck can produce in the majority of our breeds of dog or in selected examples of them a very complete range of primitive behavioural habits. I am often astounded at the qualities which still remain unspoilt in the best of our dogs.

WHITE COAT AND RED EYES

Everyone knows about white mice or rabbits with snow-white coats and red eyes. It is difficult to imagine a dog looking like this but anyone who wants to see one can do so in Karlsruhe Zoo. Birkmann, the director of this zoo, has succeeded in breeding a strain of albino dingoes.

Not only is this of general zoological interest but it also provides a further explanation of the diversity of our dogs. Earlier I conducted certain breeding experiments in which I mated artificially reared albino mice with normal-coloured wild mice. With further inbreeding all sorts of colours appeared—black mice, yellow mice, brown mice, grey mice. There were also noticeable behavioural changes; I had produced a strain of increasingly aggressive mice; they ultimately became so fierce that the strain died out, since husband and wife bit each other to death instead of mating. I even produced mice with only four pads on their hind feet instead of five, the foot remaining completely symmetrical and efficient. This is reminiscent of Arta's connected pads. On one occasion, using albino and normal-coloured golden hamsters, I even produced a pug-faced hamster, which, however, did not live long.

It is therefore possible to produce almost everything conceivable by crossing a normal-coloured animal with an albino and then carrying out very close inbreeding. This is fascinating and one begins to wonder whether it is not enough to possess an albino of whatever animal species one wants in order to be able to breed every sort of domestic animal so far known.

For a time, in fact, I wondered whether the appearance of albinos did not provide the ultimate explanation for all the changes associated with domestication. Albinos are not solely bred artificially as in Karlsruhe; they are to be found in nature. Albino giraffes and zebras have been discovered; the 'white stag' and albino roe-deer, martens, squirrels and moles have long been known. There is, in fact, no animal species in the world in which albinos may not appear; human albinos are not so rare, though among primitive peoples, at least in earlier times, their appearance was concealed and the baby killed at birth.

How do albinos arise? We now know that it is a form of mutation; we know something of the physiological changes in the albino and of heredity in albinos. But we do not know what leads to such mutations. It may be that close inbreeding, such as sometimes happens in small isolated communities living in the natural state, may be the answer.

We do know, however, that albino animals have always aroused the greatest interest among primitive peoples; even today the excitement caused by the appearance of a white stag (usually endowed with a shining cross between its antlers) shows how medieval superstitions persist. The ancient Egyptians, like the Chinese, who were expert breeders, regarded white mice as heralds of good fortune and in prehistoric times this may well have been so. Possession of a living albino animal must have turned any medicine-man or high priest into a demigod in the eyes of his

White Coat and Red Eyes

fellow-countrymen; the theory, therefore, that albinos may have played quite a considerable role in the domestication of our dogs cannot be altogether dismissed. It cannot have been easy to find an albino mate for the high priest's white wolf and so he or she may have been provided with a natural-coloured mate—and there we have all we need.

A further factor is that albino animals are generally far easier to tame than those of normal colour. If you hold up an albino mouse on a piece of board, for instance, it will stay there quite calmly, making no attempt to jump off as the natural-coloured mouse will do at once; albino rats can become remarkably tame. In short albinos are almost 'naturals' for domestication.

This opens up an interesting subject of some importance for our understanding of the dog. It is clear that natural-coloured and albino animals not only differ basically in behaviour, but also that colour mutations resulting from a cross between them are indications of behavioural differences. Colouring and behaviour are undoubtedly linked; this is nothing extraordinary since both the nervous system and the skin originate, in the early embryonic stage known as the gastrula, from the outer layer of cells or ectoderm. This outer layer of cells also develops the brain and the rest of the nervous system as well as the skin with its hair and pigmentation. It is perhaps true to say that colour is the outward and visible sign of the entire 'nerve apparatus'.

Alsatian experts frequently maintain that a 'pigmented' dog, in other words one with black in his coat, is livelier than lighter-coloured alsatians. The black panther is said to be particularly dangerous—at least that is what the travel-books say and much is made of the fact if one is produced in a circus. If a particularly difficult stallion figures in a horsy story, he is usually black. In some way black animals seem somewhat sinister to us; one has only to recall what Goethe says in *Faust* about the black poodle. In justice to the dog, however, it should be added that the animal mentioned definitely has nothing to do with our modern poodles; Goethe was referring to the old German sheep-dog poodle which was savage, dangerous and half a wolf by nature.

It may be objected that all this is merely due to the fact that from time immemorial black has always been associated with sinister mysterious things, perhaps a throw-back in the memory to 'black night', so dangerous for early man. This is of course possible but very recently precise proof has been forthcoming that there is something in this connection between black colouring and temperament, at least in dogs. Zdenko Martinek of Prague, who has been carrying out research into behaviour, developed a method of measuring activity in dogs and this showed that the black specimens of a certain breed were livelier than those of other colours.

The matter is by no means so simple, however, and naturally one cannot say that all that is necessary is to see what colour the dog is to know what its character will be. There may, for instance, be latent in light-coloured dogs the factors which should lead to black colouring but they may not be perceptible in its hereditary disposition. In such cases—and Zdenko Martinek's experiments have proved it—light-coloured dogs may possess the temperament for a 'black disposition'. This will become clear if such a dog is mated with another of equally 'black' but recessive tendencies; two light-coloured but particularly active dogs will almost certainly produce black puppies.

Like albinos, black animals are also to be found in nature—witness the black panther. Equally, however, yellow animals are to be found in the natural state as are other colour mutations; in moles, for instance, all sorts of markings are known. Everything shown by my experiments with mice, therefore, is to be found in nature without any intervention by man. We habitually refer to 'domestic colours' but I fear that we shall have to relearn our lesson; alternatively we should use the term 'self-domestication' to indicate the appearance of domesticated attributes in nature when man has had nothing to do with the breeding.

It is widely known that more and more blackbirds in built-up areas are flecked with white and recently I heard of one which was reddy grey in colour. This finally brings me to a subject which preoccupies many dog-breeders. The regulations for many of our breeds of dog prescribe that there must be no white patches on the chest, the stomach or elsewhere, no white tip to the tail and no white paws. These are counted as faults. If this is explicitly laid down in regulations, it implies that such things occur or have occurred occasionally.

I have already pointed out that my dingoes do have such white

White Coat and Red Eyes

'markings', as they are usually called. I have deliberately tried to breed these markings out, but must admit that I have made little progress. Only the magnificent Paroo seems to be well on the way; he has no white tip to his tail, the patch on his chest is quite small and so is the white on his paws.

These 'semi-albino' markings should also be considered as features of the domestic animal and it is known that they appeared very early in the domestication process. As the example of the white-flecked blackbird shows, however, they clearly do not necessarily depend on any intervention by man. I have myself come across, in a small remote marsh in central Norway, a totally isolated community of water-rats (they should more properly be called water-voles); most of these animals had white claws, some white pads to their feet and white tips to their tails; one which I caught even had some white hairs on its forehead. This was therefore another example of 'self-domestication' in the wild state.

These and other observations gave me an idea about the etymology of the dingo which may possibly open up fresh perspectives for research into the canine species. I assume that the dingoes which accompanied the aborigines to Australia were not domestic animals but wild dogs. There would certainly not have been very many of them; as they multiplied over the centuries much inbreeding, and therefore 'self-domestication', must obviously have taken place. This may be the origin of the 'domestic markings' on the dingo.

What sort of wild dog, therefore, was 'naturalised' into New Guinea and Australia at this time? We know that the aborigines came from south-east Asia. In that area is to be found a form of wild dog which has hardly been the subject of any research—a reddish-brown dog. He was placed in a separate genus because he had fewer molar teeth in the lower jaw. The *Cuon* is still retained as a genus, although like dogs, wolves and jackals, these animals have forty-two teeth. The 'adjag' (*Cuon javanicus*), the species of this animal which lives in Malaya, Sumatra, Java and Borneo, is almost indistinguishable from a dingo in build, size and colouring; similarly in these same areas are to be found indigenous dogs unmistakably descended from the red dog. Much more attention should be paid to these red dogs; it would be lamentable if the strain died out before the investigators have made up their minds to do so.

INDIVIDUALITY OF OUR DOGS

It is clear, therefore, that there is a whole range of possible explanations for the hereditary diversity of our dogs. And I have not yet even mentioned the fact that many of our present-day breeds of dog originate from a cross between two, three or more highly bred species. Production of a permament breed of dog is a highly specialised art of breeding. It demands much ability and a very great deal of time and patience—in addition to a whole packet of money! These new breeds, however, are comparatively easy to explain and understand; basically they have little to teach us about changes due to domestication since breeds already existing were used as the initial material. It is easy to see, however, why they are particularly susceptible to deficiencies of instinct, frequently far-reaching.

A further source of differences in canine behaviour is the so-called retardation or inducement of juvenile qualities. We shall understand this better when we come to deal in detail with the development of the dog and his behaviour in infancy.

Observation of the normal development of behaviour in the young dog opens up a further source of behavioural changes and these, of course, are not hereditary. I believe that these influences exert a far more decisive effect on the varied individuality of our dogs than does heredity. We already know that, even in the wolf-pack, certain differences between individuals can be observed and these are certainly not all inborn; they have been acquired during youth. This is normal and undoubtedly produces certain advantages for the wolf-pack. In the case of our domestic dogs, however, the hothouse methods so often used can lead to derangements of behaviour and even to a whole range of neuroses. A voluminous literature exists on this saddest aspect of canine existence and many veterinary surgeons specialise in the subject. I once read with a shudder a long treatise on this matter by Ferdinand Brunner, the 'dog psychiatrist' of Vienna; it was exactly like a report from a human psychiatric clinic. In ninety-

Individuality of Our Dogs

nine cases out of a hundred such regrettable psychological disturbances are due to a disturbed upbringing.

We cannot do better than study with care the normal development of a young dog subjected to no upheavals or changes of treatment. The subject is one of the most attractive in the whole study of behaviour but it also contains the key to everything the dog will do when grown up. He is, after all, the product not only of his hereditary disposition but of his youthful development. It can be stated without doubt that a dog of bad disposition but with a good upbringing will be a better dog than one with the best possible hereditary disposition but an inadequate upbringing. It may be that many modern breeders, who set more store by pedigrees and prizes than by the dog himself, will hardly be able to believe this. Anyone who pays attention to what I can relate on this subject, however, will ultimately agree with me.

4 The Puppy's First Weeks

The caterpillar which emerges from the butterfly's egg is totally different from its winged parent both in appearance and habits; neither their anatomy nor behaviour would give one to think that the two were related. If we want to know the breed of butterfly to which a caterpillar belongs, we have to wait in patience until the caterpillar has grown, shed its skin for the last time, turned into a chrysalis and finally emerged as a butterfly. This succession of differing forms of the same individual, widespread in the insect world, is known as 'metamorphosis'.

The best-known vertebrates which undergo a similar transformation are frogs and toads. Tadpoles, as they are called in their early stages, clearly differ both in anatomy and habits from their parents. In their case, however, transformation is not so sudden. The tadpole initially consists only of a head, to which is attached a stomach and a tail to act as rudder, but gradually front and hind legs develop, the latter growing longer and longer; finally the tail retracts and the tiny frog or toad climbs out of the water to live henceforth on land. This is therefore a far smoother transition from one stage of adolescence to another. Frogs and toads are not full-grown for several years, not until they become capable of reproduction.

The sight of a new-born puppy reminds one of all these things.

A HALF-FORMED LITTLE DOG?

With great care the mother nibbles and licks at the amniotic membrane and there emerges a little creature bearing not the slightest resemblance to a proud alsatian or elegant greyhound. It is a fat little barrel with short stubby legs, a round outsize head and an insignificant little tail. The latter seems to have no function but the broad rounded head makes certain motions; it oscillates from side to side. No sooner has this curious little creature been licked dry than it sets off questingly along the floor. Its method of

A Half-formed Little Dog?

progression, however, resembles a salamander's crawl. It is a remarkably awkward motion as if the little legs were only able to push the heavy body and large head forward by exerting all their strength. And so it remains for the next fortnight.

The new-born foal or calf is quite different. Though his

Two views of a new-born dingo puppy

proportions are not precisely the same as his parents', he is recognisable from the first moment as a little horse or little cow; the similarity is great. After about half an hour and a little practice with his somewhat lengthy legs the foal moves exactly like a horse and the calf like a cow; all other movements are basically similar to those of the parents.

The Puppy's First Weeks

Here we see two different dispositions of nature, two methods by which animals are adapted to their living conditions. Horses and cattle live in herds and, being herbivores, cover considerable distances daily. Their young are born among the herd as it moves slowly along and must be able to move with the herd as soon as possible if they are not to become an easy prey for all sorts of predatory animals. Only in the middle of the great herd can they be safe and protected. They come into the world, therefore, well enough equipped to keep up with their full-grown companions.

The problem is quite different for the beasts of prey of the canine variety—wolves, jackals, coyotes, red wolves, foxes and the rest. They live in small communities, many in fact simply in pairs. The young are born in a safe hide-out—usually a hole in the ground dug by the parents—and there they remain for some time.

It must be remembered that the carnivore, which hunts a fleeting prey, cannot afford too long a period of gestation. If the she-wolf, for instance, carried her five or six young so long that they were big enough to accompany her on foraging expeditions, the unhappy mother would eventually be so immobile that she could not even catch a mouse. Why, then, do these animals not have a single offspring like the herbivores who live in herds? This again stems from the nature of the carnivore's existence; they cannot live in herds since sustenance is nothing like so plentiful as it is for the herbivores of the steppes. For a small community the struggle for existence is incomparably more severe and casualties are far more frequent. The larger number of young, therefore, guarantees the continuance of the race; the 'large family system' is another of nature's adaptations to conditions.

In 1941 the Russian scientist Severzov made certain calculations, based on detailed observation, which showed how essential it is that these animals should have litters of at least five puppies or cubs. He studied the mortality among young wolves and estimated that 45% of wolf-cubs come to an end in their first year and a further 32% in their second year, in other words a total of 77% of all young wolves. Since a wolf is not capable of reproduction until the age of 22 months, if a litter consisted only of three, the likelihood of any one of them contributing to the continuance of the race would be extremely small. Such figures also illustrate how savagely selective is the law of survival among these animals.

A Half-formed Little Dog?

For the carnivores of the canine species, therefore, the best solution is that the puppies or cubs should come into the world as soon as possible so that they do not hamper the mother in her forays. Every dog-breeder knows that a bitch shows practically no sign of pregnancy during the first 30–35 days; the embryos grow quite slowly at first and are no hindrance to her. The remaining 30 days are characterised by a very rapid growth of the foetus; yet, though carrying five or six puppies, the bitch is not noticeably stouter and she is in no way hindered in her movements. She cannot be expected to carry her puppies any longer, however, and so they exchange the protection of their mother's womb for an equally well-protected lair.

To understand more of the new-born puppy's equipment, we must take a look at this lair. Ognev, the Moscow zoologist, writes: 'The lair of the wolf is very simple. In the peat-bogs and expanses of the north the wolves, who live in pairs, look for dry spots in marshy inaccessible areas. The nest itself is a simple shallow depression without any soft bedding. On the steppes wolves make their lair at the bottom of a gorge or the foot of a steep slope or bank where cover is provided by brushwood or creepers. It is of interest that in desert areas or on the semi-desert steppes wolves sometimes live in holes; on occasions—on the Baikal steppe, for instance—they appropriate the holes of the tarbagan (central Asian marmot).'

This shows that wolves look first for a secure hide-out and then, within this hide-out, create a shallow depression.

In this secure hide-out the puppies can be left alone for hours while the parents go hunting. Now the inadequacy of the puppy's equipment proves its worth; it is incapable of leaving the nest when it would be in danger of falling victim to other predatory animals. The depression is so shaped that the puppies gravitate towards its centre; they are incapable of straying outside. In other ways too the hide-out is so well suited to them that they find life outside it most unpleasant. If, by accident, a puppy actually does get out into the open, it will squeak piteously, thus warning its parents who then take it back inside.

The puppy should not, therefore, be considered 'half-formed'. It is in fact perfectly adapted to the first stage of its existence and the conditions thereof—exactly as is the tadpole to its life in the pond. The fact that the bitch does not carry her young until they are fully developed, as does the mare or cow, does not mean that they leave her womb as semi-embryos. Nature has in fact provided them with all they need for their first few days of life, during which they prepare themselves, in complete security, for further development.

THE FIRST FEW MINUTES

I now propose to explain what is to be seen during the first few minutes of a puppy's life and to do so by describing two canine deliveries, the features of which were very different.

The first delivery took place over twenty years ago and was the first which I had ever been able to observe. 'Xanthi', my alsatian

Head of a new-born alsatian puppy

bitch, had been named after Socrates' notorious wife but she was no 'Xanthippe'; she was devoted to her husband Xingu. He was snuffling around excitedly and I had to remove him; once I had done this Xanthi, who was affectionate and accommodating, had no objection to my remaining with her during her hour of trial. I stayed up most of the night and she eventually rewarded me with six healthy puppies. I was no more experienced in these matters than she was (it was her first litter); in contrast to me, however, she 'knew' precisely how to nibble the wriggling puppies out of the membrane, which she did carefully and expertly. I was so enthralled that I hardly dared move and no doubt it was better

The First Few Minutes

that way, since otherwise I should have disturbed her. So, after a full three hours, there were six puppies, all licked dry; the bitch had cleaned herself up and everything had gone very well.

I was now confronted by a difficult question. The custom in Vienna at the time was to restrict to four the number of puppies in a litter which could be given the coveted pedigree papers; moreover experienced breeders maintained that in the case of a comparatively young bitch with her first litter, she should not be allowed to keep more than four. What was I to do? How was I to choose?

It had to be done during the first few hours. How was I to know, however, whether the puppies on which my totally unfounded choice might fall might not develop into the best and finest dogs of them all?

The choice is easy, of course, if the litter contains puppies with definite faults such as large white patches. Occasionally puppies are born crippled, deformed or particularly small and again selection is no problem. But faced with six healthy puppies, each looking like the next, what should one do?

While ruminating over this question, I observed the little creatures in turn and saw how they were endeavouring to reach the warm belly of their mother, who was still licking them, and push their stubby little muzzles into the hair of her coat; occasionally the mother helped a little with her nose and soon four of the puppies were attached to her teats, sucking happily. The remaining two, however, were still lying near by; they were moving their heads from side to side; from time to time they would stretch out a little front leg and draw up a hind leg after it; but they did not seem as hungry as their brothers and sisters. One or two of the puppies had tried to reach their source of milk before all had arrived but the bitch had pushed them away since she was too busy with the actual process of delivery. One of the two puppies which was not sucking was the last to be born and the other the second or third; the latter was a dog puppy.

Suddenly the thought occurred to me: if these two have not yet reached the teats, their life has not really begun in the right way. So I took them and carried them out of the room, unobserved of course by the bitch who was still very busy.

The second delivery took place twenty years later. Again it was a first litter, this time from Buna, my dingo bitch. When Buna began her preparations I had five other people in the room. Naturally everyone wished to remain and eventually I had to explain somewhat forcibly that the bitch would only be disturbed by their presence. This is what all the books about dog-breeding say: under all circumstances a bitch must be left in peace while having puppies. The most sensible of the five (a lady) started, somewhat unwillingly, to leave the room, whereupon Buna jumped out of her box, licked her hand, whined and showed quite clearly that she wanted the lady to stay. The same thing happened when the next person started to leave and so on with the third and fourth; then we gave up and all stayed with the bitch who was now completely happy. I dictated details of the delivery to my secretary and took a series of flashlight photographs. Buna produced three puppies in fifty-nine minutes. Puppy No 2 had reached one of his mother's teats and was sucking four minutes after birth and twenty-one minutes before the arrival of No 3. The sucking noise was clearly audible.

And what of the other two puppies? They searched around a little but failed to find a teat. We placed them up against one but they did not suck. At 6.55 p.m., twelve minutes after the birth of the last puppy, No 1 weighed 312 grams, No 2, 310 and No 3, 305. At midnight the weights were No 1, 309 grams, No 2, 310, No 3, 285. Forty-eight hours later I put No 3 to sleep since it was down to 235 grams and a little later No 1 which now only weighed 242 grams.

By this time No 2—now named Tanila and a mother herself—had reached 402 grams, in other words had put on 92 grams since birth. Tanila developed into the liveliest dingo bitch I know. She turned into an incredible versatile, intelligent, merry creature of tireless energy.

Here we come to the core of the matter. Tanila's energy is not the result of some specialised upbringing or some refined vitamin diet. She has grown up like all my other dogs—without pills and potions, without the much-valued vitamins, without any human attempt to improve the animal produced by nature. Tanila's energy is solely the product of a happy combination of hereditary qualities in her parents. And this energy was clearly visible in the very first moments of Tanila's existence.

Based on many other deliveries which I have been able to

The First Few Minutes

observe besides these two, I have reached the following conclusion: those first few minutes of a puppy's life show clearly 'what is in him'. Let me repeat: the new-born puppy is not just a small dog; it is a creature in its own right, passing through a phase of development limited in time, to which it has its own methods of adaptation. We cannot and must not judge what it does by the criteria used for a young dog two or three months old and still less by those we apply to a grown-up dog. We must therefore find some yardstick by which to judge the puppy's capacity for adaptation to the peculiar transitional phase which is one of simple mass production.

The hereditary qualities of a puppy are not simply a mixture of those of his father and mother; the two ingredients of heredity can influence each other in many ways. In our highly bred strains of dog, where close inbreeding has been resorted to, this influence may show itself in a negative sense. Degeneration processes may easily appear and these can be passed on to later generations, damage having been done to the stock of genes.

It would have been no great problem to rear Buna's puppies artificially. Suppose I had done this—Buna's breed was very popular at the time and I could have sold the puppies at a good price. Suppose that I had been a calculating salesman and had said to myself that a solitary healthy puppy was not enough. I should then have sold three puppies, all looking magnificent and all with a good pedigree. No one would have suspected that I was a swindler—a swindler both to the buyer who would have believed that he was buying a perfectly healthy well-bred dog and a swindler to the dog too!

If, within its first few minutes of life, a puppy does not do its utmost to reach one of its mother's teats, then something is wrong with it. External conditions cannot be held responsible for this. I have seen bitches give birth in a warm room or in several degrees of frost and the behaviour of the puppies was no different. Provided they were healthy and as soon as they could put their little feet to the ground, nothing mattered except this overwhelming urge to seek the source of milk.

The new-born puppy is a brisk little creature who makes it quite obvious that he is glad at last to be in the world. My splendid dingo bitches, who are unadulterated dogs of nature, do not regard giving birth as anything particularly alarming and so on several occasions I have been able to observe and photograph the actual emergence of the foetus. In some cases the membrane had already been torn before the puppy was completely in the world. Even in these few seconds the little head was waving from side to side as if already searching for the teats. At once the little mouth opened wide—the hind legs still being inside the membrane—and the first thin squeak could be heard. At this point the mother naturally wants to lick the puppy dry but he clearly finds this as tiresome as some of our children do the washing process. He does his best to evade his mother's tongue and make his way to the warmth of her body.

Adaptation to the outside world must therefore be completed during the actual process of birth, perhaps even before; the puppy does not lie there surprised or taken aback. Instead all indications are that he can hardly wait for this moment; all his energy has piled up and he is only waiting for the moment of liberation to do all that has to be done. I imagine he arrives terribly hungry and wants to fill his stomach. His movements are still very clumsy and uncoordinated but nevertheless he succeeds in making his purposeful way towards his mother's body. He clearly has a marked sensitivity to heat and cold; warmth seems to him the most desirable essential in this new phase of his life. He also has a very pronounced sense of touch which causes him to burrow his nose deep into his mother's coat as soon as he reaches it. By burrowing around he eventually discovers a teat, for which he also has an innate perceptive faculty. Here again he 'knows' what he must now do; hardly has his nose touched the teat than he sucks it deep into his little mouth and with a loud sucking noise draws out the milk.

There are two other hereditary reflexes, as those who do research into behaviour call these innate habits of movement. The first is the kneading motion, the alternate pressure against the milk gland with the two forepaws which stimulates the glands' activity. At the same time the puppy is adept at bracing his little hind legs against the floor in order to give that thrust with his muzzle which equally serves to raise the milk production.

None of this does the new-born puppy learn; he can do it already. Capacity to do something, however, is no good if one does not exercise it. This postulates a stimulus and what is that? Earlier it was thought that everything that an animal does is no more than a reaction to some external stimulus. In our case this would imply that the new-born puppy is merely reacting to the stimuli provided by its mother's body.

A perfectly simple test, however, will prove that this is not so. If, for instance, one takes a new-born puppy and places it in a box, which provides no stimuli and in which there is nothing bearing any resemblance to the body of the mother, her teats and so forth, the puppy will nevertheless do everything which I have described above. It will search around, raise its head and wave it from side to side—with such energy that the whole forequarters wriggle first to the left and then to the right; it will brace its hind legs against the floor; in short it will do everything, including giving increasingly piteous squeaks. Less obvious but always visible after a time will be the motions of sucking and kneading 'in a vacuum'. These two motions are more pronounced when carried out against the mother's body. For their full development they do need the necessary external stimulus.

This reflex means, therefore, that there exist internal motive forces which cause the puppy to make these motions so essential to its continued existence. Research into the physiology of behaviour, primarily that conducted by Konrad Lorenz and Erich von Holst, has shown that these innate forms of movement stem from the excitation of certain endocrine glands. Impulses are generated in certain centres which translate these hereditary reflexes into action. In the new-born puppy these nerve centres are in a high state of excitation and the puppy is simply forced to do all these things even though no external stimulus is present. The external stimuli, such as the warmth for which the puppy seeks, merely determine the direction in which movement takes place.

The sucking and kneading motions only become more pronounced, either when the puppy has found the source of milk or when he has been debarred from it for a long time. The reason is that, in the case of these instinctive movements, the more highly developed nerve centres constitute a blockage and the products of the excitatory glands are only released when some external stimulus is present. The external stimulus acts like a key opening a lock: all the energies are now released and visible movement results. If no key is discoverable over a considerable period, however, then excitation may build up and become so overwhelming that it breaks through the barrier and movement will take place *in vacuo*.

This, in simple language, is the explanation of the hereditary reflexes, the innate components of behaviour, the sum total of which we are apt to call instinct.

It must be remembered that some hereditary tendency, some transmitter of information, is at the root of every component of a movement. Once this has deteriorated, as can easily happen in the case of our domestic animals as a result of inbreeding, the movement will not be made correctly; alternatively the production of the excitatory glands is too small. Once damaged, genes cannot be cured; they can at best be repressed or eradicated by judicious breeding measures.

This is the reason why I regard the first few minutes of a puppy's life as so important. Actuated by no previous experience but simply and solely by the hereditary instincts implanted in him, the puppy is caused to move by his innate motive forces. We can judge fairly accurately how strong these forces are since, during the first few minutes, they are evidenced by the vivacity of movement, the energy and rapidity with which he finds a teat and begins to suck. Moreover during these first few moments the differences between the members of a litter can clearly be seen. These are differences between individuals; they have nothing to do with environment nor are they dependent upon external contingencies, learning or experience; they are simply and solely hereditary. These first few minutes offer us a possibility, never to be repeated, of estimating precisely the innate vitality of the puppy and therefore of the future dog.

If anyone wants a good new word for this puppy vitality, I recommend that coined by G. Ewald—'biotonus'; it seems to me more meaningful than the well-worn 'temperament', 'activity' or 'vitality'. Whatever one calls it, it is one of the most remarkable and impressive subjects for study.

BIRTH WEIGHT

The new-born puppy, therefore, comes into the world with a certain definite stamp of behaviour, the motive forces of which stem from the nervous system. Individual differences are detectable even in the first few seconds after emergence from the membrane. So far I have only dealt with hereditary differences in biotonus and have suggested that any biotonus deficiency should be considered as a sign of degeneration.

Might it not be, however, that in the case of a large litter—and many dogs have litters as large as twelve—or if the mother is in bad health, certain of the foetuses simply do not develop properly? One or other of the puppies might turn out to be a weakling because he had been badly placed in his mother's womb; in this case there is clearly no fault of heredity. Finally it must be remembered that during the bitch's period of heat the eggs ready for fertilisation do not descend into the oviduct all at the same time. If the bitch is covered several times, therefore, it is possible that the puppies are of slightly differing ages. Here is another possibility of differences in development not attributable to heredity.

In such cases it might be expected that post-natal behaviour would give evidence of reduced biotonus and this would not be due to heredity but governed by development.

By keeping a check on birth weight combined with biotonus, however, I have become convinced that this cannot be so. I have known puppies considerably lighter than the others of their litter at birth but which were in no way inferior to them in biotonus; they soon caught up the others in weight, unless of course they were by nature smaller built. This also happens very frequently and it is then, of course, difficult to decide during the first few hours what the trouble is. In such a case it is best to check growth by regular weighing. If, after two or three weeks, a puppy is still noticeably lighter than his brothers and sisters, he will never catch up with them. In order to maintain the prescribed size of breed, he will not be used for breeding.

I have often been asked whether one should handle a new-born puppy at all. My answer is: ask your bitch—if she bites, she does not want you to do so. Unfortunately there are in fact many bitches which, at the time of delivery and sometimes for days afterwards, display an over-developed defensive reaction and are very savage if one tries to have anything to do with their puppies. Surprisingly enough this happens more often with highly bred species than with the more primitive. My dingo bitches have never objected to my removing puppies immediately after birth. They become very agitated and try to get the little one back but they have never become savage.

My view is that there should be sufficient confidence between dog and man that no difficulties should arise when one examines the puppies. I think that bitches which bite their master or mistress if they touch the puppies are not normal but hysterical; they should not be used for further breeding in order to check this unfortunate tendency.

Let us suppose, therefore, that we are present at the birth of some puppies, have a pair of scales ready and, one after another, place the puppies upon them. They can be perfectly ordinary kitchen scales; accuracy to within a gram is quite enough.

Most people know how to dintinguish between dog and bitch puppies; anyone who wants to make doubly sure can do so from two of the sketches in this book. Further differentiation between puppies may be difficult—if all are uniformly black, for instance. It will help if small marks are made at a suitable spot in the coat with a fine pair of scissors. If there are only two dogs in the litter or two bitches, then, of course, it is enough to mark one of them. If there are three puppies of the same sex, one remains unmarked, one is marked on the left side and the other on the right. It is really not much trouble!

Obviously we have ready a sheet of paper on which we can enter everything quickly, with date and name of bitch at the top. It is best to have a separate sheet for each puppy. This allows adequate space for subsequent weighings and also for such things as: time of birth, estimate of biotonus, special markings (or mark made) and birth weight.

Time of birth is required, not so that we can cast the puppy's horoscope but because we thus record the intervals at which the puppies come into the world. This tells us something about the breeding value of the bitch (more of this in the final chapter of this book). The estimate of biotonus can be made by a simple system of allotting marks. If a puppy makes active efforts to find the source of milk immediately on emergence from the membrane or even struggles while still inside it, he earns a One. The puppy which lies still for a time before becoming active gets a Two. The puppy which tries to reach its mother's body but cannot manage to find a teat and has to be placed in position before he begins to suck, gets a Three. So does the puppy which only sucks for a short time and then gives up. As for the Four—we hardly need note him down; any sensible breeder will put so inactive a puppy to sleep; he would anyway die within twenty-four hours.

Now we enter the birth weights and compare them. Differences of ten or twenty grams can be disregarded; they tell us nothing

The different sexes (Björn and Bente aged two days)

and are entirely normal except in the case of miniature dogs with an average birth weight of 50 grams. In that case a very small difference may be significant but anyone breeding such dogs is likely to be an experienced breeder who needs no advice from me.

If there are considerable differences in weight within a litter, one must consider, of course, whether to keep alive the puppies with too low a birth weight. If, for instance, five of a litter weigh between 395 and 430 grams but the sixth puppy only 315, there is no need to think for long, even if the estimate of biotonus is good. So under-weight a puppy must be put to sleep.

Let us now look at a concrete case chosen from my records, because it is in many ways highly informative (table of weights on p. 70). This was my fourth litter from my elkhound Binna, then four years old. The father was once more Björn, her own son by the dingo Abo. The litter, consisting of three dogs and three bitches, was born between 12.55 and 3.18 p.m.; whelping therefore took 2 hours 23 minutes, a normal time for Binna. In the attached table only four puppies are shown since I made a certain selection and put two to sleep immediately on birth.

The remaining four were weighed again twelve hours later. With the exception of No 115 all had lost a little. This is quite normal. In the first place, at the initial weighing the puppies are still wet and at the second weighing dry—this makes quite a difference. Secondly the milk produced by the bitch during the first two days has a slight purgative effect and with healthy puppies much of the meconium—the residue left in the gut from the gestation period—is evacuated. A puppy will only put on weight at this stage if he absorbs an abnormal quantity of milk or is slow in clearing his gut.

Next day, another twelve hours later, three of the puppies had put on weight; only the second bitch was still 5 grams below her birth weight. On the other hand she had initially lost most of all and so she needed a little longer to catch up; there was nothing to worry about here.

Since I wished to keep a specially accurate check on this litter, I weighed once more that day, some thirty-six hours after birth. This showed that the two dogs and bitch No 2 had put on weight satisfactorily but bitch No 1 was still 11 grams below her birth weight. Usually this is enough for me to put a puppy to sleep; moreover my notes showed that this bitch had a biotonus rating of −2. In this case, however, I decided to see what would happen with a puppy like this. The bitch did not exceed her birth weight until the fourth day; she then continued to gain less than the other three puppies, reached her maximum weight on the seventh day, then fluctuated and by the eleventh day had sunk to 433 grams, only 8 grams over her birth weight. She lay completely inert beside her large brothers and sister, looked exactly as she had at birth and had no further prospect of living; she hardly moved at all; if one placed her on a teat she would suck lifelessly two or three times and then relapse again—a piteous sight. She would undoubtedly have died within the next twenty-four hours had I not put her to sleep.

By the end of this first phase of existence a puppy should quadruple his birth weight. Checking against this litter, it will be seen that dog No 1 reached the required 1648 grams on the evening of Day 20, dog No 2 his 1396 grams between Days 17 and 18 and the bitch her scheduled 1464 grams on Day 23.

It should be observed that dog No 2's birth weight was extremely low; his biotonus rating, however, was very good; he accordingly put on weight rapidly to catch up his brother, which he had done, more or less, by Day 17. This, therefore, confirms what I have already said about differences in birth weight: a healthy puppy will catch up the rest of his litter if the difference is not too great. Conversely the bitch was clearly going to remain small, nothing unusual if the parents are mother and son. This bitch, however, did not become a miniature like Stina who comes of the same parentage.

THE VEGETATION PHASE

It is convenient to divide the puppy's further development into 'phases', although I agree with the reader that the word is neither very pretty nor very good terminologically. It is a practical word, however, and it has now become customary with the dog experts concerned with youthful canine development. Obviously all the timings given in this connection are averages only and may be longer or shorter depending on the early or late development of the dog concerned.

For some people the criteria for a dog's behaviour are merely the term used and the development of his method of locomotion, but if we wish really to understand, we must follow his development from puppy to full-grown dog. In this way not only shall we progress from the simple to the more complex, but we shall also realise how we should behave towards the growing dog, what we

The Puppy's First Weeks

Mill Canine Research Establishment
16 June 1970
Fourth litter from Elkhound bitch BINNA
by half-breed dog BJÖRN

Registered number and sex	R 113*	R 115*	H 117*	H 118*
Time of birth	13.45	15.08	12.55	13.07
Birth weight (grams)	412	349	425	366
Biotonus rating	1+	1	−2	1
12 hours	408	353	415	348
24 hours	419	376	426	361
36 hours	439	397	414	377
Day 2	463	422	420	387
Day 3	511	483	420	414
Day 4	573	530	427	450
Day 5	617	580	454	492
Day 6	652	644	450	534
Day 7	717	682	479	584
Day 8	789	765	447	642
Day 9	830	807	468	687
Day 10	879	857	474	714
Day 11	939	906	433**	764
Day 12	1012	972		817
Day 13	1102	1034		870
Day 14	1227	1127		922
Day 15	1255	1195		957
Day 16	1362	1289		1050
Day 17	1366	1368		1097
Day 18	1454	1429		1152
Day 19	1564	1509		1243
Day 20	1630	1610		1280
Day 21	1702	1678		1325
Day 22	1787	1789		1412
Day 23	1840	1822		1477
Day 24	1870	1905		1525
Day 25	No weight check made			
Day 26	1997	1975		1605
Day 27	No weight check made			
Day 28	2057	2059		1692

* R = dog, H = bitch   ** Puppy H 117 put to sleep on Day 11

Methods of Locomotion 71

can demand of him at various phases of his life and what we cannot. We shall then be in a position to be to the full-grown dog what every dog-lover would like to be: a master or mistress to whom the dog is devoted.

By doing this we shall also be able to see how the canine parents behave to their children and we can learn much from this. I would emphasise that in this case I mean both the bitch *and* the dog. All my puppies live a proper family life. This is most unusual since practically all our well-bred dogs grow up in fatherless families. Even experienced dog-breeders, when they saw the father-dogs playing with their puppies in my pens, have asked me whether the dog did not eat his children. This idea is so firmly established that many people have been unwilling to believe that the system works very well even after seeing it with their own eyes.

Since the breeder normally gets rid of his puppies at eight weeks, the fact that they have been reared in a fatherless family is no tragedy. But this presupposes that man will so gear his behaviour as to do that which the canine father would normally do. Admittedly most of the established rules for bringing up small dogs accord very well with what I like to describe as the canine parents' 'educational methods'. Most of these rules have been laid down by experienced dog-breeders because they have proved efficacious. Moreover, by observing the complete canine family, we can learn why we should do things in a certain way and no other and also see much which we could perhaps do better or have not thought of. Even if we learn nothing, however, observation of a normal canine family is an exciting experience and is worth while if for no other reason than the pleasure derived from it. Sometimes, for instance, I see my good Björn lying on the roof of his kennel and gazing down with interest on his little daughter who is trying to catch his twitching tail which he has deliberately left dangling there. On such occasions I find it easy to forget that I am theoretically carrying out research into behaviour, the strict rules of which forbid any 'humanisation of the animal'. All I see is a loving father and a playful daughter.

METHODS OF LOCOMOTION

Nature has given the puppy everything essential for his first few weeks; more or less everything else is left on one side. For fourteen days—the duration of the first phase—there is little change apart from an increase in size and weight. The mother's solicitude compensates for any deficiencies in his physical or behavioural equipment; he is entirely suited to remain in the little depression which is his nest.

The lateral searching movements of a new-born dingo puppy (not yet licked dry)

The two main functions of the puppy are drinking and sleeping. He must therefore be able to move far enough and efficiently enough to be able to drink. Certain defined methods of locomotion are available to him. As I have already explained, they are all inborn capabilities.

To achieve motion the puppy lies on his stomach in a fore-and-aft posture; he is thus able to crawl in both directions. It would be nonsensical, however, if he just crawled straight ahead since he might be setting off in a totally wrong direction. Against this he has two safeguards. A puppy never crawls in a straight line but in a small circle which brings him back to the starting point of his wanderings if he has not encountered his mother's body on the way. The litter-box being narrow, the probability that he will fail to find his mother is small; this again shows the value of the small depression in which the wild puppy is born, since it is difficult for him to leave the centre of the nest. We reproduce the natural conditions better if the litter-box is arranged so that its floor is not completely flat but forms a shallow depression. This presents no problem with present-day artificial heat-retaining materials.

The second safeguard which ensures that the puppy will arrive at his destination is his automatic search mechanism. The puppy swings his head fairly regularly from side to side as the three photographs, sketches of which are given here, show (read from the top downwards). The puppy is therefore 'probing' quite an area of his surroundings and, since the bitch, lying on her side, occupies most of the nest, this side-to-side probe is generally enough to bring the puppy up against some part of the mother's body.

THE SENSES

The puppy, therefore, possesses quite a considerable armoury of equipment for motion and all the methods of locomotion provide an opportunity of checking what we have called the biotonus. The point is: how active is the use made by the puppy of his various capabilities? It may not be possible to obtain a precise picture merely by looking into the litter-box; one puppy may be lucky and be lying so near a teat that he simply has to catch hold of it, while another may have quite a distance to cover. The effect of chance can be eliminated by a simple test. After weighing a puppy I lay it on the table and see what it does. If it crawls about actively with a marked head motion both vertically and horizontally, if it turns over quickly when I lay it on its back and if it recoils violently when in contact with cold glass or metal, then all is in order. A puppy which just lies there and waits to be picked up will not be viable.

Having got the puppy on the table, however, another test can be made. Place near him a heating pad warmed to about blood temperature. A healthy puppy will make strenuous efforts to reach

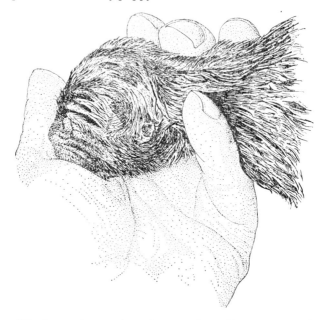

The burrowing motion of a new-born dingo puppy. His muzzle pushes upwards from below into the fold of skin between forefinger and thumb

it; this means that he can perceive warmth and that his impulse to seek for warmth is fully developed.

As soon as the puppy touches the heating pad with his muzzle, another instinctive motion should take place, that of burrowing into the mother's coat. The puppy will press the tip of his muzzle against the heating pad and then move it directly upwards for a

The Senses

short way; this he will do repeatedly. He will also do it to one's hand provided that it is warm; if the hand is cupped so that the puppy's muzzle penetrates between thumb and palm, the energy he uses can be judged. If presented with a smooth hard surface—metal or wood, for instance—he will not make this burrowing motion, even if the surface is warm. This shows that he has a proper sense of touch and can recognise something soft. The significance of the motion becomes clear at once if the puppies are watched when against their mother's body. The puppy's muzzle burrows into the bitch's coat and is then thrust upwards, thus raising the hair; in this way the puppy will discover a teat even if

Head of a two-day-old puppy with mouth open and tongue in the 'sucking position'

hidden in the mother's coat—and for the first one or two puppies it always will be. The energy and persistence displayed in burrowing is another valuable indication that the puppy has been born healthy. As soon as a puppy has one of his mother's teats in his mouth, he begins to suck. Each sucking motion is actuated by a neuro-hormonal mechanism, a reflex involving not only the passage of nerve impulses up the spinal cord to the brain but also the release of a hormone from a region in the brain.

It might be thought that, at this stage, the sense of smell was as superfluous to the puppy as sight or hearing. Troshinin, the

Russian physiologist, however, has proved by a very simple test that puppies have a sense of smell immediately on birth. Troshinin took several bitches, carefully washed their teats and rubbed them with menthol oil just before they were due to whelp. The new-born puppies, knowing no better, sucked quite happily at the teats so treated. After they had taken their first fill, the teats were washed again and now, when they next became hungry, the puppies were unable to find the teats. This means that on the very first occasion when they sucked, their mother's teats became associated with a certain smell; a connection was established in their brains between 'a good suck' and 'teat smell'—so a teat which did not smell could not be a teat. The puppy has no innate sense of what a teat

Head of a new-born dingo puppy. Eyes and ear orifices still closed

should smell like; he merely knows that it has a definite smell. If this were not so, no puppy would ever become accustomed to a rubber teat. On the other hand the smell must not be too penetrating or unpleasant. A puppy does not like concentrated aniseed, for instance; he will turn away in disgust and try to get away. If you present him with a fish, however, he will probe round to see whether he can find anywhere to suck. The puppy is therefore capable of differentiating between smells.

According to our ideas the sense of smell is linked with that of taste; we all know how tasteless the best food can be when one has a bad cold and one's nose is out of action. In the case of the dog with his highly developed sense of smell, this applies even more forcibly; his sense of taste seems to be governed primarily by his ability to smell. Dogs with no nose cannot distinguish between pieces of bread and similarly shaped lumps of mud. New-born puppies have very little sense of taste; from a bottle they will take in turn sugared milk, unsweetened tea or anything else they are presented with. For them, therefore, dog's milk carries no taste or smell for which they have an innate predilection, and they should not become addicted to any particular taste. It will then be easy to rear puppies artificially whether from birth or after they have been some time with their mother. In the latter case the problem is to accustom them to a rubber teat after they have been used to those of their mother which, for them, carry a well-known smell.

We should now consider the puppy's means of protecting himself against threats from outside. As I have already said, he will recoil from certain things which feel or smell unpleasant to him. Susceptibility to pain is also, of course, important as a means of protection. A puppy will stand a great deal and his sensitivity to pain is not particularly marked; if you squeeze him too hard, however, he will feel this and will not only try to get away but make his voice heard. This serves as a distress signal to the mother, as an expression of displeasure and pain, but possibly also of pleasure.

The voice is linked with the breathing apparatus. A word should be added here: immediately on emergence from the membrane the puppy is to be seen opening his little mouth wide, pushing his tongue right out and moving it from side to side. This may be repeated once or twice. This signifies his first intake of air and it is quickly followed by the first thin cry. In this way the breathing channels are freed. Afterwards the puppy breathes through his nose, his little mouth being required primarily for drinking.

SUCKING

In this connection the word 'sucking' must not be taken too literally. A puppy's suck is in fact a 'lick-suck'; he licks with his tongue which forms a channel in his mouth and is grooved round the bottom and sides of the teat. The tongue thus squeezes and massages the teat—at a rate of twenty times a second.

There is, in fact, an innate rhythm of the sucking mechanism geared to the milk yield of the canine teat. Numerous tests of this relationship have been made, particularly by American scientists; the most interesting results, I think, have been produced by D. M. Levy. He divided a litter of collies into three groups; the first remained with the mother, the second was brought up on a bottle with a very small teat aperture, and third equally on a bottle but the teat had a very large aperture. The result was that the puppies in this last group had not worked off their automatic sucking reaction; they would suck on anything within reach—a finger or the ears of their brothers or sisters. This means that the number of licking motions and the degree of satiety are innately geared to each other. If the puppy gets too much milk and therefore reaches satiety too soon because the aperture of the teat is too large, a number of 'lick-suck' motions remain which have not fulfilled their function and which must therefore be worked off either *'in vacuo'* or on substitute objects.

Freud, as we know, has shown that with small children, particularly those brought up on a bottle, there is a relationship between satisfaction of the impulse to suck and thumb-sucking. Recent investigations, those of Detlev Ploog for instance, have shown that in the case of premature satiety resulting from too large a teat aperture, puppies continued to suck *in vacuo* and began to squeak; they only became content when they could make good their requirement to suck by doing so on the empty bottle.

If it is necessary to bring up a puppy on the bottle, then the relationship between the automatic sucking mechanism and the quantity of milk absorbed, or alternatively the ease of extraction from the teat, becomes of importance. We may do the puppy permanent damage if we make things too easy for him. It is quite simple to test whether his sucking requirement has been satisfied: after he has drunk, place the tip of a finger in his mouth; if the quantity of milk absorbed is in harmony with the amount of sucking done, he will take no interest in the finger. If he has been sated too soon because the teat aperture is too large, then he will try to suck the tip of the finger. Sucking *in vacuo*, like thumb-sucking in children, can lead to bad habits such as 'wind-sucking' and this can be seen in dogs long since full-grown. It is not inevitable but it can happen.

Another puppy habit closely connected with sucking is the kneading motion of which we have already spoken. When sucking, puppies use their forefeet in turn to knead the area of the teat and so continuously stimulate the milk glands. This motion is so closely connected with sucking that it is safe to say that no dog sucks without kneading.

The puppy would be unable to knead with his forefeet or thrust with his muzzle unless he could brace his hind legs firmly against the floor. This is another very characteristic puppy motion; if the floor is smooth the little fat hind legs are permanently in action trying to find support. They push the puppy's whole body firmly up against the belly of the bitch and are a decisive factor in reaching—and maintaining—this position. This is clearly to be seen, for instance, when the puppies of a litter are struggling with each other in order to reach the teats. Frequently it is a brutal and ruthless battle; sometimes one of the puppies is pushed aside in the general trample to find some hind leg support.

Naturally it is not really right to use the word 'ruthless'; these tiny puppies do not yet realise that their brothers and sisters exist; they can have no feeling for them. I would even say that the more 'brutal' one of these little people is during his first fortnight, the more confidently can one visualise his future. The stronger, more powerful and healthier dogs become the best companions. The eagerness with which he sucks is the outward and visible sign of the puppy's basic energy.

Now a word about the nursing habits of the mother. During the first two days she hardly stirs from the litter-box and fusses over her little ones almost all the time. The puppies initially feed about every two hours and woe to anyone who does not allow the bitch to return to her children in good time—if one takes her for a walk for instance. She will be almost beside herself in her haste to get home to ensure that they do not have to wait too long for their food. During their mother's absence, however, the puppies are perfectly peaceful. When their mother goes out, they huddle together and sleep. They do not move until the she-wolf—or bitch—returns. If the mother is away a long time, the puppies do not crawl about the nest squeaking—another wonderful disposition of nature, for it would give away the position of the nest. If the mother never comes back, the little creatures die painlessly; sleep soon turns into coma and then into unconsciousness. Not until the puppies are older and have already left the lair do they become vocal when hungry. But by this time they are able to react immediately and hide if there is a suspicious noise or strangers approach.

In any case, during this first phase of the puppies' development the bitch has a great deal to do. She is continually sniffing them all over to see that all is well. Then she cleans their coats with her tongue. Finally she massages the fat little stomachs and so stimulates the digestion; she immediately consumes both the solid and liquid products thereof, for the nest must be kept clean.

THE PUPPIES TOGETHER

Puppies live in their nest and nestlings are pronounced egoists because, in their little world, nothing exists except their own requirements. One of the requirements is sleep. If we look into their box, we shall usually see all the puppies asleep at the same time. They just lie peacefully in their nest huddled against their brothers and sisters. Sometimes the soundly sleeping bitch sighs; now and again one of the little ones lets out a squeak of discontent because he has accidentally slipped away from his mother's belly and finds his new position uncomfortable. After a time one of the puppies wakes, stretches himself with a yawn and makes his way up to a teat. This he finds in the way we already know and he begins to suck with a loud smacking noise. If we look into the box a few minutes later, we shall find all the puppies attached to a teat. Why do they all do it at the same time? People often talk of the infectious desire to suck. This I am prepared to concede in the case of puppies which are in some form of family contact with each other but, as we shall see, this does not happen until the end of the first three weeks. In his first fortnight the puppy has no relationship of any sort with his brothers and sisters. He does not know that they or others of his breed exist; he is a solitary little being with no relationship to anybody.

There are two explanations for the fact that all the puppies of a litter feed at the same time. The first is that it is a chain reaction. The first puppy to wake works his way to a teat. As he thrashes about he is almost certain to wake at least one of his brothers or sisters. Since all the puppies are sleeping as close as possible to, if not half on, their mother's belly, as he braces his hind legs he is fairly certain to tread on one of the others. That puppy then wakes up, naturally feels hungry, works his way to a teat, waking one of the others in the process—and so on.

The second explanation is the scent of milk which probably also has something to do with the fact that the puppies wake about the same time.

The fact that the puppies lie in a heap does not mean that they desire company. It is simply that a puppy requires to lie up against something, as is proved by the fact that he will be quite happy with any suitable substitute object.

The puppy's requirement for warmth certainly also has something to do with the fact that they sleep huddled together, but it should not be concluded from this that they must under all circumstances be kept very warm. Their body temperature at birth is very low and the number of red corpuscles in their blood is far smaller than in a full-grown dog; they have a 'variable temperature'—almost like reptiles, though fluctuations are not so violent. If they become very cold when the mother leaves the nest, this does no damage provided they are warmed again on her return; their own heat generation is very small. If they get very cold their activity is reduced and they sleep.

One morning Alfred Seitz found outside the hut in which one of his dingo bitches had her litter-box, a tiny puppy apparently lying dead in the snow. He placed it in the box against the bitch, it 'thawed out' and was as healthy and lively as the rest of the litter. I have seen bitches give birth in a simple depression in the ground in several degrees of frost; this and other experiences confirm that the absolute warmth-requirement of the new-born puppy is very low and that the heat provided by the mother's body is quite enough to ensure that the puppy thrives. Were this not so, dogs would build nests offering some protection, in the same way as mice, for instance, cover their young up if they leave the nest in cold weather.

THE TRANSITIONAL PHASE

Acquisition of the senses of hearing and sight marks the beginning of the transition from the initial puppy stage to that of young dog. The suckling confined to the nest turns into an infant dog, sufficiently developed to make genuine contacts with the outside world. As with many biological processes, it is hardly possible to draw a sharp dividing line. For this reason J. P. Scott, the American socio-biologist who has conducted research into canine behaviour, refers to a transitional phase between the two stages of existence. During this period physiological and behavioural development leads to a gradual change; the new abilities can be seen developing on different time scales both in the same puppy and between puppies.

The opening of the eye-slit marks the beginning of this transitional phase. The process may take twenty-four hours and one eye may open somewhat earlier than the other. Much has been written to show how large individual differences in timing can be. According to some accounts puppies have been known to open their eyes on the ninth day while others may not do so until the nineteenth day. Both these timings are, of course, exceptional; in most cases the eyes open between the twelfth and fifteenth day. Eisfeld observed two jackal cubs which opened their eyes on Days 10 and 11 and two others which did so on Day 14.

It should not be forgotten that the puppies of a litter are not usually all of precisely the same age but that their periods of gestation may be different; differences in age up to eight days have been known. This is even more noticeable during the first fortnight. A puppy which does not open his eyes until the fifteenth or sixteenth day, therefore, need not be classified as a late developer, though he may be. In any case we should make precise notes of such details and also observe with care further developments in behaviour during the transitional phase. Combined with a regular weight check, this will tell us much about the qualities of our puppies.

The opening of the eyes does not mean that the puppy can yet see. The pupils react and the watery light-blue eyes can move. All is very uncoordinated, however; most puppies squint horribly, giving them a particularly 'dumb' expression. At first sight one is apt to think that they are defective. It is possible to check when a puppy can actually see by holding a torch close to his eyes; if he retreats when it is lighted or otherwise reacts against it, then we know that he can now see. Capacity for sight should in any case be fully developed by Day 21.

Hearing is not as a rule developed much before the twenty-first day. Then the puppy will react to noise either by movements of the ears or, far more definitely, by recoiling and showing fear (crawling away). We should always remember that for the puppy, which has come from a silent world into the world of noise, any new sound—a bang, a shout, rushing water, etc.—must initially be sinister. We should take care not to frighten him deliberately, for there is a distinct danger that fear of a certain noise may be

Puppies aged twenty-three days biting at each other

implanted in the animal for ever. The dog is as susceptible as the human being to the shock effects of frightening experiences when young.

THE NOSE

The earliest sense to develop is that of smell. By the 16th, 17th or 18th day the puppy can be seen snuffling around his brothers and sisters; he will snuffle at a finger held close to the nose. He is thus beginning to take cognisance of his surroundings and, since the dog is a 'scenting animal', it is not surprising that the nose should be the first organ to become operative. For the full-grown dog the world is composed of sensations gathered primarily through the nose rather than the eyes or ears. We depend upon our eyes but the dog upon his nose and he collects most of his information from the currents of air which pass across his nasal membranes.

The normal dog will be told by his nose as much about his

surroundings as we are told by our eyes assisted by field glasses and a magnifying glass. How many of our highly bred strains of dog, however, bred for good looks—or what are supposed to be good looks—have been deprived of their most important capability, the sense of smell! A dog with a poor nose experiences nothing. He goes through life like a man nearly blind; the man is in fact better off since he has a highly developed brain which can bring the world alive for him by its power of thought and imagination. For the dog, however, the world around him is reduced to a few crude impressions; admittedly he still has his eyes and ears but, even if fully efficient, they do not produce for him a picture of his surroundings as complete as does his nose. The whole canine brain is geared to deal with sensations gathered by the organ of smell and it is these which form his real existence—which we must allow the dog to have. Eyes and ears are auxiliaries only, like the ears and even more so the nose in our case. We are, as the expression goes, optically orientated; all our thoughts and ideas spring from visual experiences. The dog's orientation is olfactory; his mental processes are based on 'smell pictures' as those of the dolphin are based on 'hearing pictures'. The close connection between these differing brain functions and the products of the senses is shown by the fact that we are compelled to refer to 'smell *pictures*'; highly developed though our brain is, we have no other way of expressing the idea. Even the blind man, who works on his sense of touch, mentally turns the impressions gained into pictures because his brain is geared to the sense of sight, is 'optically orientated' in other words.

How is it that the sporting fraternity can tell such astonishing stories about their dogs' intelligence? The restaurant tales of Sunday sportsmen can be disregarded but the old forester, who in the last analysis is dependent on the efficiency of his dog, can be relied on. More or less all sporting dogs are bred for nose; the greatest importance is attached to a highly developed sense of smell. With such dogs it may be expected that they will use their brain to produce intelligent action and in some cases the intelligence is truly astounding.

If a dog with a reasonably well-developed nose spends all day in a house where he knows the scents so well that he is bored with them, if he is merely trotted round the corner as often as necessary, he is getting nothing out of life. We have our work and our problems; we go to the cinema, look at pictures, read newspapers or books; we telephone to people or meet friends. But how many dogs live in prisons, in an environment offering no stimulus, in which there is nothing to enliven their existence? Obviously the dog needs physical exercise, his little runs or proper walks; but he needs mental exercise even more. The importance of the walk to him is not so much the exercise involved but the opportunity for adventure. For him the world is so full of scents, a glorious variegated carpet of scent lines, scent circles, scent waves, scent boundaries or however else it may look—or rather smell—to a dog.

It is worth quoting some figures produced by physiological research into the canine senses. In the first place it can be proved that, since he is carnivorous, a dog's nose is far more sensitive to animal matter than to vegetable. A dog can detect, for instance, the minute quantity of two milligrams of meat essence and he will react to five milligrams of a bitch's urine; he can detect acid in a solution one hundred million times weaker than that detectable by man. Compared to such accomplishments we are literally 'smell-blind'.

The structure of the dog's organ of smell is therefore naturally complicated. In the upper part of the nose is a membrane in which the olfactory receptors lie; each receptor has a nerve which enters the olfactory bulb of the brain. In the case of man the size of this membrane is approximately that of the narrow side of a matchbox (slightly under 1 sq. in.); in an alsatian it is the size of nine matchboxes side by side (an average of 25 sq. ins.). The membrane is also considerably thicker in the dog (0.003 of an inch) than in man (0.002 of an inch). These are the anatomical characteristics which provide the dog with his excellent sense of smell; he is a 'great olfactor'.

HEREDITARY REFLEXES AND POWER OF LEARNING

As far as movement is concerned, the initial stomach-crawl develops into a genuine crawl and thence to a real running motion. This throws valuable light on development of the instinctive movements; the gradual growth of the movement mechanism develops in parallel with instinctive reflexes connected with motion; practice is a further factor. While initially the puppies do nothing but feed and sleep, during the third week an increasing requirement for motion is to be seen. The puppies begin to move aimlessly about the nest—it can only really be called motion because one knows that it must be, and very shortly will become, genuine movement. A real running motion, however, would never develop unless the impulses from the puppy's nervous system gave him an urge to test and exercise his growing capacity for movement.

Other activities follow a similar course. The main stimulus for all this is what we call curiosity. Curiosity is the stimulus for all learning. Under natural conditions the dog has a life-long desire to learn—and it must be maintained; it is the prerequisite for survival.

Curiosity stirs about the 16th–18th day, obviously in connection with the sense of smell. If the tiny puppy was not curious to know how something smells, he would not use his nose. In fact the greater his curiosity, the more he learns and the more he becomes acquainted with the happenings and conditions of the world around him. The puppy's behaviour towards the end of his third week, therefore, will give some indication whether he will be a 'star' or whether he will merit the notation 'born dumb and has learnt nothing'. Of course he may be a late developer who will not 'spark' until the following week. The time at which this happens is perhaps not so important as the degree of curiosity which he shows.

The degree of inquisitiveness is therefore what we are trying to observe and very soon we shall find a great deal to see. First, the puppy will snuffle at everything—his mother, his brothers and sisters, the litter-box or master's hand. Then the tongue comes into action and everything has to be licked—including his own paws. Finally the puppy will gnaw at everything which can be gnawed. During this process he learns among other things that there is no object in sitting in front of the side of the box and trying to gnaw it—the smooth surface will not go into his mouth. Much more fun is to be had, however, with the ear or nose of one of his little brothers.

And now he learns another lesson: his brothers and sisters do the same and, if one lays hold of an ear, the owner of it starts to do

Hereditary Reflexes and Power of Learning

all sorts of things. He tries to withdraw the ear, he strikes out with his paw and finally he squeals angrily. The puppy discovers that his own ear can be seized and that this is uncomfortable. It is exciting to sit nose to nose and open your little mouths wide. If you are quicker than the other fellow, you can catch his nose and he will squeal. If he opens his mouth too, however, then you can try to catch him by the lower jaw; since he is doing the same thing, you have an amusing romp. It is fun as long as you do not get caught by the other fellow.

Signs of pleasure can now be given quite clearly. The little short tail waggles like a duck's rump and soon this will turn into proper tail-wagging.

All these movements—pawing, the beginnings of the biting game and snuffling around—are done in slow motion; they look extremely comic and deliberate. The eyes still react very slowly; the puppy will gaze at something which interests him for a long time before fumbling with it. It is all very amateur and immature.

As far as noises are concerned, there is now less squeaking, presumably because the puppy's increased capacity for movement allows him to avoid unpleasing situations. By the end of the third week he has learnt to growl but not yet to bark. If one is not on terms with the puppies by this time, they will retreat into the furthest corner of the kennel when one puts one's head in to look at them and growl savagely and menacingly. This is, of course, ridiculous since growling is associated with the threat to bite at any moment. The puppies, however, are quite incapable of biting and, if one now puts a hand out to them, they will flatten themselves against the corner of their box paralysed in terror or alternatively they will squeal loudly.

By the end of the third week the puppy is beginning to gnaw at everything he can find; his incisors are beginning to grow and the needle-sharp milk-teeth are dropping out, as one can discover by inserting a finger into his mouth. The puppies will gnaw at pieces of meat although they are not yet able really to eat them. Instead the mother will regurgitate semi-digested food which they will gobble up greedily. During this period I think it best to give the mother special food rather than try to feed the puppies. Very good puppy-food is to be had, and anyone possessing a bitch whose maternal instincts fail in this respect should use these foods. But the supplementary nourishment which nature provides for the little ones is the mush regurgitated by the mother. She should therefore be given a varied diet rich in protein and fat. Fat is clearly of great importance for a dog. I have seen a bitch—and a dingo bitch guided by instinct—eat not very fresh-smelling pony grease in preference to sweet-smelling horseflesh and then regurgitate it for her puppies. When I then presented these puppies, which were twenty-four days old, with small pieces of meat and lumps of yellow grease, they fell upon the grease with enthusiasm. Beef suet is very suitable and also fat from the smaller animals—sheep, rabbits or hens. The bitch will also turn offal such as the heart, liver or kidneys into a first-class nourishing porridge. Carbohydrates should be fed sparingly—as always when feeding dogs. They produce well-covered but fat puppies. At this point the bitch should be given numbers of small animals such as mice to eat since this most nearly reproduces the natural conditions. It is not possible for everyone, however, to follow this back-to-nature rule.

The regurgitation of food creates a new relationship, not only between the mother and her puppies but also between them and the father. It is not generally known that the dog takes part in the feeding and there is often real competition between the parents. A touching story is told of 'Trigger' and 'Lady', a pair of wolves some ten months old, reared by the Crislers, a husband-and-wife team engaged on research in the remotest parts of Alaska. These two wolves brought up some wild puppies; although totally inexperienced and quite young themselves, the sight of these little new arrivals aroused in them a maternal instinct normally only associated with highly domesticated animals. They would go twenty miles to find food for the little creatures. Each of the pair vied with the other to be the first to produce food. Erik Zimen once told me that his first she-wolf would regurgitate food for younger wolf cubs when she was only four months old—and she could not have learnt this habit since she had been taken from her mother when very young and brought up on a bottle. Many of our present-day bitches, and even more dogs, have lost this instinctive reaction.

The young—whether wolf-cubs, jackal cubs or dog puppies—make begging gestures to cause their parents to regurgitate for

Hereditary Reflexes and Power of Learning

them, stubbing their noses over and over again against the corner of their father's or mother's mouth. Dog puppies will do this from Day 22 onwards.

It is of interest that this begging gesture is made, not against some indeterminate portion of the parent's mouth but always against the corner. There may be some connection here with the puppy's habit of yawning. If one strokes the corner of a three- or four-week-old puppy's mouth with a finger, he will open his little jaws wide and give a great yawn. It may be that the stimulus provided by the puppy's nose at the corner of the parent's mouth causes the latter to open his or her mouth and regurgitate food.

This thrust of the muzzle into the corner of the mouth and the regurgitation of food are of definite significance in the puppy's development as a creature which lives a communal existence; this will be dealt with further in the next chapter. Towards the end of the transitional phase the puppy's begging gesture must be regarded as the reaction of a gregarious animal; it is a request designed to lead to the bestowal of some favour. It is an action entirely distinct from the kneading or thrusting against the milk glands which are completely instinctive and unconscious. It is, of course, perfectly conceivable that this begging gesture is merely a development of the thrust against the teat, directed to a different spot as experience has shown to be profitable. We shall be referring later to a similar transformation of the kneading motion.

5 Imprint for Life

When the puppy first leaves the nest a new phase of life begins; it lasts until about the end of the third month. The first three weeks spent in the seclusion of the nest were a sort of continuation of life in the womb, although under entirely new conditions. Now the puppy begins actively to wrestle with the world. For the first time he really sees daylight.

This first excursion into the wide world, however, is not all pure joy. Their father in fact shows them that life outside is by no means so comfortable and happy as in the security of the nest. He does not, of course, mean it seriously and is in the best of humours —but the effect is considerable. In the happiest and most playful mood he bounds from puppy to puppy, seizes each one by the scruff of its neck and tosses it around like a ball until eventually it turns over on its back squealing to high heaven. If the dog then leaves it alone, it crawls hastily back to the kennel; there at least it is safe from its father's rough methods of play. Soon all the puppies are back in their box after their first excursion. Woe to the puppy, however, which shows any sign of weakness at this moment; if, for instance, it has not developed or cannot make the innate gesture of submission, if it is not astute enough or strong enough to escape its father's playful pursuit and make its way back to the kennel, it is lost. The father will go on playing with it until all its strength is exhausted. The mother does not come out to fetch it back. She no longer recognises the puppy which does not return to feed. So for many a puppy Day 21 is the last of its life. It is a decisive day in the puppy's life when a selection is made which undoubtedly has much influence on maintenance of an hereditarily strong and healthy breed.

This entry into the great world, although initially perhaps restricted to a short period daily, implies for the puppy a complete fresh orientation. So far his existence was 'automatically' regulated; the alternation between intake of nourishment and rest proceeded in an orderly manner governed by the puppy's innate habits and the mother's nursing arrangements. Now all at once, almost with violence, thousands of new things impinge on the puppy. He finds old bones, dead leaves, pieces of stick, stones and sand; he experiences wind, rain-drops and the warmth of the sun; shadows move just like his brothers and sisters but they cannot be caught. The parents come and go; they rest and allow him to play with them. All this and much else penetrates through the senses into the little brain where it is processed. In the wild—and we must start from the natural state if we are to learn the background to canine behaviour—there are also great dangers. Just as the puppy first learnt to run away from its father and make its way back to security, now it is essential to run from danger and always be on the watch.

To give a single illustration—the puppy must now observe its parents' behaviour. From the outset the little creatures know the meaning of a soft sneezing noise from their parents; it means: Look out! Back into the lair at once.

Eisfeld's term for this 'warning sneeze' is 'panting' but then, in the case of the jackal, he describes it as 'a short sharp sneeze'; my dingoes make precisely this noise whenever a stranger approaches their pen; in the next second all the puppies have vanished. The movement of the head is similar to that made with a genuine sneeze, as if it was caused by some irritation of the nasal membranes. By a process of thought transference the smell of a dangerous animal such as a bear might set up an irritation and the dog might attempt to sneeze it away, thus producing a warning signal. In contrast to the normal sneeze the warning is given in a definite direction and is therefore aimed at something. The head movement indicates to the family the direction from which this 'revolting nasal irritation' comes.

This is just one example of the completely new circumstances with which the puppies are confronted. To enable them to deal with this situation they possess a whole range of innate habits of behaviour; if they had to learn everything, their first excursion into the world might well be their last. There can be no question, for instance, of learning the meaning of the warning sneeze. The process of learning what this curious noise made by their parents meant would be dangerous, if not fatal. This sneeze causes the puppy to disappear absolutely 'automatically' into the lair where he crushes himself into the furthest corner. Moreover in this reaction he cannot be imitating his parents since they usually run out to meet the threat and then 'mislead' the enemy; by making a great show of running away they attract attention to themselves and so lure the enemy away from the lair. This process can be seen even in the restricted conditions of a pen; here too the grown-up dogs do all they can to divert attention to themselves and under no circumstances run back to the kennel.

By the beginning of his fourth week, therefore, the puppy will display a whole series of behavioural habits which we have not hitherto seen. At the same time, however, he will be learning more

A four-week-old dingo: Tanila trying to jump down from the table

and more, much of it with astounding rapidity. Primarily as a result of the studies of Irenäus Eibl-Eibesfeldt we know that dogs have an 'innate disposition to learn', something of great importance in the life of an animal. By nature the dog is equipped with a special capacity to learn easily and extremely quickly things vital to his existence. In most cases this gift of learning complements and increases the efficiency of hereditary reflexes which the dog already possesses. To some extent this capacity creates difficulties for the observer since he can very easily overlook this rapid

The Imprint Phase

learning process and emerge with the impression that all is dependent purely on instinct.

During their fourth or fifth week puppies will give evidence of almost all canine behavioural habits except those associated with mating. It would, therefore, be possible for me to set out, in the next chapter, a complete catalogue of canine behaviour. The special features of this particular phase, however, would be swamped in the plethora of material, and subsequent phases of the young dog's development would appear as a summarised rigmarole, without background support. In each phase of development my purpose is to highlight those aspects of behaviour which will play or have played a more important role in subsequent or previous phases. This should be stated beforehand since otherwise, having read the next section, the reader will think that I have omitted at least half of all that is to be seen during these weeks. In recent publications the period from first emergence from the lair to the end of the third month is referred to as the socialisation phase. The first part of this phase, however, lasting approximately until the end of the seventh week, is characterised in particular by this phenomenon of learning—and by the innate aptitude to learn. This I propose to examine as a separate subject. After this period socialisation is far more dependent on the initiative of the puppy himself and his learning upon the acquisition of knowledge from other members of his breed. It therefore seems justifiable to treat the two periods separately. Accordingly I propose to differentiate between an 'imprint phase' (fourth to seventh week inclusive) and the true 'socialisation phase' (eighth to twelfth week inclusive).

THE IMPRINT PHASE

Many readers unfamiliar with the terminology of behavioural research may be doubtful of the meaning of the word 'imprint' in this connection. Coins are moulded or imprinted; both sides of the metal then bear the indelible impression of the mould or imprint; when a certain idea is imprinted on the mind, in normal language this means that it is not easily forgotten.

Some considerable time ago Konrad Lorenz was rearing by hand every conceivable variety of bird, including the grey goose. This is the best way to find out innate habits of behaviour. The little bird which emerges from the egg has never seen one of its own kind before and will not do so later; it can therefore have learnt nothing from its own kind and everything it can do must be hereditary. If on emergence from the egg, and entirely unaided, the chick picks up corn, in current terminology this is an instinctive action.

Konrad Lorenz's experiment showed, particularly in the case of the grey goose, that a bird hand-reared from the egg thought of itself as a species of man and continued to do so throughout life. A grey gander reared in isolation will never understand that he is of the same species as a grey goose; he remains attached to men and does not recognise others of his species. I once knew a hand-reared turkey which only wanted to mate with human beings and would kill any turkey-hen. These birds, therefore, have no innate picture of what their species look like; they do not need it since under normal circumstances the first living things they see when they hatch are the older birds. To ensure that this impression remains with the chick for life, nature has endowed it with a special attribute of learning even more effective than the innate capacity for learning to which I have already referred. The picture of the older bird of his species is so firmly imprinted on the mind of the chick during his first few hours that he will never make a mistake in later life even when confronted with a bird very similar to his own species.

If, unexpectedly, man is the first living thing that a bird sees when hatched, the appearance of the human being is imprinted on his mind—and this imprint can never be eradicated. Konrad Lorenz refers to the 'irreversibility' of this imprint and considers it an important criterion for the expression 'imprint'.

Many examples of such irreversible imprints can be quoted in the case of fishes and birds but in that of mammals the position is not so clear. Anyone researching into behaviour should be careful about referring to processes of learning as 'analogous to imprints'. If a dog is reared in isolation from birth, it too will regard itself as a member of the human species; if it never sees another dog, it will be quite happy and one day will make its proposal of marriage to some human being. But from the moment that it meets another dog, it will realise that here is another of its own species. In this case the imprint has been eradicated; it was therefore no imprint in the strict sense of the word.

Lorenz himself discovered the explanation why mammals are different in this respect. A cartoon in a newspaper provided the answer. It showed a dachshund circling a tree and 'meeting' its own back ends; he smelt them and found to his disappointment that they were his own. So here was the solution: mammals are primarily dependent on their sense of smell while birds are entirely dependent on their eyes. Mammals can smell themselves. A bird cannot look at itself and therefore cannot know what it or its breed looks like. A mammal, however, knows what one of his own kind smells like. The dog knows that there is a difference between his own smell and that of the man who reared him, even if he has never seen another dog. The first dog he meets has a familiar smell, similar to his own. He will therefore at once be attracted to another of his kind because the smell is familiar.

IMPRINT OF MAN AS A MEMBER OF THE BREED

In the case of the dog there is a definitive form of imprint which can never be eradicated. This is an exceptional case, but nature did not allow for a number of things; it did not allow for broody coops or behavioural research, for instance; nor did it foresee that one day there would be intimate partnership between man and dog. This particular imprint, however, works in the opposite direction: if no human imprint has been made, there can never be true partnership between man and dog.

I can prove this by citing a concrete case. One dingo litter I deliberately brought up in such a way that between their third and seventh weeks, the puppies had no contact with human beings. They could see people but no one ever touched them or played with them. Result: they developed into shy wild dogs which hid whenever anyone came within ten to fifteen yards of their pen. All attempts to gain contact with them after their seventh week failed. They could only have been tamed with a great deal of patience—like wild animals. At best one might have removed their fear of man but genuine partnership, such as normally links man and dog, was no longer attainable.

My jackals provide another illustration. It is well known that, if taken very young, jackals can become as trusting and faithful as dogs. My jackals were born in a pen with no artificial floor covering.

These animals develop very quickly and by the time they were no more than five weeks old they had already dug themselves a trench, which by the end of the sixth week, was two and a half yards long. They slept all day in this trench, only coming out to their mother at night and so avoiding all contact with human beings. When they were precisely six weeks old, we collected them, but it was already too late. With the help of Sascha, our alsatian, we got so far that they could stand the sight of a man and did not immediately become timid if approached. But they would never let us catch them; if one tried, they bit savagely.

People will say: well, of course; these are wild dogs. My dingo experiment was not a haphazard affair, however; I was led to make it by the results of trials carried out with innumerable dogs in the United States. There is in Bar Harbor, Maine, a scientific institute known as the R. B. Jackson Memorial Laboratory which studies the psychological performance of dogs. They have there, among other things, a number of large enclosures in which various pedigree breeds of dog live and rear their puppies with no interference from man. There are fox-terriers, beagles, collies and basenjis. All the puppies brought up there behave exactly like my dingoes—they are shy and remain so. This was the starting point for my dingo experiment. By further trials I hoped to obtain an even clearer picture.

My next experiment was as follows: we left one dingo bitch puppy in the pen with her mother for three months without ever touching her after her twentieth day; then she was taken into the house and kept with some very tame puppies, some younger, some the same age and some older. The entire kindergarten was allowed into my study every day and they romped and played gloriously with Uncle Sascha. The dingo bitch, however, remained shy; she would hide and run away if one tried to catch her; even living in close contact with people under these conditions, she could not be tamed. Sometimes she would even avoid the other puppies, for whom contact with human beings was obviously sheer joy.

Finally let me cite a third, somewhat differently arranged experiment. Two of my puppies, Kor and Kira, were born in a hole in the ground during an arctic spell of weather. They were weighed every day until Day 20 but between then and Day 50

Imprint of Man as a Member of the Breed

only four times. Otherwise, after Day 20, we only had contact with them occasionally. During their seventh and eighth weeks they were taken into the house twice so that they could play with the other puppies and with Sascha. When they were ten weeks old we fetched them into the house from the pen every day and continued this throughout the week. When they were five months old they came into the house permanently. What is their attitude to man? They wag their tails in a friendly way but only give a pretence of a welcome, coming up quite close and raising their muzzles in the air. There is a small difference between the two in that Kira will sometimes come right up and on occasions shyly lick one's hand; this Kor never does. After thus signifying that they are pleased to see one they withdraw a short way, still looking friendly and wagging their tails but with the tails right down; they then wait to see what will happen. If one sits quietly down in a chair they will soon resume their games with the other puppies, sometimes coming up casually to register submission, Kira perhaps being bold enough to nudge one's hand with her nose. Kor and Kira make a definite distinction between me and Eva, my kennel-maid. Since she feeds them, Eva has a 'positive grading', and since she is obviously with them far more frequently they are more forthcoming to her; Kira will often allow Eva actually to stroke her.

By further experiments I could produce a record of all the intermediate stages ranging from total refusal of contact through more or less marked shyness to unconcealed pleasure at contact with human beings. It all depends solely and exclusively on handling the puppies at a certain age and on the frequency with which one does so. I cannot, with any certainty, give precise timings; to do this further experiments are necessary. It is clear, however, that the critical phase begins about the eighteenth day and that it does not extend much further than the seventh week. In addition comes the problem of expanding the picture of the human being, as I like to call the process.

What I mean by this is that, when the critical phase opens, the puppy regards as a partner only his handler, the first person with whom he comes in contact. Initially he shows fear of other people but he will very soon lose this if they play a lot with him at an early stage of the imprint phase. If they only enter his life after the eighth week, he can quite well become attached to them, but not in the same way as if he had been in contact with numbers of human beings at an early age. In the case of some breeds puppies remain permanently attached to their initial handler if they have no other contacts with human beings over a period of twelve or more weeks; their picture of the human is then restricted to this one person and cannot be expanded. Breeds may differ in this respect; it is well known, for instance, that at any age alsatians find it easy to transfer their loyalty, or at least far easier than do many other breeds. Nevertheless the imprint period is at least a factor, if not a decisive one, in this problem. Usually puppies make the acquaintance of several people during their first eight weeks; they therefore realise that there are many human beings with whom they can play and so come to regard man as another breed of dog.

Here is the nub of the matter: during these vital weeks the dog gradually acquires an imprint not of *a* man but of *men*.

Stray dogs try to contact human beings even though they may be strangers; they 'just arrive', people say. Every day calls come in to police stations and dogs' homes saying that 'a dog has turned up'. These are all dogs who have acquired an adequately broad picture of the human being during their socialisation phase. Dogs whose 'man-imprint' is too restricted will not 'arrive', although they may not run away if one entices them. Depending on their upbringing there are, of course, all sorts of intermediate grades of behaviour, as has been made clear above. Dogs whose imprint is too restricted tend to look exclusively for their master and in extreme cases will approach no one else. If they are caught after failing to find him and are adopted by some new owner, they will seize any opportunity of running away.

Some years ago I took in a black alsatian from a dogs' home. He was the exception to the rule that the alsatian is everybody's friend; even a month later (he was three years old) he showed no real desire to make contact; he accepted me as a provider of food but that was all. For my part I was continuously on the road looking for him far and wide until one day I failed to find him. It should be emphasised that this alsatian had clearly been on very good terms with someone since he knew all the normal words of command, although when given by me he obeyed them grudgingly —in his eyes I was still a stranger. The fact that he obeyed them at all, however, showed that he must have had a very good relationship with his master; there was no trace of cringeing in his movements. Many alsatians who have had a stern or unsympathetic trainer literally shrink into themselves when they hear a word of command even if given by a stranger or even if addressed to another dog.

On this whole subject much is still unexplained. This much, however, is certain: a dog's first experiences of man are decisive for the future development of his character. In this field we do not know what is truly hereditary and what is imprinted during these vital weeks, but what we are apt to call a dog's 'nature' is considerably affected thereby.

BUYING A PUPPY

Anyone intending to invest in a small dog should look for a breeder living, if possible, not too far away who has just reported to the breeding association that a new litter has arrived or that he is expecting one shortly. The prospective purchaser should contact the breeder and visit the puppies in their initial imprint phase, so that he can play with them a little. If, while still with their breeder, the puppies obviously have adequate opportunity to expand their picture of the human being and broaden their contacts, then no more than one or two visits need be made before the time arrives to take home the puppy selected. If this is not the case, every effort should be made to maintain contact with the puppies by visiting them as often as possible up to their eighth week. I would never buy from a breeder a puppy which runs away on my approach. Puppies which have been properly introduced into human society will rush up to a visiting stranger without the least sign of timidity and with every expression of pleasure. The puppy which first jumps up to you offering you a nose-nudge or a lick is the one to choose.

This shows clearly enough, I think, that if one is to have a dog as a friend for life—generally his own, far too short life—one should know about these things before buying; only a good breeder will provide one with a good friend. There is no other way—unless, of course, one does one's own breeding.

There are unfortunately many people who have never given these matters a thought; they think that they can buy a dog like some trade-marked article with the quality guaranteed by the producing firm. When buying a car destined to last for the next three or four years most people examine, consider, test and study long and hard before deciding on their purchase. For a dog, however, they require only the famous papers showing that it is pure-bred and has several champions in its pedigree; they may perhaps ask casually whether it is healthy or even demand to see an inoculation certificate; they then simply put the little creature under their arm and take it home.

Some breeders refuse to sell a dog to such people. The genuine breeder is very proud of his puppies and will be only too pleased if the prospective purchaser clearly takes interest in them before the day comes when he takes his puppy away. I really do not believe that there will be difficulties if my advice is followed. At worst look for another breeder who shares and appreciates your interest. You will not regret it.

PAW-GIVING

During the imprint phase the bitch no longer invariably feeds her puppies in the nest; more often she does so in the open. Frequently she will sit and later stand, like the Capitoline she-wolf. Just like Romulus and Remus, therefore, the puppies now have to suck with their heads in the air. The small puppy finds it difficult to put up both forefeet at the same time and so he uses only one for the teat-kneading motion, supporting himself on the other.

I have described this in some detail for two reasons: first, it illustrates how some puppy habit—in this case the kneading motion—develops into a definite element in the behaviour of the growing or full-grown dog; secondly it gives us a little more insight into canine methods of expression.

Rana, my alsatian bitch, has a somewhat tiresome habit. Whenever she is let into my room, she rushes up to me and places a paw at least on my knee, if not higher. She does this most intently, repeating the motion several times and using first one paw and then the other in eager salutation. Since she has usually come straight from the kennel, the resulting mess on my clothes can be imagined. I have been most hesitant to try and break her of this habit which has been hers from a puppy. When carrying on research into behaviour one is frequently tempted not to do something which any normal dog-owner would do as a matter of course. If necessary I can always make research the excuse for the

A puppy feeding in the sitting position using one paw for kneading

fact that my dogs are 'untrained'. I was genuinely interested, however, in Rana's passionate paw-giving, a habit which no one had ever taught her. In Rana's case paw-giving is a definite sign of submission, in other words a prophylactic attempt to allay any possible expression of ill-temper on my part.

Almost every dog I know will give a paw if one has occasion to scold him soundly. Its effect, combined with the characteristic look of guilt and devotion, is disarming and touchingly human. It is a method of expression, however, which dogs use between themselves and it carries for them the same meaning; it is not a man-taught movement. Practically every dog-owner trains his puppy to give a paw. Naturally he then thinks that, when his dog is trying to placate him, it is making rational use of the trick which it has learnt and he is overjoyed to find that his dog is so clever.

But there are other ideas about this. One of my friends, for instance, once told me that his beloved poodle bitch's children had inherited from her the paw-giving trick which she had learnt. He was quite cross when I told him that this was an old wives' tale, long since disproved. As 'proof' that he was right he maintained that all his poodle puppies were able to give a paw on their own without having been taught.

My answer was that all dogs can do this by nature; it is not necessary to teach them *how* to do it, only *when*, in other words on what word of command; they can also be taught always to give the right paw—like a man shaking hands.

On this subject Eisfeld says: 'This movement indicates good-humoured submission.' When used between dogs it does not necessarily involve actual contact; it is simply a gesture which the other understands perfectly. It may well be a development of the 'pawing' which I have often observed between my dogs. In this case the paw actually touches the other dog, usually around the head or neck. It frequently takes place between dogs and bitches as a sign of affection; puppies will do it to the full-grown dog. The dingo dog in particular insists on unquestioning obedience from his children, though otherwise he will play lovingly with them. If the father goes for one of his youngsters, the puppy turns on its back squealing loudly (one would think that it was about to be eaten!); as soon as the father ceases to be menacing, however, and the puppy plucks up courage again, there will almost certainly be a full-scale ceremony of apology in which paw-giving and pawing play an important part.

The puppy thus obtains 'good marks' from his parents and he

uses the same method when dealing with man. I emphasise here the word 'obtain', for it brings us back to the teat-kneading motion.

At first this may sound surprising but it is easy to explain. We only have to look at a puppy—say in his sixth or seventh week—feeding from a bitch in the standing position. He cannot make his kneading motion in the same way as he did when lying in the litter-box—but he makes it nevertheless. He continually raises a paw and taps against the teat with it. This reproduces precisely the paw-giving motion; in this case, however, he is obtaining something else—a flow of milk.

When the mother brings the puppies their food, giving the paw can be seen as a begging gesture, as a request to be given some of the food. Here again it is a development of the teat-kneading motion. In the animal world begging motions are frequently used as placatory gestures; with men raising the hand serves the same purpose. On this subject Eibl-Eibesfeldt says: 'Chimpanzees offer their hand just as we do. The junior in rank takes the initiative; he offers his hand, open and palm upwards, to the more senior. The gesture originates from the baby's attempt to make contact. The senior chimpanzee stretches out his hand and this reassures the other'.

NOSE-NUDGING

There is another puppy habit which reappears in later life with a new function. This is the burrowing motion which the new-born puppy uses to search for and find his mother's teats. It develops into the familiar nudge with the nose which an affectionate dog will give when he wishes to be stroked. From the point of view of the study of behaviour this is an interesting case of transference of an expressive motion from one functional area to another; if insistent nose-nudging is used to indicate that the dog wishes to be fed with scraps from the table, it is a sign of bad training. In any case, when the cold muzzle is thrust against one's hand, the dog wants something; he is asking for something. A nose-nudge, as can be clearly felt, is given upwards from below—precisely the motion used when burrowing into the mother's coat. If he wishes to be stroked, the dog may even succeed in pushing one's hand across his head; alternatively he will push his head underneath the hand, having first raised it with his nose.

Binna, my elkhound bitch, loves being fussed over; she has brought this request for stroking to a fine art, laying her ears back so tight that they almost disappear into the thick coat of her neck; with an adoring gaze she presents one with a 'stroke-worthy head', looking more like a seal than a dog. Binna's nose-nudge simply is not to be denied.

Head-stroking is generally preferred by the long-eared breeds, the dachshunds and spaniels; a good alsatian—my Rana, oddly enough, is an exception—generally does not like it very much if one passes the flat of the hand from the nose back over the head. There is here a clear indication of character; an alsatian which likes this form of stroking is noticeably submissive, its master's devoted slave, a docile instrument for the domineering and prepared to follow any stranger who is friendly to it. I refer here to full-grown male dogs. In the case of a bitch this should not be taken quite so literally, particularly if she is looked after by a man and still less if she is on heat. I was recently told by an alsatian expert who judges at guard-dog competitions that he places a strict ban on head-stroking. I do not think that he is opposed to it because a dog lying beside its master with its ears back does not make a pretty picture; his main reason is that a dog with pointed ears cannot be on guard unless his 'sound aerials' are in position. A good guard-dog cannot be at ease if his sensory organs—nose, eyes and ears—are unable to keep watch all the time on the world around him. An alsatian with his ears laid back and his nose and eyes permanently directed on his master's face can neither hear, see nor smell anything but his master.

The nose which nudges too insistently, of course, should be quietly pushed aside—for instance when the demand becomes impatient because, although the lead is in our hand, we are being dilatory in going out for a walk. His master must remain the dog's pack-leader and he must be the one to decide when a walk takes place. If nose-nudging means that the dog wants some of our lunch, however, he should be rebuked sharply; that merits no sympathy.

Any normal dog will understand quickly and easily that nose-nudging must be reserved for the functional area from which it originated and that, provided it is used as a sign of a friendly desire for contact, it gives pleasure.

As I have already pointed out, the purpose of these behavioural habits implanted in the dog is intercourse, not with man but with other dogs. 'Affectionate nose-nudging and snuffling in the region of the head, neck and shoulders' is part of the courting ceremonial, as Alfred Seitz observed in the case of jackals and coyotes. R. Schenkel also observed wolves acting in this way. My dogs do just the same; the dog and bitch burrow their noses into each other's coats from the side of the head, along the neck down to the shoulder; there are numerous variations ranging from a short nudge to a prolonged and apparently pleasurable burrow into the other's coat. This burrowing is accompanied by an audible snuffling which, however, in origin has nothing to do with nose-nudging. We shall be dealing later with this habit of sniffing at another dog's head and neck since it is connected with an aspect of canine behaviour which many dog-owners find distressing.

Finally, between dogs, nose-nudging may be used as an invitation to a game, usually the sort of game which follows the demonstrations of affection associated with mating. Between dogs which know each other well, such as mother and daughter, brother and sister or dogs which have long lived together and are on very good terms, a nose-nudge may be an invitation to a gentle biting game, the jaws of the nose-nudger usually being softly gripped by those of his partner. A dog must be very confident if he is prepared to place his sensitive muzzle between the other's gleaming teeth.

With human beings the hand is usually the object of nose-nudging instead of the face or neck; similarly the 'muzzle in the jaws' game can also be played with the hand. If a dog takes gentle hold of the hand with an almost imperceptible chewing motion, this is an expression of affection (not always pleasant if done by the inexperienced puppy with his pin-like teeth). If the hold becomes a little firmer, a request is being made; the dog wants a game. It is the same with puppies; their nose-nudging develops into a biting game. A firm hold on the hand followed by a little tug, therefore, is an invitation to play; sometimes it can be an appeal for the usual walk to take place at long last.

When Binna or Rana invite me to take notice of them by nose-nudging, I often put a couple of fingers into the mouth, bending them to simulate a bite; this must be done gently so that, by turning its head, the dog can rub its jaw against the crook of the fingers; then it will understand what you mean. Why should it always be the dog which is expected to learn and understand human behaviour? We can sometimes well make an effort to talk in 'dog language' without losing any of our authority.

SLEEPING

I now propose to examine a totally elementary aspect of behaviour, namely sleeping, which at this age still plays a great part in a dog's life. First let us look back to the period of early puppyhood.

The puppy's anatomy—the splayed legs, for instance—dictates

She-wolves lying huddled together—an exceptional position showing great attachment

that he sleeps on his stomach. He nevertheless insists on contact with his mother's body or at least with his brothers and sisters. A puppy unable to nestle up against something warm, soft and similar to a dog's coat does not sleep but squeaks loudly and continuously.

Lying in close contact is a habit not only of early but also of later childhood and is only given up gradually during the first year. The full-grown dog does not like sleeping in contact with another dog, not even one of whom he is very fond. When Rana was eight weeks old she became very attached to Sascha, then aged eighteen months. As already mentioned, Sascha loves puppies and often adopts an almost maternal attitude towards them. He took to the little alsatian bitch in a most touching way and would play with her as often and as long as she wanted. When, however, Rana was tired after a game and lay down against him puppy-fashion, he could not tolerate this for more than a few minutes; he would get up, leaving Rana sleeping by herself, and lie down a yard or so away. Rana is now almost ten months old and occasionally she still feels the need to nestle up to Sascha when she sleeps. Though the two dogs are devoted to each other, Sascha still gets up and lies down somewhere else.

The full-grown dog normally sleeps curled up; he lies half on his side and half on his stomach, the body forming a complete circle with the muzzle near the root of the tail; the tail itself

Rana, the alsatian bitch, lying curled up

encircles the head. In this way the body surface is reduced and the more sensitive parts are well protected. It is a highly practical position, giving protection against wind and weather (my elkhound-dingo crosses curl up and often allow themselves to be completely snowed in, like huskies).

The stretched-out position resembles that of the tiny puppy; the dog lies on its stomach with the head between the forelegs stretched out in front. Generally one hind leg is tucked under sideways so that both hind legs appear on the same side. Many dogs, however, sleep precisely in the puppy position, stomach flat on the floor and the hind legs splayed out behind. My Binna adopts this 'hearth-rug position' for preference and so do some of her dingo-cross offspring. Anyone whose dog does not do this but would like to see it has only to go to the zoo. All bears, particularly polar bears, lie in this position for hours.

These are the three typical positions of the dog in repose. Binna has discovered a fourth: she likes to lie on her back with her backbone slightly curved and her legs bent; she even manages to sleep in this position. Dogs can adopt the most extraordinary

Binna in the 'hearthrug' posture

postures which the human being finds it difficult to think can be comfortable.

During his first ten days the new-born puppy does not attempt anything other than the polar bear position; with his clumsy uncoordinated little legs it would be very difficult to get up from any other posture. He is also intent on lying in contact with his mother. Something else is to be seen when a puppy sleeps: the paws and sometimes the tiny ears twitch occasionally.

Everyone has undoubtedly seen this in the full-grown dog; frequently these movements are accompanied by noises which sound like a muffled bark or howl. A man who talks in his sleep usually does not do so very clearly and it is the same with the dog; the reason is the same too—a dream.

A dog undoubtedly dreams exactly as we do, though naturally about his own world; scents possibly play an important part in his

Sleeping

dreams. Sometimes a dog may be dreaming very deeply. If one wakes a dog who is clearly dreaming about chasing the neighbour's cat, one can actually see him finding his way back to reality from his dream. The process is much more rapid with the dog than with most men since, even when deep in sleep, a dog's senses are not in suspense as are ours. While still asleep, for instance, a dog notices if one approaches; I even think it possible that this becomes woven into his dream. From personal experience I know how the tinkle of the alarm clock can be woven into a man's dream before he wakes up. It is a known fact that the brain reacts more quickly while dreaming than when awake. The dog must therefore dream very vividly and the approach must be made almost imperceptibly if the moment of puzzlement at the sudden change in the situation is to be seen. Moreover anyone who has become familiar with his dog's behaviour over the years will almost certainly be able to tell what the dog is dreaming about. There can be no proof of course —but guessing is rather fun.

Sleeping is therefore not only an agreeable but a profitable occupation; it is preceded by an urge which we usually call 'becoming sleepy'. This urge causes the dog to go looking for 'sleep-producing stimuli'. H. D. Schmidt refers to this as 'an acquired desire directed towards localities possessing qualities which the animals know from previous experience'. In other words the dog jumps on the sofa because he knows from experience that he sleeps comfortably there. Alternatively he does not do that because he remembers that it is forbidden and that he has his own place, the only spot where he will not be met with an angry 'Off' or be otherwise disturbed. Many dogs may often hear their masters give a sigh of relief when they finally go to their place after hours of rushing around.

Having reached his place, the dog usually turns round in a circle several times before lying down. Even Charles Darwin, founder of the modern doctrine of heredity, referred to this motion, citing it as an example of an instinctive action inherited by the dog from his wild ancestors but still present in the domesticated dog though without function. For the student of canine behaviour, however, this turning round before lying down provides a shining example of 'unintelligent' deduction made from a hereditary reaction: ever since Darwin people have maintained that this turning motion comes from the necessity to flatten the grass and that by inherited instinct it is still performed even when there is no grass. This sounds like an obvious solution, but it is not right. It is equally incorrect to say that the motion is intended to scare away 'snakes and scorpions'. This sort of thing can only have been dreamt up on some office stool, for anyone who knows about snakes and scorpions would realise that this would be the stupidest action that a dog could take. The dog has no need of instinct to protect himself against such animals—his good nose is quite enough if he is really condemned to live in an area inhabited by snakes or other poisonous animals.

Kurt F. König, who has carried out a number of remarkable breeding experiments and has become known for his breeding of the 'Hovawart'* and other strains, has never been able to bring himself to place much credence in these theories. He has therefore made a number of extensive experiments using not only dogs but also wolves, jackals, foxes, martens, minks and racoons. All these animals he caused to run in a treadwheel, first for a short time and then for a long time; he then watched how they lay down. The result, as König told me in a letter, was 'that after a long run the animal had to turn round more often before achieving the curled-up sleeping position; after a short run one turn-round was enough'. Here is the solution; this turning round is designed to achieve no more than the correct curvature of the spine for the curled-up sleeping position which is the one most generally used. If the muscles of the spine are tired after a run, several turns are necessary in order to achieve the correct position. Moreover a dog which has been asleep a long time and then gets up and lies down again, turns round several times since obviously the backbone has become stiff. As everyone knows, when he finally gets up, he copes with the situation by stretching, just as we do.

In our dogs ancient instincts are closely linked with intelligence. They are not one-track-minded creatures obeying their instincts unthinkingly and flattening down non-existent grass! Sleep and rest are things which we automatically associate with a house or home. The same applies to animals, although in their case security

---

* *The 'Hofwart' was a medieval breed and has recently been revived. The 'Hovawart' is a popular present-day breed.*

comes before comfort. This should be remembered when we bring our eight-week-old puppy home. We should think beforehand where in the house a place is to be found in which the dog can be really undisturbed—not only when a little puppy but later when full-grown. He will be more ready to obey the command 'basket', 'box' or 'bed' if he likes his place and so it should be made as pleasing to him as possible. The best is a kennel-like box with a flat top, completely open in front since he likes to be able to look around from his place. Height should be sufficient to ensure that he does not hit his head on the roof when he gets right up, as he will do on hearing his master's step in the passage. There are many dogs which prefer to sleep on something raised so that they have a better view of things. For this reason I recommend that these 'indoor' kennels' should have a flat top so that the dog can sleep on it instead of using the sofa. There need be no more than a plain blanket in the box. There is no upholstery in the dog's natural lair, only the bare earth. When, as an experiment, I placed hay or straw in my dog's kennels, they invariably preferred the holes they had dug in the pens.

CHILDHOOD IMAGE AND INDUCED JUVENILITY

Grown-up dogs clearly recognise a puppy; moreover they can equally differentiate between children and grown-ups and will adapt their behaviour accordingly. Many examples can be quoted

Infantile face of a two-day-old dingo puppy. Note the vertical searching motion of the head

of otherwise savage and dangerous guard-dogs allowing themselves to be seized and pulled about by little children—children whom they did not even know. All the savagery normally shown by such a dog often vanishes when he is faced with a small child.

We shall be dealing later with methods of expression instinctively understood by other dogs. Detailed analyses by students of behaviour have shown that there are invariably certain quite simple components of these methods of expression which serve as 'key stimuli', which in other words evoke or inhibit a certain response; this means that the ganglion of instinct reacts only to a simplicist, broad-pattern picture of any overall expression. To explain by means of a very simple example: draw two circles; in the lower third of one draw a line curving upwards at the ends and in the other a line curving downwards. Everyone will see a sad face in one and a smiling face in the other. One evokes thoughts of sadness and the other of merriment. Here we have the key to what Konrad Lorenz has called the childhood image. A glance at the world of vertebrates, including man, will show that the young animal displays certain special features. The head is very round—quite the opposite to that of the full-grown animal; it is usually strikingly large compared to the diminutive body attached to it. So at once the optical signal 'Baby' is hoisted. But this is not all: the large round eyes give the face a distinctive expression; the little nose is barely in evidence but there are large chubby cheeks and there is the round suckling's mouth. All this distinguishes the baby's face from that of the grown-up. Anyone desirous of studying this phenomenon should look at the display of dolls in a toy shop. The makers so design their dolls that the features liable to evoke maternal instincts are pronounced if not exaggerated. They are often 'sweeter' than real children. The grown-ups naturally respond to this attraction and this is transmitted into an urge to buy; the children play with the dolls—or to use a more technical behavioural expression, display maternal instincts. Thus human beings are doing exactly what seemed so astonishing in Zimen's little she-wolf. Childhood's image is therefore recognisable to young animals or, to put it more precisely, it exercises an evocative effect upon them. They respond 'automatically'.

The tiny puppy, with its short fat legs, silky coat and general awkwardness possesses the same features as those to which we react in the human child. Its appearance touches the same chords of emotion; we want to go up to it and stroke it. All this happens quite unconsciously; we are simply responding to the evocative mechanism of the childhood image.

Childhood Image and Induced Juvenility

The dog, therefore, reacts in exactly the same way, particularly since the puppy must also certainly carry an infantile scent picture. A dog will first sniff at a puppy before being quite sure and starting to mother it. The childhood image also has another function: it protects a small puppy from attack. This is not an invariable rule, however, since protection of the dog's own brood from competition may, in certain cases, give rise to violent impulses which break down the barriers. The threshold of stimulus is not always at the same level or conditioned by the situation—this is one of nature's safeguards against an unbalanced, over-rigid functioning of its mechanisms. It is known, for instance, that wives of the Australian aborigines, who are nomads, will kill a new-born baby without scruple if the tribe is threatened with starvation. Like mothers everywhere they are tender and affectionate to their children, but there are situations in which the mechanism of motherhood gives way before even stronger impulses. Similarly a nursing bitch will kill a strange puppy mercilessly; in its case the childhood image is no longer effective, although it remains fully in force as far as her own puppies are concerned.

Nevertheless it is possible to introduce a strange puppy to a nursing bitch by ensuring that it lies among the other puppies for some time. It will soon have acquired the smell of the nest and, since dogs cannot count their puppies, the bitch will not notice the subterfuge when she returns.

The childhood image is therefore highly 'generalised', in other words its basic features are similar in all animals. This explains why it is possible to use a bitch as foster-mother for young of another species. There are many examples: foresters have reared fawns on a retriever bitch and there is the famous boxer bitch in a circus which brought up a litter of lion cubs; they still regarded her as 'mummy' even when full-grown.

How powerful the childhood image is in producing the reaction 'attractive' or 'sweet' is shown by those curious breeds of dog in which the features which actuate this emotional mechanism have been turned into permanencies. Take, for instance, the much-abused pug; in this case, as with pekinese, toy terriers, griffons, maltese and so forth, the breeder's art has turned the childhood image into a breed characteristic. 'Oh, if only he could stay so small and sweet and not grow into a St Bernard'—how many dog-lovers have said something like this and thousands of years ago the breading speculator took note of it and he has bequeathed us these 'living dolls'. In these cases the breeders' object has been to retard the development of certain features, in other words the growth of certain features is either reduced or suppressed altogether. The little puppy muzzle does not grow and so there appears a pug-faced dog; the brain, however, is not dwarfed and so the head remains round with large eyes like a puppy's. The 'puppy-fat' of the silken-coated pug is an invitation to cuddling and the maltese, with his

The rounded head of an Italian greyhound. The infantile expression is the result of miniaturisation and is emphasised by the comparatively large eyes

long soft silky coat, is also a natural object of stroking and petting.

It is an apt question whether this retardation is restricted only to physical features or whether our dogs display certain juvenile qualities of character. This is certainly the case and it occurs far more frequently than is supposed. There are two possible causes of retardation in behaviour. In the first place hereditary changes may take place as a result of which certain character-development processes never occur. One such clearly hereditary retardation is the incredible playfulness of a pug which has been reared intelligently and not allowed to degenerate mentally by being used as a mere object of stroking. There are many other breeds which do

Childhood Image and Induced Juvenility

not become so stolid when full-grown as does, for instance, a bulldog. Obviously retardation of this or that attribute may differ within an individual breed.

Konrad Lorenz has pointed out that in certain cases the effects of retardation can be extremely good. The puppy's inquisitiveness and desire to learn may be retained right through to old age. Pugs are extraordinarily quick to learn whether as puppies or old dogs; the latter in themselves present a striking contrast for it seems odd to see an animal which is clearly of considerable age but still retains not only his juvenile appearance but the merry youthful disposition of a young dog.

The other cause of juvenility is not hereditary: an individual dog may retain his puppy habits. The part this can play in the relationship between man and dog should not be underestimated. The following should be remembered: the initial imprint made by man on a dog's mind is that of another form of dog. The puppy's initial picture of a dog is provided for him by his brothers, his sisters and his parents. But there is an important difference between the two: the parents provide food, the brothers and sisters do the opposite—they take it away if they can. In this respect the dog's large two-legged human companion has much in common with his parents since he produces food. When the young dog is nine or ten months old he cuts loose from his parents and goes off on his own; he becomes independent and at latest by this time must obtain his food for himself—not always easy for a dog living wild. We, however, take over a dog as a puppy and for him become the food-provider and father-figure; this we remain, not only because we give him his food and even prevent him obtaining his own, but because we remain in close touch with him. Separation from the parents is brought about, among other things, by the fact that they have no further intention of providing food for the adolescent lout; instead, by growling and baring their teeth, they give him clearly to understand that he is now old enough to look after himself. This is just what we do not do and so, between us and our dog, a large proportion of the parent-child relationship remains throughout life. This definitely reacts in many ways on the dog's mental development; and for this reason—provided we behave properly!—he will retain a large part of his childish respect for parents or recognition of parental authority. I trust that this will give us better insight into the part we should play in our dog's life—to the pleasure and profit of our relationship with him.

THE SOCIALISATION PHASE

From the ninth to the end of the twelfth week new factors enter into the dog's development. Now all those things have to be learnt which form the basis for the more advanced communal activities so important in the lives of animals high in the scale of those living in families or clans.

So far the puppy has been allowed to do as he likes. The parents tolerate anything with long-suffering forbearance and understanding—he is still a child and allowances must be made. He must first develop, must discover and practise his movement capabilities; he must have reached a certain maturity before the parents assume the role of trainer.

All this now changes. Now it is time to educate the youngster into a sensible effective dog who will later find his or her mate and in turn bring up puppies properly. Incredible as it may sound, there is actually a graduated, well-considered programme of training and it is not 'anti-authority' but extremely authoritarian. It should be added that canine authority is something quite different from the spurious authority which developed in certain western societies and which was characterised by a master-and-servant relationship between father and child. The word 'authority' leaves an unpleasant taste in the mouth as a result. In the canine family authority is clearly not only the secret of successful survival in the struggle for existence but is a complete necessity for the young dog. He looks for and automatically accepts his father's authority and later, in the case of wolves, that of the pack-leader. A dog which does not recognise his master as the authority, registers a protest. He becomes a 'difficult dog'—that is his form of protest and it is often not understood. If the leader of a wolf-pack fails to exert his authority, he is torn to pieces—he must be killed to ensure the pack's survival. When old, worn out and no longer capable of leading the pack, he would bring ruin upon it unless he was got rid of. There will be more to say on this subject when I come to deal with aggressive action, both its possibility and necessity.

Introduction into the Human Community

What I wish to deal with here, however, is something of far greater and more decisive importance for a communal existence than any form of aggression—the behavioural characteristics leading to the formation of groups. In this connection I would refer to the book *Liebe und Hass* [Love and Hate] by Eibl-Eibesfeldt which deals with the fundamentals of the social bonds between animal and man. Observation of the dog, whose social structure is so similar to that of man, can produce much instructive information on this whole complex of problems.

The early imprints on the dog's mind are conducive to the formation of groups. They establish unalterably who is to be regarded as a member of the breed; in the specialised case of the dog reared under human care there are, as already explained, two 'members of the breed', although a clear distinction is made between the genuine member and that which man has become. Since, in the wild state, dogs differentiate between members of the tribe and strangers to the tribe, in principle this is not difficult for him: he has joined the human tribe and feels himself a member of it; other dogs, which do not belong to the tribe, are merely strangers to the pack and as such may, as in nature, be taken as mates.

INTRODUCTION INTO THE HUMAN COMMUNITY

Membership of a tribe necessitates—in addition to innate habits of behaviour compatible with a communal existence—a whole series of procedures designed to form the group and render it cohesive. Wolves, for instance, are as pliable and adaptable as men and must be so in order to survive; their communal existence cannot, therefore, rest on instinct alone—as with bees for instance. For this type of animal, therefore, the scope of development is larger. To some extent the animal learns from training. This is an important factor in the habits of behaviour which promote the coherence of a group.

As can be seen to perfection in my 'family pens', the canine father comes to the fore at this point as trainer. I was particularly interested in watching the two alsatians, Sascha and Rana. Rana is one of Sascha's daughters and when she was eight weeks old we took her away from her mother and handed her over to Sascha for training. While in the pen with her mother she had established excellent contact with human beings; she is very attached to me and is friendly with anyone who shows goodwill towards her. Sascha accepted the little girl with his customary benevolence. He joined in all Rana's games, taught her other ones, guided her and indulgently tolerated all her pranks. The two dogs were together all day; in the evenings they usually spent some hours in my study with me and Eva, my assistant. We never took Rana for a walk; there was no point since she could rush about in the open with Sascha to her heart's content. All Rana learnt from us was the meaning of 'Pfui' (the word of rebuke) and to be clean in the house. We did nothing else. Rana is meanwhile full-grown. She never misses an opportunity to demonstrate her affection and friendship to us. It is impossible to play with her, however, nor can one teach her anything. It is hopeless; at the smallest attempt she tucks in her tail and cringes.

Exactly the same reaction is to be seen from any one of our other dogs which has been brought up solely by its father and has not learnt, from the eighth week onwards, that man is not only a kind of being whom one likes and whose hand one licks affectionately, but is also a being with whom one can play and collaborate. If, during the socialisation phase, the sole trainer has been a dog, the social conduct of the youngster will be basically attuned to that of dogs. If man has been the sole trainer, the dog will be geared to man and will not be at his ease with other dogs. Dogs which have an opportunity, at least occasionally, to meet and play with other dogs, develop into what I would describe as a 'normal dog'. What sort of a dog can it be which is not at ease with other dogs! Conversely Rana is not a 'normal' dog because she is unable to assimilate herself to the human community. She can attach herself to it—that is part of her imprint—but she cannot really enter into it because that was not demanded of her during her socialisation phase. With other dogs she is splendid—very good with puppies and friendly with any strange dog she happens to meet.

Sascha, her trainer, however, is completely and absolutely integrated into human society. He is a dog whose principal joy in life is to play with you or learn some new trick. He literally turns himself inside out in his desire to collaborate with man. He thus demonstrates a group-forming aspect of conduct which I would

Introduction into the Human Community

like to describe since it provides an excellent illustration of the concept.

Sascha loves it if you throw a piece of stick; he rushes after it, retrieves it and brings it back to the thrower or preferably someone else; in fact he selects the person who has so far taken least part in the game. Since Eva works and plays with him a great deal because he is her dog, his close relationship with her is, in his eyes, so to speak an understood thing. Of his own accord he looks for contact with other human beings, for, after all, a society consists of several people, not merely two. When Eva and I are together, he will never bring her a stick and ask her for a game (unless by chance she has not played with him for some time) but on principle he brings it to me. If a visitor is present, the first thing Sascha does is to bring him a stick; he places it in the visitor's lap and sits down expectantly, looking the man straight in the eye. If there is no reaction, he becomes impatient, takes back the stick, carries it round held high in his mouth, places it ostentatiously on the lap once more and nudges a hand with his nose—'Come on, get going.' Unmistakably he is trying to form a bond, to expand and consolidate his acquaintanceship.

Rana never asks human beings for a game. She adheres to her baby ways—paw-giving and hand-licking—despite the fact that Sascha provides her with a daily example of collaboration between dog and man. If one throws a stick for her, she simply looks at one uncomprehendingly. If Sascha rushes after a stick, however, she will chase after him and try to take the toy away.

During the socialisation phase, therefore, depending on his upbringing, the dog will become attuned to playing, and so forming a group, either with others of his own kind or with human beings. If we have a 'lone dog' we should ensure that he sometimes has opportunity during this period to play with other dogs, otherwise he will become an unbalanced man's dog who will later have difficulties with other dogs. This can be unpleasant when out for a walk and catastrophic if another dog comes into the house.

If the dog joins the family somewhat later in life, say about the twelfth week, it is wise to check on his upbringing. A breeder who has perhaps fifty dogs on his hands, usually has no dog for sale which has had much to do with people. If one tries to play with the dog, it will at once be obvious whether, during this vital period, he has developed adequate social contact with human beings by playing with them.

PLAY

By studying the games played by dogs not only do we gain valuable information about canine behaviour but, even more important, we can discover how we ourselves can enhance our social contact with the dog by playing with him. Animals' games have long been

Twelve-week-old dingo puppies playing the biting game

a subject of study for psychologists and students of behaviour. I propose first to outline the main features of these games, relying principally on Eibl-Eibesfeldt.

The first thing to note about puppies is that when they romp around, chase each other about or stalk some object, this is not done in earnest. It is not a serious affair. Suddenly, of course, a game may become serious; that is to be seen often enough when,

Play

for instance, during the hurly-burly one puppy bites the ear or defenceless stomach of another too hard. He may get properly cross; he squeals loudly, shows his teeth, growls and soon there is a real rough-and-tumble in progress with tufts of hair flying. Yet it all began with a happy game. But these are mere incidents.

The next thing to notice is that a game does not consist of an exercise in capturing a quarry rehearsed through from A to Z; the individual components of such an operation are included at random. Even actions which have nothing to do with the case but belong to the category of social behavioural habits may be included. The game is kaleidoscopic, as things happen to occur. Certain aspects of behaviour make their appearance out of context and are pieced together with no definite system. This applies both to the hereditary reflexes and to actions which the puppy has learnt.

It is generally recognised that a puppy's games serve to teach him all those things which he will require in later life. Playing is a form of preparation for the future serious business of existence. This we shall see quite clearly when dealing with the individual types of game.

Eibl-Eibesfeldt describes as follows the connection between inquisitiveness, playing and learning: 'There is an obvious disposition to play at the root of which lies the urge of curiosity; in other words there exists a mechanism which induces the animal to look for new situations and experiment with new things. Disposition to play and disposition to learn in fact have a common root. Playing is an active form of learning.'

In his desire to learn, which gives rise to all his playing, the puppy shows just the same inconsistency as the small child who continuously wants to do something new and shows no capacity for persistence. Something which at one moment is extremely interesting is pushed on one side in the next second because something else has come in view which suddenly seems more interesting. Watching a puppy's development, however, it soon becomes clear to us that his inquisitiveness increases and that more and more time is spent on *one* thing. This, of course, applies primarily to playing with objects. The puppies' games together are full of change since every movement made by one of the partners in the game may open up new avenues of play.

This means that a single toy is not enough for a puppy. The range of animal activities is wide and advantage should be taken of this since playing with objects is important for the puppy's development. Such play, of course, can never replace all those communal games which teach him how to associate with others of his kind and also provide practice in the various motions which serve in hunting some quarry.

It may be objected that the domestic dog, the family dog, has no need to associate with others of his kind and will never be required to hunt for his food. But what would become of a child who was shut up in a pen with fifty rabbits with which he could play to his heart's content but was never given an opportunity of playing 'his type' of game with other children? This would be no healthy upbringing; children inherit certain habits of play and acquire others; this child could satisfy none of his natural desires. He would never be able to integrate into human society—he would be a Tarzan.

We have already seen in another connection how important it is that innate habits of behaviour should be allowed to develop unchecked. Constriction of the natural impulses, prevention of normal development of innate habits and other frustrations are no basis for the evolution of the dog's personality. Playing with others of his kind is an integral part of his natural upbringing, and if this is prevented far-reaching disorders in his mental make-up are the result. This means, of course, that much can be done for a puppy's development if account is taken of his requirement for play and allowances made accordingly for the new member of the family. Most people cannot stop themselves playing with a puppy; but the game can be much better and more successful if one knows the meaning of each of the puppy's forms of game and what their purpose is under natural conditions when the dog would be hunting in a pack. This stimulates inventiveness and makes the game more varied—for the man as well as the dog!

Here we shall have to abandon the timetable. Habits of play do not lend themselves to compartmentation or division according to age-groups. It will therefore be necessary sometimes to look back at previous phases of development and sometimes forward to later ones—those of seniority classification and pack formation, for instance.

Some years ago Hanns Ludwig of the Veterinary Institute, Giessen University, studied the playing habits of boxers. It must have been a highly amusing business since, if you have available all at the same time nine puppies together with their parents, things tend to happen. It cannot have been easy to disentangle individual motions from a milling mob of eleven mouths, forty-four legs and twenty-two ears. Nevertheless Ludwig did it and I propose to make use of the results of his efforts.

The most frequent form of puppy game is the fighting game. This should not lead one to think that among dogs fighting is one of the first principles of existence or that it plays a major part in their life. Playing is not only an active form of learning; it also satisfies a highly important urge for movement designed to develop the muscles, sinews and joints. How can this be done better than by measuring one's strength against others of one's own kind, in other words by fighting games?

These are started either by using one of the forms of invitation of which we already know or by a challenge issued by rushing at the other dog with exaggerated body movements—in bounds, at a gallop, waggling the back ends. There are no preliminaries such as the tiptoe or threatening approach to be seen in the case of a real quarrel—after all it is just a game; as it proceeds, however, all the methods of biting used in serious battle are employed. There is no real biting, of course; sufficient control is kept of the bite to ensure that no damage is done. If, in the heat of battle, however, someone goes too far, he is rewarded with loud shrieks of pain. One can be sure, however, that this is vastly overdone—rather like footballers after a foul who give one to think that they will die any minute.

Growling is part of the game but it sounds quite different from that of a serious fight. It is short and higher-pitched, whereas in a serious fight it is deep-throated, prolonged and sounds savage. It is easy to tell when a puppy really gets angry in the middle of a game.

One form of game is to jump at each other and then do what Ludwig calls 'boxing'. The two place their forepaws against each other and try to push each other away; the position somewhat resembles that used in the so-called 'standing fighting posture' when the opponents clasp each other round the shoulders. The 'standing position' differs from 'boxing', however, in that the two animals stand on their hind legs, clasp each other and try to seize the throat. When 'boxing', puppies usually lose their balance, one of them runs off and then a fresh game of catch-as-catch-can begins. Biting games in the standing position offer many variations. The two dogs may stand against each other, for instance, and try to seize each other by the throat, or they may try to bite the other's leg or they may use the 'neck and throat hold' when a foreleg is placed on or over the opponent's neck. The whole thing is a trial of strength using the weight of the body; the object is to push the other away by thrusting the chest against him or to press him down, in which case the whole weight of the forepart of the body is used to hold him to the ground.

All fighting games demand skill, instantaneous reaction and use of all the forces of the body; all capabilities are exercised. The puppy learns to know what he can do and how strong he is; he discovers that relative strengths differ, that his parents are far stronger than he is, for instance, and some of his brothers and sisters weaker. Fighting games, therefore, give rise to the relationships which will later find expression in seniority classification.

By simulating the motions of the fighting game in so far as we can, much can be done to lay the foundations of a sound relationship between us and our dog. Physical contact is essential for a fighting game. The hands are excellent for the purpose and can even do the work of two other puppies. If, for instance, the puppy tries to bite one's right hand or prevent it seizing his throat, then the left hand can 'bite' his hind leg; he whirls round to confront this new assailant whereupon the right-hand partner in the game uses the neck-and-throat hold to throw him on the floor, press him down and hold him there. When the tiny puppy has grown into a bulldog or St Bernard, then we shall need both hands and so can only provide one playmate for him. By this time, however, the dog will have learnt that he must keep slightly more control of his bite when playing with master—a man's skin is not quite so tough as the ruff of another dog's neck.

The dog learns by playing. In a fighting play with man he learns in particular that he can never—never!—beat us, that we are far stronger than he is and that in a game we are always in the lead.

This he finds easy to understand because he was taught exactly the same in his original canine family: his parents were always and in everything superior. What he learns by playing, however, produces no inferiority complex. During a game, acting the defeated is very amusing and, as Ludwig observed with his boxers, dogs play winners and losers; it is just as good fun to play inferiority and subordination as superiority. So here we have the best and most natural method of habituating our four-legged friend from his youth, without using force and without conflict, to the fact that we are the predominant partner.

I have often noticed that men are inclined to leave the puppy's upbringing to their wife and only concern themselves with the dog when he is old enough to be trained. This is not right. The reason is not that women are unsuitable for this job—that is an unkind insinuation usually advanced when the man has not been as successful as he would like with the subsequent training. This is usually what happens, however, when there has been a division of responsibilities during the development period. The dog cannot suddenly be expected to change from childish games to the serious business of life. Under natural conditions there is invariably a gradual transition from the games of childhood to the serious requirements of existence, which include seniority classification.

The main point to remember is that the games played during the socialisation period establish once and for all who is a playmate and who is not; if his master takes no part during this period, this is a fact which, from the dog's point of view, governs his attitude in the future. The canine father, who spends much of his time as teacher and trainer, also plays with his puppies; he is adept at using a game to turn his lessons into fun. In this we ourselves can learn from the dog. Development into a good sporting dog or a performing dog which will do all kinds of tricks with genuine pleasure begins in the socialisation phase. Only at this period is the puppy susceptible to learning the joy of learning. Only if account is taken of this natural evolution can a healthy attitude to learning be inculcated and there will then never be difficulties later when something new is demanded. In this connection I am reminded once more of Rana who would allow a dog to train her but not a man. When she walks to heel she does it because she has to and has learnt that resistance is useless. But this sort of obedience is not what we want from a dog.

Undoubtedly a good experienced handler given charge of a grown-up dog will be able, by his understanding and gift of empathy, to establish his authority in such a way that the dog will accept it willingly, even gladly. But there are only a few men who can do this. Many difficulties will be avoided if one begins, while the dog is still a small puppy, to knit the bonds of confidence and establish one's own position of predominance and command authority by means of a merry game. Then the dog will show no antipathy to the new demands which change his existence but there will be a gradual transition from playing to all those other things which a good dog should be able to do.

Full-grown dogs also play with each other; the games usually seen are fighting games. In all my pens the dogs live in pairs and, apart from times when the bitch is nursing her puppies, the dog is in every case indubitably master in his own house. At least twice a day, however, in the morning and in late afternoon, violent fighting games between dog and bitch take place; I have the definite impression that they are of some significance for maintenance of the order of seniority. During play the fact that the dog is the senior partner emerges clearly; he is the one who decides when there has been enough play. Here is another factor to be exploited in our relationship with our dog: for the grown-up dog play is undoubtedly more than a mere outlet for stored-up energy; it fulfils a function in holding the group together in that seniority can thereby by 'exercised playfully'.

Another category of play has been christened by Ludwig 'food-procurement games'. We will deal first with the hunting game.

In the case of this game I have been struck by the fact that it is frequently the senior dog which acts the role of quarry, which volunteers, in fact, to act the 'terror-struck fugitive'. In the kindergarten it is usually the strongest puppy which does this or, in the case of dogs living a family life, the father. Sascha and Rana, my two alsatians, give me a daily display of the hunting game—two grown dogs of whom the male is undoubtedly the leader. Sascha takes up position some eight to ten yards in front of Rana and gazes at her fixedly; Rana thereupon crouches down as if lying in wait, her neck stretched out and her head held low, gazing back at him. Suddenly the dog leaps to one side and rushes off; Rana is up in a flash, her joints working like coiled springs, and she hares after him.

All this is typical of an animal stalking its prey. The wolf steals up to his victim which, sensing danger, is alerted; the wolf adopts the lying-in-wait posture, lowering himself slowly until he has reached the best position from which to spring. He fastens his eyes on his victim, which gazes at him in terror—and suddenly springs to one side to seek safety in flight. Its pursuer must act in a split second; he must jump just as quickly and without delay. This demands extreme rapidity of reaction and continuous training. One must keep oneself on the top line!

I do not know whether wild wolves play hunting games when fully grown; the actual process of catching their food gives them plenty of practice. It is possible that our dogs continue to play until an advanced age simply because they have no opportunity to follow their natural instinct and obtain their food by hunting. Undoubtedly the pent-up hereditary impulses require a safety valve; the games of youth may be continued as a substitute for the real thing—capture of some prey. In the case of cats which have no opportunity to go mousing there may even be 'dummy-run reactions'; the pent-up impulse is so strong that the cat will stalk and jump on imaginary mice. In the dog's case the principal movements employed in the capture of some other animal are undoubtedly hereditary reflexes but between them there are major gaps which must be filled by experience; this allows the fixed components of the system to be adjusted to the situation or the type of animal being stalked. Since we are dealing here with hereditary reflexes, there is clearly some innate stimulus, some urge demanding satisfaction through action. Many dogs display a disposition to return to nature: they steal quietly away and poach until they meet the barrel of some sportsman's gun. His furious reaction is understandable; a poaching dog is a competitor in his domain; hunting is, after all, an age-old occupation and defence of territory is as essential a feature of it as ever.

A question not without its importance: what can one do to stop one's dog going off hunting or rather poaching? The first and most important thing is to provide him with substitute activities on which he can work off his innate impulses. We know the main features: hunt—stalk—lie in wait—jump—pursue—catch—shake the life out—carry home.

As we know, the individual hereditary reflexes need not necessarily and in every case follow each other in a fixed order, as they would do when used in earnest. The games a dog plays have shown that each action can stand on its own and all can be mixed up at random; the object is to work all these impulses out of the nervous system. So here we come back to the game, the planned, purposeful, 'therapeutic and instructional' game between man and dog.

Hunting, in other words the tracking down of some animal, may be done by scent or, in the case of dogs primarily dependent on their eyes such as Mediterranean staghounds or greyhounds, by sighting some moving object at a distance. Naturally the ear too can play a part in hunting. The important factor, however, is not which senses are used but the fact that there is a desire to hunt based on the impulse to obtain food. This normally stems from hunger; even a well-fed dog, however, may show a desire to hunt if his pent-up impulses get the better of him.

Heinz Bäsche, an alsatian expert, once told me how he trained a difficult dog to follow a scent. What he did was in fact 'applied behavioural research', although he did not know it. He had taken over an eighteen-month-old alsatian which he wished to train for competition. Though perfect in every other respect, when he first placed a 'seek-and-find' harness on the dog, then two years old, the dog began to tremble all over. Clearly he had once had some highly unpleasant experience with a harness; perhaps something had hit him during one of his first tracking exercises or he had suffered some shock now inseparably bound up in his mind with the harness. This being so, there was clearly no hope of putting the dog on a scent. He simply ran away terrified. Heinz Bäsche first accustomed the dog to the harness by putting it on him when out for a walk or while playing. The dog accordingly overcame his fear of the harness but he still refused to follow a scent. All efforts were fruitless.

Bäsche then worked out a new method which was in fact a resounding success. First he starved the dog for three days; this was not in the least cruel; such a thing is good for a dog's health since it corresponds to the natural feeding habits of the wild dog.

I would like people to starve their dogs at least once a week, if not twice; most dogs one sees on the street are, to put it baldly, overfed. Over-generous feeding is a crime against a dog's health. No wild dog eats every day and he frequently has to survive periods of severe hunger. But by the natural process of selection he is adapted to this and our domestic dog also needs a period of starvation to remain healthy. Heinz Bäsche's course of fasting, therefore, did his alsatian no harm; instead it activated his predisposition to hunt, as would happen in nature. No predatory animal goes hunting unless his stomach is rumbling; he has no wish to work harder than necessary. This dog was therefore certainly in a state when the threshold of his desire to hunt was very low.

Heinz Bäsche led the dog to the prepared trail, indicated the start of it (a three-foot square trap) by making a fuss and walking round and round, tied the dog to a tree and took a package from his pocket. It contained good juicy pieces of beef. One was given to the dog at once; in sight of the dog Bäsche then placed the others every ten yards along the track which was some fifty yards long. The remainder he put back in his pocket, went back to the dog, put him on the lead and led him to the start where was the first the first piece of meat. For the first time the dog made no attempt to leave the track but followed it with genuine interest from one piece of meat to the next; at the end he was given the remaining pieces as well as much congratulation. From now on following a scent was connected in the dog's mind with something pleasurable and so the way was now open to teach him all that was required in this field.

This is the way to teach a dog to follow a scent; it conforms to the nature of the dog, and the sportsman will, of course, follow it logically through. A sporting dog following a trail illustrates the point even better. If an animal is wounded it will lose blood as it tries to escape into the undergrowth and this blood forms the trail. As it hunts the dog will naturally find this trail attractive and will follow it until it has discovered the animal. The dog will get his reward if the hunter breaks up or rather disembowels the animal.

Basically, therefore, following a scent is something which the dog's instinct tells him is pleasurable—a function connected with obtaining food. A guard-dog, however, follows a scent for a different purpose. In this case the dog must learn to follow the scent of a man whom he does not know at all and not one shred of whose clothing must he touch when he has tracked him down. Here, therefore, is a form of conduct which has been divorced from its original function and related to something that means nothing to the dog. What happens is that the dog is first taught to follow the scent of his own master; this is more easily comprehensible to him. Then he is taught to follow the trail of one of his own kind. Following a scent thus becomes connected either with

The English Pointer, bred 'for nose'

his social existence or with reproduction. From this point it is no great transition to pursuit of the scent of a strange man. Meanwhile, moreover, the dog has learnt the relevant words of command such as 'Seek' and has realised that for some reason it is of importance to his master that he should follow a certain trail.

For those who have no wish to train their poodle, pug, dachshund or terrier as a guard-dog I can recommend a splendid game which the dog will enjoy from the outset. His master or someone else the

Play

dog is fond of goes some distance away—start with a short distance only—placing at the start of the trail and the half-way point a handkerchief, glove or some other object which has been on the person for some time and so carries his or her scent. The person laying the trail hides at the end of it and keeps quite still. The other person then brings the dog on the longest possible lead—ten to fifteen feet will do for a small dog—to the start of the trail and calls out 'Seek'. There is great rejoicing when the dog finds his friend at the end of the trail. Initially the dog should see the first person move off (it must be someone he wishes to go with) but he must never see more than the first half of the trail or he will seek with his eyes—and he must be made to use his nose. When a dog will follow one definite scent and no other, this is known as steadiness on a scent. In the hide-and-seek game this happens automatically since it comes naturally to the dog to look for the person of whom he is fond. What, for instance, does the sportsman do when he wishes his bloodhound to follow no scent other than the fresh trail of a deer? He finds some soft ground where are the tracks of a deer which he can see are fresh and causes his dog to work along them, encouraging and congratulating him. When he reaches the end of the trail the dog will be rewarded by a piece of deerhide, a fresh deerbone or a piece of venison. Whenever the dog takes off, even momentarily, on another scent such as that of a roedeer or hare, he will be called back sharply and scolded. If he is obstinate there is a well-tried method of preventing him following other scents— and it can be used to stop our dog poaching or raiding our neighbour's chicken-house. I refer to the spiked collar which is in fact less severe than its name might imply. It is merely a square-linked chain which does not chafe the dog if he is going properly on the lead. If he goes off on the scent of a hare or roebuck, one simply lets the chain run out (it must be at least thirty feet long) until it is taut; at that moment one rebukes the dog sharply and jerks him back. The sudden tightening of the links of the chain will make him feel that he is really being punished. If this is done three or four times, the scent of the animal concerned will become connected in the dog's mind with the punishment meted out by the chain; that particular animal will acquire a negative flavour. The dog will no longer go poaching or even glance at the neighbour's hens if they are connected in his mind with this sort of treatment.

This, therefore, is one method of eradicating the bad habits of the incorrigible poacher or poultry-thief. But we must not be content merely to impose our will upon him. We must find some substitute outlet for the dog's innate desire to hunt. I have already described how we can satisfy his urge to seek. Next in the category of hunting functions come stalking and lying in wait. Here I must admit that I do not know what games one can invent but this can quite happily be left to the dog—he will think up something when opportunity offers. As we are strolling along, for instance, he will take us by surprise and jump at us from one side; he will select moments when he can be certain that his beloved master is ready for any form of fun. If a forty-kilo St Bernard is too much for you and you fall over, that is the best fun of all from the dog's point of view!

After stalking and lying in wait the next action in hunting is to spring on the prey. An entertaining 'substitute satisfaction' for this is 'doing the high jump' with Master. Care should be taken with a young dog; do not make him jump too often or too high; he should be trained up slowly—he cannot be expected to jump a six-foot hurdle in his first year. It is far far more important that he should do what we ask, even if he only jumps over a stick held a foot from the ground. Provided he does not have to exert himself unduly, it will remain for him a game that he likes and he will still like it when one day, after slow, careful and progressive training, he can jump through a burning motor-tyre, over six three-foot hurdles in a row or down from the climbing wall.

This is, of course, 'advanced training'. It will be clear, however, that everything that we can teach our dog is basically no more than utilisation of his natural capabilities. He is endowed with certain methods of movement and he requires to exercise them; he uses them of his own accord as a puppy and enjoys doing so. Here, therefore, are pointers to the dog's training; basically it is no more than happens in nature: the game becomes serious business and the capabilities exercised in play and expanded by learning are used in the struggle for existence. We remove from the dog the struggle for existence; we must therefore do something to provide an outlet for his urge for activity. Training the dog is a necessity not just for the police and frontier guards; it is a necessity for the dog. A dog which has no opportunity to learn something, to develop his capabilities to the full, becomes stupid, mentally atrophied, a pitiable creature.

I have deliberately dealt with these questions of a dog's education and training under the heading 'Play' since the services rendered by the trained dog, such as tracking down criminals or finding people buried in an avalanche, must from the dog's point of view remain play; the game, however, is played within definite limits set by man and in a way which man has taught.

Today those who train dogs for a definite service prefer not to use the words 'drilling' or 'teaching' because they carry an implication of the brutality used in the old days when the whip did duty for the intelligence. Unfortunately there is still much prejudice— we train our animals, the circus drills them. I would advise many ambitious dog-handlers to watch one day what happens in a circus. There people are mostly dealing with animals which have not the patience of our dogs. For years I went every morning to the so-called 'exercise manège' of the Krone circus and saw how the animals were 'drilled' there. The 'drill-masters' showed a sensitivity, an understanding and love of animals which made me realise how merciless and impatient many people are when dealing with their dogs. Training for the circus is done slowly and progressively, as if it were an amusing game with rewards provided— titbits or congratulation; there is neither coercion nor competition to have the 'turn' ready as quickly as possible. Training lasts as long as the animal finds necessary. It therefore likes what is asked of it and does its 'work' as a game, with pleasure and interest. I have never seen a circus animal show signs of servility or fear during its display; at dog-shows, however, I have seen many animals display both to a shattering degree.

If a dog has been well brought up and is healthy, one can teach him anything one likes, always provided, of course, that it is within his capacity. Eva and Sascha demonstrate this daily. Quite quickly he and she have worked out a real 'turn'. It begins with the dog refusing to obey orders; she can call him, kick him, pull him about and slap him but he just lies there and will do nothing she says. It is very effective since it looks exactly like a fit of disobedience. He just stays there and waits until Eva appears with a wheelbarrow. He jumps into it and is carried to the playground where are motor-tyres and other articles of equipment. This is the start of the 'turn'. Eva only has to put a hand on the wheelbarrow or one of the tyres and Sascha is beside himself with joy. He can hardly wait for the 'turn' to begin; he rushes off and comes back carrying some other piece of equipment and is heart and soul in the business. If Rana, to whom he is always extremely polite and affectionate, disturbs him during his game, he can be really savage with her and growl at her furiously.

For Sascha, therefore, it is real joy to work with his mistress and he does so with his head high, his eyes bright and his ears pricked. The tail, the morale barometer, indicates 'high' and if some change in the routine is made or something new introduced, his interest is even keener.

Sascha's greatest joy, as I have already said, is retrieving pieces of stick. He can play this game till he drops. Whenever one comes out of the house he comes galloping up carrying some piece of wood, sometimes half a tree-trunk, sometimes a tiny twig—whatever he has been able to find in his hurry. He is always bitterly disappointed if his invitation is unanswered. So here we come back to the substitute game: this represents the catching phase in the capture of some prey.

Young dogs often play with some object quite by themselves; they throw it sideways or upwards and then catch it again. It is particularly good fun if the object is round and rolls away; then it can be chased. Balls of wood or solid rubber are excellent dog toys and there is a good choice in the shops. Recovery of some object which has been thrown—retrieving—is no invention of man but a game peculiar to the dog. It can easily be explained: the object he pursues represents his prey which he hunts, catches and carries home. Retrieving is a form of play which can be turned into a 'duty'. It is worth spending some time on this because it provides a good practical example showing how to prepare for later serious training.

The basic rule is not to try to teach the puppy to retrieve but to wait until he asks for this game on his own. This should happen in the eighth to ninth week at the latest. Of course one can assist by rolling a ball which will naturally be chased with enthusiasm. Now take the ball away and throw it again; never demand that the dog bring it back; he will do so of his own accord sooner or later and certainly as soon as he has realised that the game with his

Play

master will only go on if the ball is taken away from him. The puppy will very soon bring the ball or stick back without being asked. When he does so he is rewarded with congratulation; as he rushes off, call out 'Bring' and congratulate him when he does so; only start using the command 'Bring', however, when it is certain that the dog will come back and proffer the object thrown. If the puppy is more than four months old and will retrieve an object on demand, a more controlled form of game can be instituted. The dog can be required to sit in front of us with the object in his mouth and wait until it is taken from him; he can be made to sit 'to heel' when the stick is thrown. He will thus learn that he may

Young alsatian playing at retrieving with a rag

only run after it on the word 'Fetch'. All this can be done without shouting, without a cross word and without smacking; it simply develops from an amusing game and in the dog's mind will always be connected with the enjoyment of this game even when he has to do it as a grown-up dog on the training ground. Anyone who turns to account the puppy's enjoyment of a game, shows some sensitivity and works out a comprehensive training programme based on the various forms of game, will never have difficulty in training his dog for more serious business. The desire to learn must be inculcated while the dog is still a puppy, between the eighth and twelfth weeks. At this point the desire to learn is at its greatest; at this period too the desire to play with others develops and the enjoyment of a game with man is especially great. If we make adroit use of all this, we have laid the foundation for the future. The puppy learns to regard man as a partner with whom one can play wonderful games and he realises that these games give equal pleasure both to him and the man—we must always show him that we are pleased with every little advance. We can also show him, however, that we are not pleased when he does something wrong; a reproachful 'Pfui' is all that is required. I would not recommend slapping a puppy of this age—it is not necessary. Such methods need only be used after the twelfth week and then only when there is no alternative. By this time we have reached the 'seniority classification phase', as I call it; the puppies of a litter will have established a definite order of seniority among themselves and at this point the man must definitely insist on his position of authority if he does not want to lose it.

Now let us look at one or two other canine games; in most cases it is obvious what can be made of them. Puppies often wrangle happily over a 'capture' such as a piece of rag which they have been given. A real tug-of-war develops and we can naturally play the same game with our dog. The significance of the game is obvious: if one holds his 'capture' fast, the dog can nevertheless tear pieces off it. The guard-dog under training does the same when he holds the padded sleeve of the man representing the criminal. Here is an instance of a game developing into collaboration with man. The dog should hold on until he gets the word 'Dead' from his master.

Another category of game is concerned with movement; such games are designed less to practise some function in life than to harden the muscles, develop dexterity and train for speed. It will often be seen that the puppy will carry out certain movements over and over again until he can do them to his own satisfaction; only then will he do something else. In this case, therefore, the exercise has a definite purpose and the reward is undoubtedly the pleasure he derives from his ability to do the movement in the end.

Puppies are often to be seen playing sexual games, though Ludwig rather questions whether they are genuine games. Even very young puppies, however, are so often and so clearly to be seen mounting each other, though obviously without any real sexual intent, that it seems reasonable to refer to regular 'mounting games'. Even full-grown dogs play the same game. I remember some comic scenes when Sylvia, a long-haired dachshund bitch, and

Buna, the dingo bitch, were both in season simultaneously. They had lived together for some time, were very good friends and used to play all sorts of games together. When they came in season they suddenly began to mount each other, as one sees heifers doing in the field. One may say that this was no mere game since the sexual urge was there but the two were, after all, both bitches.

Finally Ludwig mentions wolf-pack games. This is not in fact a separate form of game; all the different types of game are played by the whole litter as a pack, with the parents often taking part as I have frequently seen happen in my pens. From the twelfth week onwards, sometimes a little earlier, real disciplined co-operation between the animals can be observed. One of the litter plays the part of an animal on the run while the others hunt him in concert. Interestingly I have often seen the father challenging his puppies to chase him. By such 'catch-as-catch-can' games the puppies gradually learn to work together in a coordinated fashion; sometimes they encircle their 'quarry' or descend upon it adroitly from both sides. This is how the wolf-pack's hunting tactics develop.

As time goes on these games become increasingly disciplined; there is now a definite object: to train the dogs to work together in real life like a football team. It should be remembered that at this age nature has conditioned the puppies for the seniority-classification phase and for tactical co-operation with others of their kind; mentally they have developed to the stage when they will accept discipline. This is therefore the time to begin planned obedience training; it is part of the young dog's education even if he is living wild.

It is amusing to watch such pack games based on the pursuit of an animal. The dog playing the part of the hunted criminal uses special evasive tactics which may, after all, come in useful in real life. The father introduces these tactics with a very definite purpose. He reproduces all possible situations which may occur when hunting an animal and so, even at this age, is giving effective 'instruction'.

Sascha, whose instincts are highly developed and who is a talented father and uncle, gave me a particularly good illustration of these hunting games. When his daughter Rana had reached the right age he would play hunter and hunted with her every day, showing astounding imagination. The game began with Sascha bounding away from Rana or attracting her attention by one of the usual forms of invitation to play. Sometimes he would fix her with his eye, as already described. When Rana started to chase him, he would use all sorts of tricks to get away from her. Frequently, for instance, he would hide behind a wood-pile and watch to see which way the little bitch came round so that he could creep round the other way. After one or two games Rana rumbled this and went round in the opposite direction so meeting the discomfited Sascha face to face. He allowed this to happen once or twice but then did exactly the opposite, running round the pile in the reverse direction so that this time Rana was outwitted. Rana now had to use all her wits. She did not now run round straight away but spied out the ground first; excitement increased. Finally the two dogs were waiting, each at a corner, to see which way the game would go. Sascha then made as if to run left-handed, causing Rana to go right-handed to meet him; but Sascha had only been bluffing; after a few paces he ran back right-handed round the pile, so Rana was caught out again.

One can spend hours watching dogs at play. It is a continuous pleasure and shows that we can act as a substitute in many things —but not in all. Young dogs should therefore always be given an opportunity to play with others of their kind. Most breeds of grown-up dog also like to play with each other and an exemplary dog like Sascha loves playing with puppies.

DISCIPLINE

As we have seen, the canine father not only plays with his puppies but most explicitly demands their obedience. Here again we can learn a great deal from him. His training methods are severe, tough—but just. When Father administers a hiding it is accompanied by much squealing from the puppy, but the next moment they are back on the old terms and the father is playful and affectionate again as if nothing had happened.

During the socialisation phase the canine father begins to give his puppies a good shaking once to three times a day; this seems to do the young rascals a great deal of good since the result is a certain 'subordination' which, however, shows not a trace of fear or obsequiousness. In his own family, therefore, the puppy learns

Discipline

to respect the size and strength of his superiors without turning into a neurotic cringer as can so quickly happen with a dog-owner who thinks he can instil respect into his young dog by use of the stick. If a dog refuses to conform, in most cases the reason is that

How to carry a four-week-old dingo puppy

he was not properly brought up at the right age. Subordination is instilled during the socialisation phase; if this not done, the best we can hope to achieve is submission to coercion.

We should therefore take a lesson from the male dog and do our best to take his place with this puppy which we have brought into a human community at the age of eight weeks. He is at an age when not only does he understand good order and discipline; he actually requires it, since it has been implanted in him by nature.

We have already seen that in play the hand is a very useful substitute for a dog's jaws. So do not hit your puppy; bite it—and in the nape of the neck. Seize him by the scruff of the neck and pinch with finger and thumb; give a quick shake with a word of rebuke—it is the first step in teaching the meaning of the word. Do this three times and the hand will no longer be required; the word will be enough.

By this method the puppy learns very quickly and he reacts without frustration to our list of prohibitions since such a thing is quite usual in his natural surroundings. The puppy is, of course, an inquisitive being and frequently, in fact almost always, he wants to know for sure that it is forbidden, for instance, to gnaw the leg of a chair. He tries it out under our very nose and then waits for our reaction—thereby compelling us to take extreme measures! He requires this to be repeated several times in order to be quite sure of our opinion about chair-leg gnawing.

It may be, of course, that the puppy will try this on so frequently that the word of rebuke alone is clearly not enough. We must then take action but this time seizing him by the scruff of the neck and shaking him will not do. Seize the miscreant by the scruff of the neck, hold him up high and shake him hard or seize him both by the scruff of the neck and the backside and hold him up high. All this must of course be done immediately after the crime and be accompanied by the word of rebuke.

In my pens I have often seen the male dog obviously and deliberately create situations enabling him to demonstrate his authority to the puppies. He sets up, so to speak, arbitrary 'taboos'. The favourite object used is a bone. It should be mentioned that at this age the parents are still giving preference to feeding the puppies over feeding themselves; the youngsters are still allowed practically to take food out of the parents' mouths without the latter becoming savage. In the case of this particular bone, however, they are not allowed to touch it. For them it is taboo and the father keeps a sharp eye on it even when he has apparently left it casually lying around somewhere in the pen. Hardly has a puppy approached this bone than he is sharply called to order by his father. Unless

Discipline

one knows the implications, it all looks most odd since the bone is usually an old one, gnawed clean, which has been lying about in the pen for some time. I have seen something similar happen with a piece of wood.

Another disciplinary measure is insistence on prior approval of new objects by the father; only after him, and possibly also the bitch, may the puppies approach them. If a leaf falls from a tree and comes down near a puppy, he is in real trouble if he has the temerity to sniff at it before his father. The old man rushes at him bellowing, the puppy screams to high heaven and one would think that it was a matter of life and death. After his inspection the dog withdraws and then the puppy may sniff at it. This is in fact a wise and sensible arrangement since it could be something dangerous. Discipline, therefore, is a contributory factor in self-preservation and the creation of taboos by the father is an ingenious method of education.

This also demonstrates the male dog's position of superiority; within his family he is the pack-leader. Rudolf Schenkel, who has produced much valuable information on the behaviour of wolves, tells a story which shows how this type of action can be expanded into a demonstration of authority over a community. He saw the following in Whipsnade Zoo where the wolves are kept under very good conditions in a large area of woodland: on waking in the morning the pack-leader walked around sniffing the ground. At a certain spot he stopped and dug up a large bone. This he carried 'proudly', with tail held high, past his pack. The other wolves now got up, formed a circle round him and performed a begging ceremony. The leader growled and then continued his peregrination. Then he let the bone fall and took no further notice of it. The others now formed a circle round the bone for a moment; no one took it, however, and they then dispersed again. Schenkel emphasises that the other wolves were not really begging for food; it was all symbolic. The bone was merely a 'prop' for the leader and his pack, used for a 'ceremony of harmonious social integration'.

It is tempting to draw parallels to this story from the ancient traditions of the human race, but our business is with the young dog, to whom we wish to be an equally good pack-leader, a person whose authority he will accept with pleasure once he is grown up.

We have no need to turn some old bone into a taboo or carry it demonstratively around. A well-kept house and the flower-beds in the garden offer more than enough possibilities of creating taboos. Permission to eat can also be used in this connection: it is no crime against a dog's nature if we place an inviting sausage in front of his nose but do not allow him to eat it until we have lifted the taboo by some signal or some specific word. Such demonstrations of authority are, after all, the prerogative of the pack-leader. The essential condition, of course, is that the dog accepts us as such.

It is an interesting and instructive fact that, if a male dog displays willing obedience to a man, without any action by the man he will pass this on to his children. From him they have learnt subordination and they now perceive that he, the great father to whom they are subordinate, is himself subordinate to us. This applies equally to puppies brought up by the bitch alone. Subordination to man instilled into a young dog in this way is something highly satisfying since much experience and sensitivity is required to educate a dog to that degree of unconstrained subordination which can be achieved by the dog or bitch. The conflicting tendencies in poor little Rana's disposition are a good illustration here: taking her cue from Sascha, she will obey very well and quite willingly but one can really do nothing with her because, at the socialisation age, she never learnt to recognise man as a trainer and playmate. She is happy if she can show her appreciation and affection but is in agonies if something is asked of her, be it only the most innocent game. Naturally she cringes terribly if scolded because she has done something wrong, for she has never learnt to accept well-merited punishment from a man. Equally it is impossible to teach her that men have certain possessions; she steals like a magpie because, during her school-age, she never learnt not to; she stands in awe of Sascha's bones but not of the kitchen cupboard. Sascha, on the other hand, will stalk proudly about among the dishes prepared for visitors and never even put a nose near the inviting slices of sausage or legs of chicken. For him they are taboo.

People talk of 'subservience' or 'an air of inferiority' and the like. What the properly brought-up dog displays is better described by the words 'demonstration of allegiance'. In my canine families

Discipline

I have often seen puppies demonstrate their allegiance to their parents: a puppy which has been punished does not creep to its father on its stomach as one sees many dogs do when scolded. He goes up to his father with his head high and demonstrates his attitude by one of those infant gestures which, as we have already seen, denote supplication or propitiation such as a nudge at the muzzle or corner of the mouth or paw-giving; they signify respect for an authority which exercises discipline sensibly, appropriately and justly and to which one is therefore gladly subordinate. Only if our dog reacts to well-deserved punishment in this way can we feel that we are a really good master to him. He must not obey out of fear; he must show that he recognises our authority openly and willingly. We must promote his self-assurance and self-confidence and this we can do by playing with him and disciplining him, always provided that we do not ask more of a puppy than he can be expected to understand at his age.

What he can understand are the prohibited things, as I have described. He can also understand that at certain times we are willing to play with him and at others are not. He will develop no complexes if we suddenly stop playing in the middle of the most glorious game; if during a biting game he becomes too violent, as often happens, and we suddenly break it off as a result, he will quickly learn how far he can go. He will not be able to understand, however, if he is suddenly punished in the middle of a game; this is no way to deal with his high spirits; all it will do is to give him a sense of insecurity since he cannot understand the connection between the two things. It is a different matter with a grown-up dog who has known for a long time how far he can go; if he forgets himself and gets a smack, he will know exactly why. A ten- or twelve-week-old puppy, however, will merely register that man is an incalculable being—and at this age the impression will go deep.

From the outset one should adhere to the principle that punishment is only administered when something forbidden is done, never when a young dog, who is after all still immature, fails to do what we wish. As I have already said when discussing retrieving, we shall only obtain all we want from our dog and do so without dissension, if we show pleasure at what he does—visible pleasure, for the dog will soon learn to know our expression—and if we congratulate him. The result will be that he will find working with a man to be pleasurable and will seek to do so of his own accord. Anger, rebukes and still more blows because the little dog does not at once do what is expected of him are the surest way to turn him into a creature lacking self-assurance and self-confidence which will later obey us solely out of fear of our strength. If at this age we show impatience in training our dog, he will merely become head-shy. We must remember that our puppy, even if he comes of a particularly expensive strain, is no infant prodigy. The process of maturing implanted in him by nature presupposes a very prolonged training period and we are merely overtaxing him if we think that he ought to be able to learn everything all at once and as quickly as possible.

At the socialisation age disciplinary measures should contribute to consolidation of the bond between master and dog and creation of a basis for absolute confidence. The little dog looks by nature for a firm hand; he is still in need of protection and only feels secure in a community led by some strong experienced being. He will react entirely favourably to suitably exercised discipline.

I must now refer, however, to certain disciplinary measures which run counter to the dog's nature. There are certain habits of expression which we shall find fully developed in our puppy but which, unfortunately, we cannot tolerate. I refer to the tendency to lick one's face and jump up in order to show his affection. Schenkel observed these demonstrations of affection among wolves living together; he describes them as follows: 'a lick of the face with ears laid back, a gentle nose-nudge against the lips of the more senior of the pair, finally a gentle seizure of the other's muzzle accompanied by an "affectionate" whimper. The tail was invariably tucked in but not under. Frequently the wolf would "waggle" its entire hinder ends. The movement, the uninhibited approach and still more the nose-nudge have earned this form of conduct the name of "active submission".'

If a senior wolf gazes at a more junior one from a distance, the latter may simulate the nose-nudge by raising his muzzle with his ears laid back; he merely raises the muzzle in the air, the nudge movement hardly being perceptible; it gives the impression instead of a sign of gratification.

Schenkel observed that sniffing at the coat of the neck, muzzle,

Top: Knud and Kala, children of the cross-breeds Björn and Bente, aged 30 days. Their 'submissive' attitude shows that they have still had little contact with human beings.
Bottom: Peer, cross-bred dog aged 40 days. He had long been in contact with human beings and was not in the least perturbed at being photographed.

Sascha, the alsatian dog, is very good with children and beloved of all puppies. As soon as they hear him at the door they wait eagerly for him. At once they begin to play happily with the indulgent great dog.

Top: Dingo puppies like to push their little muzzles between Sascha's great jaws, as they would do to their mother in order to get at the regurgitated food.
Bottom: Nose-nudging derives from the request for food and is a gesture of affection. Similarly 'paw-giving' derives from the teat-kneading motion. Both gestures demonstrated by Aboriginal, the dingo.

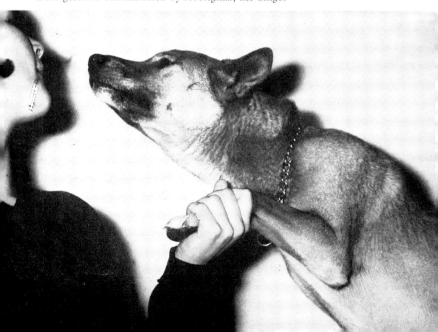

Two half-grown dingoes look suspiciously at the photographer—a new experience for them. The tucked-in tail betrays uncertainty.

Top left: Rana, the alsatian bitch, on the watch. Her expression and the position of the ears indicate excitement.
Top right: Paroo, the dingo dog, 'giving tongue'.
Bottom: Luxl, the New Guinea dingo, at his first encounter with Aboriginal. Being older, though smaller, he is quite self-assured and 'inspects' the younger dog, whose attitude and raised hackles indicate uncertainty and an 'on-guard' position.

Top: Aboriginal meets an alsatian for the first time. Although he is the smaller dog, he approaches stiffly and menacingly with hackles raised and a low growl. The friendly alsatian is uncertain in face of his threats.
Bottom: During a game Rana and Peik have overpowered Pira, Peik's sister. She turns on her back in a gesture of submission.

Binna, the elkhound bitch, and Suki, the dingo bitch, both in season at the same time and therefore aggressive towards each other. They clasp each other's shoulders and show their teeth with muzzles wrinkled.

Two half-grown ridgebacks (South African lion dogs) want to play with this small girl, who runs away screaming. Children who are afraid of dogs have been badly brought up.

Top: Having retrieved his stick, an alsatian jumps a burning pole. Such a high degree of training can only be reached through the closest co-operation with the handler.
Bottom: The alsatian Schlapp must have had a difficult upbringing for he shows every sign of fear when placed against a wall to be photographed.

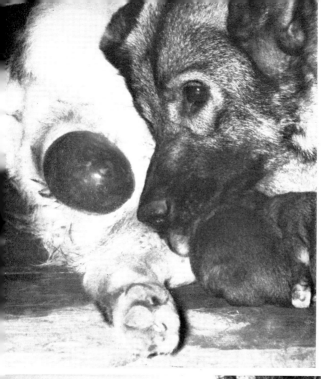

Binna giving birth.

Top: The membrane containing the foetus as it emerges, the bitch looking back at it.

Bottom: The puppy out of the membrane. Binna sniffs it over.

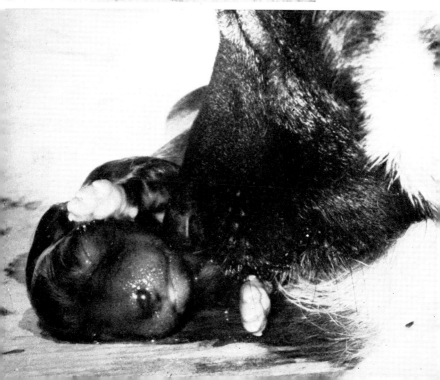

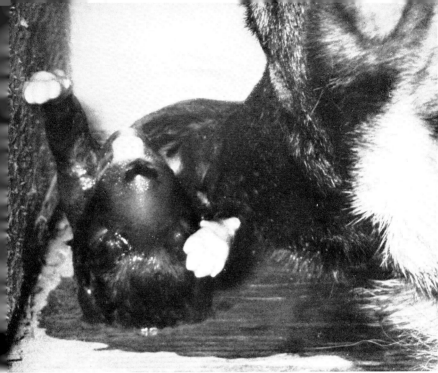

Top: The puppy puts out his tongue and takes his first deep breath.

Bottom: While being licked dry the puppy tries to avoid his mother's tongue, squeaking in protest. As soon as released he makes his way to a teat.

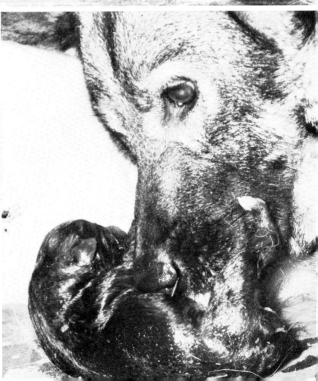

Top: Character test with Leonbergers (see p. 228): Sascha, always friendly, is on a lead beyond the hedge. After a preliminary sniff Asko invites him to play.
Bottom: His brother Arras, on the other hand, charges at the hedge barking loudly. He dislikes other dogs on principle, thus showing considerable deficiency of instinct.

Discipline 145

side of the head or corner of the mouth was generally a sign of a friendly relaxed attitude. The sketch below reproduces a photograph showing a demonstration of affection between my elkhound bitch Binna, then sixteen weeks old, and her aunt of the same name, then aged four years. The situation was as follows: the elder Binna had played for some time with little Binna; both were somewhat tired and little Binna nestled happily up against her good-natured aunt, licked her on the muzzle and snuffled her affectionately. The

Little Binna affectionately nose-nudging her aunt

ears were laid back as a sign of humility; she was thus demonstrating that she had no thought of aggression in her mind, in contrast, for instance, to her expression when challenging to a biting game. The old dog turned her head away—another typical propitiatory gesture, as if to say: 'All right; that's enough; I won't do anything to you.' Had she not turned her head at once, little Binna would have had to continue her efforts and with greater emphasis. Further persistence, however, would have been tantamount either to an invitation to a biting game or have been a sign of real hostility.

So here we have a peaceful scene such as can be seen daily between dogs which are good friends, particularly between elders and juniors. It is most frequently to be seen between mother and child.

Now we can understand what our dog is wanting to 'say' to us when he pushes his muzzle into our face. If one has the necessary self-control, one need only remain quite still; there will be a well-aimed nudge of the cold muzzle against our lips, particularly the corner of the mouth, followed immediately by the warm wet tongue drawn right across the mouth. This is a muzzle caress. Note how the ears are laid back; the good dog is undoubtedly treating us like one of his own kind and demonstrating to us that he accepts our authority gladly; he is saying that he is our affectionate servant. What more do we want? On the other hand no one particularly likes this damp demonstration of affection. One can quietly turn one's head away and so evade the caress. This is no insult to him, since the mere turning of the head shows him that we are so superior that we have no need of this gesture. But there must be no punishment—and a rebuke is tantamount to punishment. This is not 'bad manners' on the dog's part. He can quietly be shown that we understand very well what he means but do not require to be shown it quite so directly. He will soon turn it into a declaration of intent, an action not quite carried through to the end, a nose-nudge in the air.

Equally it is not bad manners if, when we come home, our dog jumps up at us in his excitement—though with a mastiff or the other larger breeds this can be 'upsetting' in the literal sense of the word. This is merely an expedient on the dog's part. If anyone asks me what he is to do to stop his dog jumping up, I tell him to go on all fours. The dog will not then jump because he has no need to; he can reach our mouth and welcome us home with his muzzle caress without more ado.

It is sad that we have to evade and forbid so many of our dog's friendly gestures, but unfortunately there is no alternative. We try to restrain the overwhelming joy caused by our return by rebuking him and pushing him away—scurvy thanks for so much love which the dog is trying to demonstrate to us in his own way. There is only one thing to be done: strictly forbid this particular method of expression but make it clear at once that it is only the form which we do not like and that we understand the intention very well. Depending on the size and temperament of the dog, it is possible to find ways in which each side can show its pleasure. Paw-giving is a very adequate substitute for nose-nudging and face-licking. A dog may have certain innate habits of behaviour but he also has the capacity to suppress them when the moment is unsuitable or substitute for them something that he has learnt. If we teach him to do some definite little trick and invariably demand that he does it whenever he wants to nose-nudge, he will soon conform and realise that in this way he can demonstrate his 'active submission'.

A dog is by no means an unintelligent creature working on instinct alone. He has his armoury of hereditary reflexes but he also has considerable capacity to employ them sensibly and control them. This applies especially to his methods of expression. After all, we too have innate methods of expression. The laugh, for instance, expresses pleasure. We may laugh because we have heard a good joke; this is a hereditary reflex expressing a certain emotion. We can also laugh at a very bad joke, however, for purely social reasons—because the managing director has told it, for instance; this is conscious use of a hereditary reflex. This brings us to the question whether a dog can think. He can, but in a way different from ours. Otto Koehler has produced a first-class synopsis of behavioural research and animal psychology which provides an insight into the higher-level capabilities of the animal brain; he refers to 'inarticulate thought', a process of thought which cannot express itself and which we must imagine as formed of memory-pictures. In the human being this form of thought is the preliminary stage in the development of speech. The small child learns its mother tongue through inarticulate thought; it situates the words which it hears and imitates in their correct places in this inarticulate thought because it realises that the individual words are always connected with a definite thing or situation. Our dog's process of learning is the same, but he is unable to imitate words and he is also unable to grasp the fact that a combination of words produces a meaningful sentence. For him—as initially for the small child—there can only be 'single-word sentences'. If, for instance, we say 'Go to your basket', what he hears is 'Gotoyourbasket'; for him this combination of words is no more than an audible signal which he connects with his basket because that is what he has learnt. Koehler, who has carried out research for decades, has taught us much about animals' capacity for thought; one can, for instance, dismiss as pure nonsense the claim so often heard that signals consisting of a number of knocks or taps enable a dog to form a sentence and that he can answer questions if expressed in this way.

We must concede to the dog, however, that, undoubtedly to a considerable degree, he is able to think, though his thinking does not work on word-symbols, as with a grown-up man who can speak, but on a combination of situations experienced. Koehler, for instance, had a terrier who worked out that it was difficult to carry at a gallop a six-foot branch of a tree if it had twigs and so always gnawed all the twigs off before carrying it; this was indubitably an effort of thinking. One can imagine the process as follows: the dog becomes conscious that a branch with twigs is always getting caught up in something. He had recently carried a piece of wood of similar length without trouble. He remembers how it looked and his memory-picture indicates to him that it had no twigs. He compares this with his unwieldy branch and finds the solution: he must make the branch like the one which he recently had. His memory-pictures no doubt remind him of the process of biting off twigs which he had done in play for no particular reason. Combination of all these memory-pictures leads him to purposeful action—he bites off the vexatious twigs. This is successful in that the branch can now be carried and so henceforth every branch is tailored in this way. This is the way to interpret 'inarticulate thought'.

The dog does not 'understand' the full meaning of our words of command; he merely relates their sound to what he has learnt. Many people are often taken aback when their dog does something before the word of command has been given. Here he is assisted by his astonishing gift of observance. We do not simply give our orders perfunctorily but, during the time of training the dog in what he has to do, we have become accustomed to adopt a certain expression. At that time we were giving each order with particular clarity and emphasis, all the time wondering 'Will he do it or won't he?' Many elements of our facial expression have become permanencies and so, even before giving the order, we put on the 'Come here' face or the 'Go to your basket' face. These are frequently tiny insignificant changes in our features or attitude

Discipline

which we should probably never even notice when looking in the mirror; our eye is nothing like so finely trained. In this the dog is far ahead of us!

I am continually being asked how a dog can know precisely the moment when his master is on his way home—has he the gift of 'clairvoyance'? The dog can do so many astonishing things that we are often lost in admiration and unable to understand how they are possible. Any dog-owner will experience something of this sort almost daily and much passes our comprehension.

This is not to say that we should be believers in miracles. During an interesting lecture by a dog-handler the words 'sense of feel' were used. This is a well-established expression among 'doggy people'; it is perhaps useful but it is somewhat misleading.

The following discussion took place between me and this experienced dog-handler:

'What do you mean by "sense of feel"?'—'Well, the dog has a special sense enabling him to understand the moods and feelings of his master'—'Right—the dog can sense our mood and adapt himself accordingly even though we have not made a sound. But here is my objection: you have told us of the sense of smell, sense of hearing and sense of sight. These are true senses in the normal meaning of the word since they are connected to the corresponding organs of sense—nose, ears and eyes. There is no sensory organ, however, which can register the mood of another dog or of a man.' The lecturer then replied: 'Agreed, but if you read the books by the great canine experts like Moss and others, they all refer to sense of feel.'

So here I was confronted by the traditional 'school', bound by the venerated theories of the 'great teachers'.

For some idea of this 'sense of feel' one should study the significance of the various forms of behaviour inside a wolf-pack. Take as an example a couple of wolves hunting in concert who have flushed some large animal. There then follows some extremely fine teamwork between the two wolves; it depends not only on great hunting experience but on close observation of what the other partner is doing. One of them sees the animal but the other, who is lying in wait, does not. He must judge from the smallest, most unobtrusive movements of his partner how near the latter has approached and when the moment has come for him to act. All this depends on the efficiency of nose, eyes and ears; in the same way, when wolves form a pack in winter and establish their order of seniority, all depends on the working of these same organs of sense. Maintenance of the keenest watch on other members of the pack is the be-all and end-all of a wolf's existence in the struggle for self-preservation.

What would be the point of these manifold and expressive habits of behaviour if they were not continuously being watched by other members of the pack? 'Watch' is in fact too simple a word since it implies something active. An animal has a perception, however, which does not depend on conscious application of the senses; the organs of sense are continuously at work, all the time passing to the brain the impressions received. The brain processes these impressions automatically and from the storehouse of its computer system picks out the necessary data which produce the necessary conclusions. As I have already said, if a dog is not sleeping too deeply, he will know immediately on waking what is afoot, because while he has been asleep his nose and his ears if nothing else have been passing their messages to the brain and the brain's data-processing centre works even in sleep. Active application of the senses is not, therefore, essential in order to register what is going on around him and in particular the attitude of others of his kind. The sensory organs are continuously at work and their output is registered and evaluated in the subconscious; all that is necessary is for the results to penetrate into the relevant channels of the mind.

Now we know that the sensory organs of the wolf and the dog are far more efficient than ours. I can well imagine that a wolf who happens to wake will know that another wolf sleeping a few yards from him will be in a bad humour when he wakes because he has had a bad dream which has agitated him and changed his body odour. The first wolf will know this, not because he has made an inspection on waking but because he has perceived it while still asleep. He will know because the computer has sent a message into the sphere of the conscious which says: 'Watch out—Dark Eyes is in a bad temper!'

This is the secret of the dog's 'sense of feel'. By associating with us he has learnt the meaning of every attitude, every expression of the face, every tone of voice or any excess production of adrenalin

Discipline

(caused by the income-tax return perhaps!) leading to a change in our scent. Frequently he has no need even to look at us; he knows it all already—if we are more fidgety or more relaxed than usual, for instance (the rustle of one's clothes, often barely perceptible to us, is audible to the dog loud and clear). So even before we know it ourselves, he discovers our mood without having to concentrate on the problem and adjusts his behaviour accordingly.

Closer examination, therefore, shows that this chimerical 'sense of feel' is no more than the combined product of extremely sensitive organs of sense and, moreover, they are the normal organs but they are connected to a highly efficient computer. Here more detailed sensations are processed than we can ever even perceive with our deaf ears and insensitive nose. It is a wonderful achievement on the part of the dog—but no super-sensory miracle.

A creature which can register with such refinement must also possess a very delicate capacity for differentiation between its various sensations. This means that a dog must feel very deeply— far more so than many human beings who kick him around like a slave. Expressed in highly simplified and somewhat biased terms, the dog differs from man primarily in that he does not possess man's complex and highly developed cerebral cortex; it is this which has produced the great divide between modern man and the animal. This is not the part of the brain, however, from which feeling originates; the frame of mind is dictated from the 'old' part of the brain, known as the diencephalon because of its position. There is no basic difference between the human and canine brains in so far as this part of the brain is concerned. Instead of making full use of our empathy we all too often rely on the astounding efficiency of our cerebral cortex.

We have now come a long way from the elementary reactions of the new-born puppy and have reached the height of canine achievement both in intelligence and sensitivity. These major achievements, as we have seen, belong to the final phase, the vitally important socialisation phase. There is good reason for this. After all, the capacity to form so close a relationship as that which can develop between man and dog stems from the fact that all the dog's best mental attainments spring from the practice of serving in a society; in this can even be included the capabilities he has developed of capturing his prey, for in the wild state the dog is only occasionally and temporarily a solitary being; for most of his life the capture of food is a communal effort.

The background to our own mental make-up is very similar. Man was once a hunter, living in small tribes of about the same size as a wolf-pack. We still possess today the habits of social behaviour which developed at that time; as we know, they are also the habits which make life difficult when men are packed close together in cities. In the early stone age, hunting was a communal affair and good discipline was the prerequisite for successful co-operation—little different in fact from that of the wolf-pack. As with the wolf, early man combined to defend his territory against neighbouring tribes or to care for his children in concert. In short there are so many similarities in the social existence of man and dog that the incorporation of this wild animal into human society demands no major readjustment on his part. In all his main characteristics he fits perfectly into the human community, whose social customs of those days were presumably far less involved than they are today when man is forced to live in an environment to which he is not suited. Man has been overtaken by the advance of civilisation and he must make an effort to come to terms with it.

It is therefore easy to see how, in those far-off days, man and dog came together. Moreover the social habits of the dog can frequently indicate to us what is genuine and what is a veneer in our own social behaviour. Again the behaviour of a dog which has been badly brought up during its socialisation phase will later bear an astonishing resemblance to that which, in human society, leads to the drop-out or the criminal. The reasons may often be much the same as those which produce the difficult dog.

We shall be reverting to this matter when dealing with aggressiveness in a dog and we shall then find ourselves re-learning two lessons: first, that since the dog is a high-grade family animal, the innate aggressiveness with which nature has endowed him is of far less significance in his existence than the habits of social behaviour which lead to the formation and cohesion of groups; secondly, that it is man's fault if this ratio is upset and aggressiveness becomes uppermost in a dog. At this particular period, when a puppy is very ready to attach himself to a group, a bad upbringing stemming from a faulty assessment of his character can produce lasting damage to his social attitude *vis-à-vis* both man and others of his own kind. For the dog life can then become a permanent misery.

6 School-time and Lessons

So far we have been following the dog's upbringing from puppyhood to membership of a community; in the next stage, from the twelfth week onwards, emphasis is laid in the wild dog family on training to become a fully effective auxiliary in the pack. The trainers are, of course, still the parents, primarily the father, whose special position of authority emerges with increasing clarity as the puppies become larger and more independent. As we have already seen, during the latter half of her pregnancy the bitch increasingly replaces the dog as the predominant partner. Now, however, the dog becomes the Number One, the senior, once more and the bitch begins to subordinate herself to him again. During the preceding month she has recovered from the exertions of nursing and the dog makes no special allowances for her as far as sharing of food is concerned. The puppies are still allowed their share without demur but the old dogs no longer allow them impudently to snatch away pieces of meat from under their noses.

The youngsters are now no longer so strictly nest-bound. They make little communal expeditions without their parents, but they still do not go too far from the lair, to which they return quickly. During these forays, of course, they discover many novelties, some of which are fatal for the over-adventurous. Responsibility for training lies primarily with the father, the old experienced dog who now, through highly disciplined games, introduces the youngsters to the arts and artifices of hunting; he also teaches them how to fight others of their kind—in defence of the family territory or in self-defence against a superior enemy. My pens cover 'only' 500–1,000 sq. ft. and so can never reproduce true wild-life conditions; they are nevertheless large enough to enable one to see all the main features of the older dogs' 'training programme'. One may be led astray by the fact that aggressive tendencies sometimes seem to be uppermost; these are no doubt the result of constriction in space and would probably develop quite differently in the open where the possibilities of evasion

School-time and Lessons

would undoubtedly reduce them. The second reason may be boredom; when dogs have nothing else to do but wait for their food there can easily be a 'build-up of impulse' which will find its outlet either in occasional fights or in a playfulness greater than would be seen in the wild state.

These, however, are marginal phenomena affecting only the fringe of puppy-training as I see it. To judge from the behaviour of my dogs which are not in the pens, what I see is broadly in accordance with that which takes place under natural conditions.

It is of particular importance that about this time the young dog should be in the hands of its future master, particularly if it is destined to be a working dog. In San Rafael, California, there is a breeding and training establishment for guide-dogs for the blind known as Hamilton Station; here the puppies are kept until their twelfth week. Until then they are brought up like normal puppies and at the end submitted to a test to determine their basic aptitude for their future work. At the age of three months the dogs selected are placed in private hands and are only trained as guide-dogs and do their final test after they are one year old. Clarence J. Pfaffenberger, director of this establishment until his death in 1968, made the following highly informative observation: puppies sent out during their thirteenth week almost all came up to expectations at the end of their first year; at the most 10% failed; of those which remained in kennel until their fifteenth week, however, only 30% could be used as guide-dogs.

These figures illustrate the vital importance of this particular age in determining a dog's future character. The dog has an aptitude for learning but it is related to certain periods of development when lessons must be learnt if they are to be learnt at all; there is no such thing as a 'second attempt'; omissions cannot be made good.

The failure of so many dogs is due, not to their hereditary disposition but to the fact that no proper use has been made of their early days. A puppy may have the best possible pedigree and the best possible disposition but, if he gets into the hands of someone who thinks that training should only begin in the eighth or ninth month, none of this will help. The decisive developments affecting the dog's future capacity to learn occur in his early days when the idea of co-operation between dog and man can be imprinted on him for all time. If, during this period, the puppy has learnt to accept man as a partner and has found by experience that co-operation with man is pleasurable, then he will be able successfully to pass the most difficult tests when full-grown. The way to learn what must be done and how one should proceed, however, is to observe what happens in the natural canine family. Wild dogs, after all, are not interested in rosettes won at dog-shows; for them training is a matter of life and death and the preservation of the race. To this everything is subordinated; this is the purpose of all the multifarious adaptations demanded of the puppy during his training for the struggle for existence and designed to turn him from an inexperienced pup into a fully equipped dog able one day to bring up his own puppies properly. Unhappily research into all this is still largely in its infancy; much still remains to be done before a complete picture can be given. Nevertheless we already know enough to ensure that, if we obey the rules, we shall enrich our relationship with our dog.

I propose to divide the period from the thirteenth week to the end of the sixth month into two phases. The first phase—until the end of the fourth month or at least until the sixteenth week inclusive—is characterised primarily by the establishment of an order of seniority among the puppies of a litter. During the second phase the puppies begin really serious work with the older dogs; they attain the status of 'associates'.

THE SENIORITY-CLASSIFICATION PHASE

Seniority is not, as a rule, a simple straightforward affair ranging from the bottom-class or 'Omega' animal to the top-class or 'Alpha' animal; at least in the case of the dog it is a highly complex business with many aspects difficult to disentangle. It is, of course, specially complicated in the case of a pack including different age-groups. For the purposes of this book, however, we are less interested in this aspect since it can teach us little about our personal dealings with our dog. Of far more importance to us is to know about the establishment of seniority among the puppies of a litter.

What purpose is seniority among puppies or young dogs intended to serve? At the age of about ten months the bitch (who

The Seniority-classification Phase

will be in season again) and the father too will drive them away and they are frequently forced to carry on life on their own; it is therefore difficult to see any very profound purpose in the prolonged and often violent scuffles which serve to establish seniority. It seems to me that there may be two reasons: in the first place these struggles for seniority may serve to bring about a second process of selection; one can well imagine that the weakest puppy of the litter might soon be so short of food compared to the others that it would no longer be able to contribute to the preservation of the race. A more likely explanation, however, seems to me to be that these struggles serve as practice, more realistic than that of a mere game, for serious battle with others of their kind. Only in certain cases does the quarrelling become a matter of life and death; as a rule it is characterised by stylised habits of behaviour reminiscent of the tournament; the male dog too, when calling his bitch to order, will never deliberately hurt her, however violent the quarrel may be. These tournaments are closely connected with battle technique and methods of self-expression; during the period of seniority classification these are developed and perfected from the raw material of the lupine hereditary reflexes.

This is the process followed by wolves when forming their packs in the winter; if seniority had to be decided beforehand, too much time and effort would be expended; the pack's killing power would be reduced as a result. When hunting in concert, after all, seniority really amounts to a distribution of duties; this depends on the specific capabilities of the various animals who, as we know, work together with a definite allocation of roles. Once the prey has been killed seniority determines 'precedence in eating' and, as I have already mentioned, this is connected with selectivity; only the most senior and capable animals have the best prospects of perpetuating the race and preserving its hereditary qualities.

In the artificially formed wolf packs seen in zoos seniority classification gives rise to much petty jealousy and a great deal of commotion; the fact that they are living in captivity is most probably the reason; wolves living wild do not display these exaggerated tendencies. In so far as I have been able to observe animals in a zoo, constriction in space and lack of activity produce a permanently aggressive disposition which in the natural state would imperil the continued existence of the group. On the whole subject of aggressiveness we are over-influenced by what we see of animals under the abnormal conditions of captivity. As I have already said, there is more fighting in my pens than would be conceivable under natural conditions.

To do justice to my animals, however, I must add something here. There is a striking difference between what I had to put up with during my early days as a breeder and what happens now. At first hardly a week passed without some form of commotion and my nerves were more or less permanently on edge. Recently all has become comparatively calm; in fact nothing really happens at all. At first I used to tell people that young dingoes certainly could not be left with the old dogs longer than the eighth month or there would undoubtedly be serious fighting. After my initial experiences of this sort I kept careful watch and removed the young dogs in good time so as to avoid such battles. Certain fortuitous observations, however, then made me suspicious and I took the risk of leaving the young ones where they were. Naturally I was permanently on tenterhooks, ready to intervene if things started happening. But nothing did! Abo, the male dog, watched with an air of boredom while Paroo, his eight-month-old lout of a son, mounted his mother Suki; she was not properly in season; it was a week too early and the young dog was merely going through the motions. When Suki was really ready Abo covered her and Paroo, the son, stood quietly by, well brought up and deferential. Yet dingo dogs are definitely capable of covering a bitch at the age of seven months.

Now, therefore, I let matters ride and, as I have said, nothing happens. Suki, for instance, lives peaceably with two sons and a daughter. Björn, Binna's son by Abo, recently covered his wife Bente, and their two children, a dog and a bitch ten months old to the day, stood to one side; sometimes they were violently assaulted but did not seem to mind—it was all only semi-savage; the two-day honeymoon was soon over and then they could have splendid games with their parents once more.

There is an easy explanation for all this: in the early days my arrangements were always changing to suit my breeding experiments. New dingoes were arriving from the zoo and I placed them arbitrarily here and there according to my breeding plans. There

The Seniority-classification Phase

were as yet no set mating periods as there are now. All was still in turmoil; the animals were grouped artificially and changed from one pen to another. Since then everything has become more settled; new generations have grown up in orderly conditions; natural families have been bred—and lo, all is now peace, or at least a great deal more peaceful than before. Here is another pointer to the importance of an orderly upbringing. If, to be able to observe them, I take a bitch into the house with her puppies as soon as they are born and do not put them back in the pen with their father until they are six or seven weeks old, the family life is nothing like so smooth as if I leave the bitch to whelp in the pen or at least return her with her little ones before the end of the third week. Family life is also noticeably upset if I take the puppies or one of the older dogs out of the pen for some time—say a fortnight or more—and then put them back again. There is no alternative—if you want to see dogs as they are, with their astonishingly sociable peaceful way of life, then you must not mess them about; they cannot stand that and they react with extreme sensitivity. When so sensitive a creature is unable to come to terms with something, a chain reaction of aggressive tendencies is let loose—one does not use a hammer and chisel on a wristwatch!

Under natural conditions groups grow up naturally together; they are not pushed around, divided or reassembled at will. Everything follows the line of least resistance according to a well-established order designed simply and solely to preserve the race. Animals which often have to cover several miles a day to find their food certainly have not the time to spend hours worrying about questions of seniority; they need their energy for more important matters. Battles for seniority among the carefree youngsters, whose food is still brought to them by their parents, are probably designed to settle these questions beforehand, so that, when the serious business of life begins, no more time or energy is wasted on them. Everyone then knows how things are done; I believe that the salutation procedure at the start of the pack-forming process is quite enough to settle all questions of seniority. As I shall show later, among dogs it is far more important to demonstrate psychological than physical superiority.

This process begins during the phase of development which we are considering. Initially struggles for seniority among the puppies are primarily a question of physical strength, but this elementary method of deciding seniority is soon replaced by recognition of self-assurance and personality. This emerges very clearly in the puppies' relationship to the older dogs, especially their father. Naturally he uses his physical strength when there is no alternative. His position of authority, however, now rests primarily on recognition by the youngsters of the superiority given him by his experience and his mature personality; their own personalities are now sufficiently developed to enable them to feel genuine respect for authority, under the guidance and leadership of which they feel secure—so much so that in the next phase of their existence the father becomes, in human terms, the 'hero'. Konrad Lorenz has observed that since dogs originate from the wolf, they model themselves, so to speak, on the pack-leader—or human leader. More on this subject later.

Here I propose to quote a most interesting example of the adolescent battle for seniority. It shows that the process is confined to this particular age, also that the aggressiveness bred into certain strains of dog carries with it certain difficulties at this time.

At Hamilton Station, to which I have already referred, it was found impossible to bring up more than three wire-haired fox-terriers together. If a litter consisted of four or more puppies, during the period of seniority classification the weaker members were not allowed near the food or were even killed. A puppy can defend itself against two others but not against three; the odds are then too uneven. The following experiment was therefore tried: four puppies of a litter were brought up separately until the end of their sixteenth week and then brought together again. Result: the four lived together quite happily; the seniority-classification phase was over and what is over cannot be recaptured. Here we see once more how scheduled and regulated is the period of puppyhood. The dog being a predatory animal with a special aptitude for learning, too much play cannot be allowed to the hereditary reflexes or they will limit his knowledge of the outside world so essential to learning; there must be a form of regulator to ensure that he learns the essentials. The dog therefore possesses an inborn 'education programme' geared to life in the natural canine family and to the parents' training programme. No Ministry of Education could lay down plans more dogmatically.

The Seniority-classification Phase

Nevertheless short cuts can be taken if some point in the system has to be omitted—if the father meets with an accident while hunting, for instance. In that case the bitch is fully capable of assuming his role. Suki, my dingo bitch, does this quite excellently. She has three half-grown youngsters and no father to help her; why and what happened is a later story. Seen from a distance one would think that one was looking at a male dog; she is an outstanding disciplinarian and rules her family with complete self-assurance. She does everything which the male dog would normally do and, if they were living wild, her youngsters would undoubtedly be as capable of coping with life as others brought up under the authority of their father.

Similarly in emergency the father can replace the mother. Naturally he cannot suckle his young but, provided the puppies have reached at least the end of their third week, he can keep them alive by regurgitating food. In East Africa a group of hyenas (admittedly only indirectly related to dogs, wolves or jackals) was seen consisting entirely of males who in concert were bringing up a litter, the mother of which had been killed. I have even heard of a young dog-fox rearing a litter of strange cubs whose parents had been killed. There is clearly a deep-rooted maternal instinct in the canine and related races. It is all the more regrettable, therefore, that we have thoughtlessly bred this quality out of our dogs, so much so that there are many bitches which barely have sufficient maternal instinct to rear their own young.

What happens to young dogs, however, if both parents disappear? In order to see this, I have kept puppies by themselves from their eighth or tenth week. It is astounding how the roles are automatically distributed between them, and a substitute home, so to speak, created. It reminds one slightly of a self-governing children's village. One of the puppies at once assumes the leadership, exercises discipline and everything goes very well. Since at each stage of life the innate requirement to learn appears, the essentials are learnt more or less.

On this subject here is another astonishing example which gave me much food for thought: it showed that even at the age of ten weeks puppies were perfectly capable of feeding themselves, evading their enemies, withstanding bad weather and basically living the life of grown-up dogs. Even more surprising—the puppies did not belong to my much-vaunted breed of wild dog with its highly developed instinct but to a highly bred strain, a breed which one would have thought the least capable of such fortitude. Some 3,000 years ago expert Chinese breeders succeeded in producing a small extremely friendly dog with a delightfully infantile face from which looked out large guileless saucer-like eyes; it was the much abused, much misrepresented pug.

The pug is connected in people's minds with velvet sofas, artificial flowers, antimacassars and good old Aunt Emily; what they really mean is that it is fat, stupid and ugly. The cartoonist's satires, however, do not portray the pug as he really is but only those unfortunates whose real nature is not appreciated and who have fallen victim to an egocentric 'love of animals' amounting in effect to brutality. All breeds of dog which suffer this fate are the subjects of similar distortions.

I was sitting in a small clearing among the pines and birches watching a couple of dozen 'genuine pugs' romping all round me. Activity was such that some thirty attempts with my camera were necessary before I could get a snapshot. They were running, skipping, jumping and racing, chasing and being chased; at one moment one of the little dogs produced a long branch which he defended against a mob of others; another was digging an enormous hole in the soft peaty ground with the industry of a mole; elsewhere yelps of pleasure gave notice of a rough-and-tumble—just as at home with my wild dogs, the jackals, dingoes and half-breeds.

When my film was exhausted, Frau I. von Keiser, the owner of this uproarious pack and formerly assistant to Erich von Holst, with the help of some sketches told me their story, which was in fact the reason for my visit.

'I had a litter of four puppies but I had not been able to bother much about them since I had a very bad attack of 'flu which kept me in bed for almost two months. When I had at last recovered, I resumed my daily walks in the woods with the dogs. The puppies were by this time ten weeks old. It was January 15, a cold winter's day with a lot of snow on the ground. Suddenly all four went off and all attempts to get them back again were fruitless. They disappeared from view and stayed lost. Of course we followed them up at once and found tracks, but there was nothing to do;

The Seniority-classification Phase

the pugs had gone.' I should add here that Frau von Keiser has been breeding pugs for twenty-five years and they have naturally had adequate contact with man during their imprint phase; they have invariably been extremely obedient and would never think of leaving their mistress. The ancestor of the strain was a shining example of fidelity; together with one or two large well-trained guard-dogs he refugeed with the family from East Prussia at the end of the war; he was the only dog to cling to his family through

All dogs like digging in soft ground (a young pug)

all the turmoil of those terrible weeks and arrive in West Germany. Frau von Keiser continued:

'The next day I went out searching with a friend and the puppies' mother, but it had rained during the night and so we could find no tracks. That afternoon one of the pugs returned but the others were still nowhere to be seen. It now began to freeze hard with temperatures down to −10· C and this went on for six days; then came rain and a thaw, though of course it still froze at night. From tracks we now discovered that two of the pugs were roaming the woods together while the third was hunting alone. The latter, as far as we could make out, covered about a three-mile circuit every day, sometimes going parallel with the tracks of a fox. On the ninth day two people in a car, after a laborious pursuit, managed to catch the pair who were roaming together. All attempts to catch the last bitch, however, were fruitless. She was very shy and suspicious, crouching down whenever she saw a man, even at a distance, and refusing to go near any of the boxes which we baited for her. I even placed her well-known feeding bowl on her beat and she came cautiously sniffing up to within two yards of it but then disappeared into the bush again. On the fourteenth day about 5.30 a.m., the time at which I usually let out my dogs, I heard a loud howl in front of the house; this is the noise which pugs make when lost in order to regain contact with the others. The fugitive had come home of her own accord. As far as I could make out, the animals must have lived on deer and rabbit droppings which contain some protein, carbohydrates and Vitamin B.'

Naturally the pugs had lost weight. The dog, for instance, which originally weighed 5.8 kilograms, was down to 5.2 kilograms, his sister had lost 0.9 kilogram and the last bitch over 1.5 kilograms. These figures, however, must be kept in perspective; according to the book pugs should have some fat beneath the skin to give them a 'more childish' expression. To judge from my lean dingoes they were merely down to normal condition for a wild dog. This seems to indicate that the pug would be perfectly capable of leading a permanent wild existence. His very short jaw, of course, would give him little chance of catching animals such as mice alive; the dog, however, is a natural feeder on offal and so it is quite conceivable that a pug could live wild. In any case, to live wild for fourteen days in frost, snow and rain is a remarkable test which one would never have thought such a 'lapdog' could withstand.

There is, therefore, an adequate range of hereditary reflexes available coupled with the corresponding learning ability to enable a dog to live under highly unfavourable circumstances. Among the hereditary reflexes are the methods of expression to which I have already referred in connection with the seniority-classification battles and the 'tournaments'. These matters are worth closer examination since we have to understand our dog's 'language' if we are to grasp what goes on among dogs. Moreover the dog also tries to make himself intelligible to us by means of his 'language'.

I have so far been somewhat cautious on this subject since we do not know in every case what is an innate method of expression, what is a hereditary reflex or what is an acquired reflex, in other words has been learnt. Much possibly stems from the special capacity for learning.

One thing is certain: the dog can learn to mimic the expressions, for instance, of a cat with which he has been brought up or of a man. At least he learns to understand; he learns the significance of certain imagery. Moreover certain dogs develop a real gift for mimicry of other creatures' habits. Konrad Lorenz has pointed this out in his handbook on dogs and has also shown that this is most in evidence in domesticated dogs whose tendency to mimicry is restricted. Lorenz accordingly infers that canine mimicry stems primarily from hereditary reflexes which will be understood by other dogs without having first been learnt.

A highly interesting experiment was once conducted in which young monkeys were reared separately and were then shown all sorts of pictures, their reaction to which was studied. They looked with obvious interest at pictures of other monkeys whose expression was friendly; when suddenly they were shown the face of a savage menacing tribe-leader, despite their total lack of experience they fled in terror and crouched in a corner of their cage showing every sign of fear. The significance of the menacing expression of one of their own kind was therefore clear to them through some 'innate intuition'.

By thousands of examples behavioural research has proved that animals' methods of expression stem almost exclusively from hereditary reflexes (exceptions prove the rule); irrespective of experience, therefore, they will be understood by others of their own kind and will evoke the relevant reactions. With no great reservations, therefore, it may be assumed that the same applies to our dogs and so I now propose to examine their 'language of mimicry'.

GESTURAL AND FACIAL EXPRESSIONS

As I have so often done in this book, I would emphasise one thing: I am dealing here with the primitive or basic repertoire of methods of expression as demonstrated by Schenkel's wolves in Basle. Most of our domestic dogs, however, are not well equipped in

166 *School-time and Lessons*

methods of expression and a dog-owner will often be unable to see the full range in his terrier, poodle or schnauzer. I have already mentioned elsewhere that with the artificial 'long-eared' breeds the expressiveness of the ears is largely curtailed. Similarly in many dogs the mobility of the facial muscles seems to be reduced or even atrophied; lack of instinct is not, therefore, responsible in every case for this poverty in methods of expression. As I have already said, gestural expressions on the part of my dingoes are comparatively few, a further reminder that the capacity of any particular type of animal for this form of expression depends on the level of its social development; the more numerous and varied the

Sketch of a wolf's face. This emphasises capacity for expression particularly when combined with the winter coat

relationships between groups of similar animals become, the more there is to 'say'. Visual methods of expression only take a back seat when replaced by the most highly perfected form of communication yet developed between living creatures—human speech; this much is obvious if one compares the gestural repertoire of a man with that of a chimpanzee.

Among all members of the canine race, therefore, the wolf, which stands high in the social scale, has the most varied repertoire of gestures and bodily expressions.

Gestural and Facial Expressions 167

This is particularly noticeable in winter when wolves combine into larger packs and explicit communication is specially essential. The winter coat with its longer hair and different markings, particularly in the region of the head, increases the wolf's range of visual expression. Bound up with this are the facial markings, for instance a dark stripe from the rear corner of the eye to the base of the ear, usually triangular patches above the eyes and a stripe on the forehead running from the back of the head to the base of the muzzle. Many of our wolf-coloured strains of alsatian show similar facial markings contributing to their capacity for visual expression. Most of the colourings and markings to be seen in the animal world are no products of chance but have a definite function for purposes of internal communication or as 'cautionary and camouflage colourings' in the event of battle with other types of animal. For reasons of domestication the colouring of most of our domestic dogs has been changed and the lupine markings have been lost in the process; this is another cause of the reduced capacity for expression in our dogs.

Significantly enough, in the case of the human being the expression of the eyes is the primary feature in all visual expression; being visual animals, for us the most important thing is invariably 'how someone looks'. Paradoxically, however, although we immediately understand the smallest alteration in the expression of a man's eyes, we find it far easier to describe a smiling mouth than smiling eyes. The reasons, no doubt, are first that the mouth, being a larger feature of the face, produces a greater optical effect, but also that our instinctive sense makes it unnecessary consciously to analyse the details which produce any particular facial expression.

Some dogs will look one straight in the eye, calm, relaxed, candid, friendly, perhaps expectant; others will shyly avoid one's eye. This may depend on the situation but it can also throw light on the dog's character. If our dog has done something which he knows perfectly well to be wrong, if he has done something badly or has failed in some other way, he will of course guiltily avoid our eyes. This is evidence of insecurity and we understand it very well since we do exactly the same ourselves. If a dog looks one straight in the eye, he feels secure and no further word need be spoken. This happens if we and our dog understand each other and there is no cause for disagreement. I refer, of course, to the normal friendly gaze; there are other possibilities, as we shall soon see. A dog, however, which never has the courage to look even its master straight in the eye but which invariably looks away, perhaps with a shifty eye, is an insecure and worried character. There may be something hereditarily wrong, but in most cases the dog has been wrongly handled; he fears his master more than he loves him. He is probably the whipping-boy for his master's moods, the victim of an unhealthy desire to dominate. All too often dogs betray the character of their owners in this way. In the wolf pack too a shifty eye betrays the whipping-boy, the most junior in rank; here it is only the most senior who takes it upon himself to look others of his kind straight and unwaveringly in the eye. He thus demonstrates his seniority; should a junior wolf dare to look a senior straight in the eye, this would be sheer challenge—as in a bygone age the fixed gaze constituted a challenge to a duel—'Sir, you are fixing your eye upon me!'

In general there are two different motives for this fixing of another animal with the eye. First, as in the case of the pack-leader, it denotes an attitude of aggression, a challenge, a demonstration of strength. This gaze can very easily become menacing and then it is particularly rigid. All attention is riveted on the other dog, for if a single false move is made, the threat, which is not solely confined to the eyes, may turn in a flash into an assault. This can easily be seen between rival dogs who are threatening each other, also if one is oneself the object of attack. The expression is characterised by a contraction of the skin of the forehead above the eyes leading to a raising of the eyelids reminiscent of what we do when we wish to look threatening.

A straight look in the eye, however, may also be an expression of affection as we know from dogs with whom we are on intimate terms. A dog and bitch who live together often look at each other in this way, particularly during the mating period. The forehead is quite smooth, the expression welcoming, frequently one of great courtesy. In a grown-up dog this attitude often reminds me of the trusting expression of the puppy aged four or five weeks. They will look both other dogs and human beings quite unconcernedly in the eye, their own seemingly fixed in an expression of friendship. The infantile face, radiating innocence, tranquillity and affection,

Gestural and Facial Expressions

undoubtedly serves to inhibit any aggressive tendencies; no older animal will regard a puppy's gaze as a challenge; it will react to the 'childhood image'. During the socialisation phase the young dog must ultimately be able to look its fellows in the eye without their becoming savage. The puppy's gaze is a further example of the way in which infantile ways can spill over into the repertoire of actions and expressions on which social affinities are built.

Other expressions of the eyes I propose to describe along with that of the face as a whole; ultimately all these components of

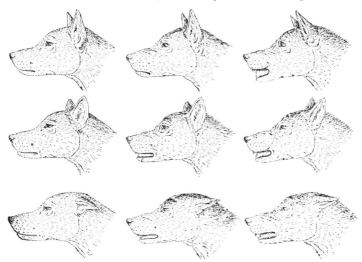

Nine possible differing expressions of a dingo's face showing the frame of mind (lay-out based on Lorenz)

expression complement each other to form an overall picture. When the assured, superior gaze of the pack-leader turns into a threat, other features of expression become involved. Under the lowering brows the eyes now glare upwards from below. The lips are curled to show the teeth, the entire muzzle wrinkled. The neck muscles are taut, the ears pricked sharply forwards. As the ultimate threat the jaws are opened wide, indicating an intention to bite.

Thus threatened, the under-dog expresses readiness to take to its heels; it puts on its 'face of fear', the forehead being 'drawn out' towards the corners of the eyes, the base of the ears and the sides of the neck. As a result the forehead is quite smooth and the eyes turn into narrow, drawn-back slits. The corners of the mouth are also retracted, making the slit of the mouth look very long. The ears are laid right back on to the coat of the neck precisely as when nose-nudging to signify 'active submission'. The head may wave from side to side, indicating great insecurity. If the senior dog continues to threaten and growls with increasing savagery, the next stage is flight.

Schenkel saw his wolves employ so wide a variety of expressions that he began to question the validity of the whole idea of hereditary reflexes among mammals. He could discover no connection between hereditary reflexes and 'the apparently limitless possibilities of graduation' in methods of expression.

Konrad Lorenz, with his experienced eye for the more profound implications, has solved the riddle and, using sketches of nine canine heads, has explained what the various expressions mean. I have attempted to reproduce the sense of his drawings, using dingo heads since this was the breed on which I was best informed. The series can be easily explained: taking the top horizontal line, the left-hand head is in repose, the next to the right evidences a degree of menace and the right-hand head a serious threat. The left-hand vertical line begins at the top with a head in repose, the next below shows some feeling of insecurity and the bottom great insecurity and preparation for flight.

Two attitudes of mind, however, may overlap. The dog is not quite sure whether to threaten more savagely or to take to its heels. At one moment the first thought is uppermost in its mind and in the next moment the second. The outward expression of these two attitudes of mind, however, is dependent on hereditary reflexes which overlap in various ways. This produces four combinations: the head in the centre shows some readiness to fight overlapping with some readiness to take to flight; that in the bottom right-hand corner shows both at greater intensity. There are therefore four further possibilities of expression combining two differing degrees of threat and two differing degrees of readiness to take to flight. By introducing additional degrees of intensity in expression the picture may be made as complex as one likes.

The Body as an Instrument of Expression

Basically the facial expression is only an adjunct to that of the body as a whole and certain elements of movement complete the picture. In the dog the 'expressive attitude' is used as a method of communication far more than the facial expression. This we must examine in more detail if we wish to understand the dog's 'language'. We have already seen in earlier sections what is the origin of these attitudes and how important they are for the communal existence of dog and dog or dog and man.

THE BODY AS AN INSTRUMENT OF EXPRESSION: AGGRESSION AND DEMONSTRATION OF SUPERIORITY AND INFERIORITY

We will deal first with aggressiveness. This gives many dog-owners a hard time. Unfortunately there are particularly aggressive types among our dogs who will attack any passing dog on principle. Usually they do so for reasons other than those of the so-called 'savage dog' who bites people. The notorious bully far more frequently suffers from a bad upbringing by man than from a morbid desire to assault others of his kind. In the case of such dogs I have often noticed either that they have a limited capacity for expression or that, if fully trained, they seem highly nervous and ill at ease.

Any normal dog can become aggressive, however, though only in certain situations and to the extent necessary. Even the sweetest bitch will turn nasty if some over-bred, oversexed dog insists on trying to mount her when she is not in season. The male dog will inevitably adopt a threatening attitude if another challenges him. This threatening posture is one of the most impressive attitudes which the dog can adopt:

The head goes up; slowly the eyes darken and the ceremonial of menace begins. The tail is held up straight, motionless as a flagpole. The leg-muscles become taut until the dog moves only in stiff jerks, as if on stilts. On stiff legs the body is higher off the ground than normal, giving an impression of increased size. The hackles rise along the neck and backbone—the hair is usually longer here; this is a phenomenon to be seen in many mammals and it invariably serves the same purpose: an apparent increase in size. The principle is age-old and the object to impress the opponent; men do likewise, though in a different form since they stand upright. The four-legged animal has to offer a side view to his enemy; the two-legged tries to make his impression by an increase in size as seen from the front—puffing out the chest—arms akimbo. Instead of raising his hackles the human being employs artifices of clothing—the guardsman's bearskin, the shoulder-boards and the breeches are all 'trappings intended to impress', as are the feathers of the Red Indian on the warpath or the plumes in the knight's helmet. The background to much of history is the need to impress but that is more a matter for the biologist.

Our dogs provide a good illustration of the real purpose of all this. The dog which feels himself superior presents his impressive array broadside to his opponent, at the same time, however, displaying to him the threatening expression on his face. He stares at his rival fixedly and unwinkingly. The first stage, therefore, is a bloodless 'duel', each side testing the psychological strength of the other. Frequently a highly impressive display of menace is enough to decide the question of superiority. Often the weaker dog will turn his head away to avoid the glare of his opponent; his threatening expression dies away and the ears are laid back; we already know how two opposite attitudes of mind can overlap. The hackles fall, the tail sinks, the muscles slacken and the whole dog shrinks into itself; perhaps it even tucks the tail between its hind legs and makes off. The resolute threat and the impressive attitude of the other dog have intimidated him; there is no fight.

These methods of exerting a threat and making an impression, therefore, serve to avoid the 'all-out battle' which may end in wounding or even killing another dog. They constitute a form of aggression offering the adversary a last chance before the fight leading to bodily injury. From the point of view of race preservation this is an important biological regulator designed to prevent unnecessary blood-letting.

The above assumes that the encounter takes place on foreign territory or in no-man's land. In this case it is obviously the prerogative of the stronger to take over the territory. There would be no sense, however, in killing the weaker dog willy-nilly; the latter is generally a younger member of the breed whose prospects for the future should be preserved. In the end, moreover, the

The Body as an Instrument of Expression

stronger dog will become old and the resulting vacant area should be occupied; the erstwhile rival, who has meanwhile become strong himself, will move into the vacant place. Then he in his turn will intimidate and expel some rival, using the bloodless methods of 'psychological warfare'.

It may be, of course, that no decision is reached in this trial of strength using only threats and impressive attitudes. In this event the adversaries come closer and closer together, the threat turns into a determination to fight; the dogs stand shoulder to shoulder and use every trick to take a hold and turn the other over, like experienced wrestlers. They push and jostle each other, leg against leg, taking the measure of each other's physical strength and adroitness in evading the hostile jaws. In addition to the threatening growl a sharp snapping of the jaws is to be heard— an attempt to make an audible impression. Many dogs begin to make a sort of battle-cry, as men do in hand-to-hand fighting. Hard words are spoken—the prelude and accompaniment to any brawl. Listening to these noises one would think that the two dogs had more or less eaten each other but in fact not even the smallest scratch has been inflicted.

Only if all this is not enough to cause one of the pair to lose his self-assurance and evacuate the field does battle begin in real earnest. The main targets are the legs, paws, neck and ears. In the attempts to evade the opponent's bite, the jaws naturally clash; lips and corners of the mouth are punctured. Dogs have fought in this way, however, since time immemorial and so Nature has arranged that the wounds heal with incredible ease and rapidity.

If, after all these introductory stages, still no decision has been reached and a really serious fight takes place, the primary target is the throat. Biting the side of the neck is not, as a rule, very effective since wild dogs have developed a thick ruff not easily penetrated by the adversary's teeth. In a serious fight the parry consists of presenting the side of the neck to the opponent since it acts as a shield. When standing shoulder to shoulder this is the best way of avoiding being bitten in the throat. In an attempt to seize the enemy's throat, therefore, the dog tries to turn him over. When this stage of the battle is reached, all becomes confusion; the contestants roll over and over; any part of the body may be bitten as it becomes accessible.

174   *School-time and Lessons*

Sascha and Susi jumping up against one another (play preliminary to mating)

The shoulder-to-shoulder battle may develop into a standing fight. In this the two dogs stand against each other on their hind legs, placing their paws on each other's shoulders. The throat is protected by turning the head aside or alternatively by lowering the head and opening the jaws wide. During a mock battle between

Sascha and a friend's alsatian bitch, a preliminary to mating, I obtained a very good picture of the complete upright battle position. Though the attitudes and noises looked and sounded menacing, all was much more playful than would be seen in the event of a genuine fight. In this case, obviously, no real damage was done; the standing position was employed to exert a threat and give an impression of great size. The object was to impress the other dog by displaying certain capabilities, by emphasising one's strength and, above all, by demonstrating superiority, mental as well as physical—we are all ready to present ourselves thus, to make an impression measurable not in feet and inches but in mental energy. Little Sven, Stina's brother, raises his hackles at the sight of Sascha but Sascha is impressed, not by the resulting minute increase in size but by the little dog's courage in thus challenging him.

We have now examined the significance of the various methods of expression which are dependent on some physical feature but in fact only make use of these features to demonstrate an attitude of mind and its intensity. Without these outlets, dogs would simply rush at each other and bite each other to death as quickly as they could. As we have already seen, from the point of view of race preservation this must be avoided. Accordingly the whole complex comprising expression and fighting technique combined with a basic tendency to aggression includes numerous built-in barriers to ensure that questions of superiority can be solved with as little bloodshed as possible.

Finally, therefore, a dog can demonstrate that he feels himself to be the loser and is ready to give up; for this purpose he has available one other method of expression, the effect of which is astonishing. As we have seen, during a fight the object is to seize the throat. As Konrad Lorenz has shown, in the animal world voluntary exposure of the vulnerable areas is taken as a signal of submission, a demonstration of subordination. This attitude immediately raises a blockage against the attacker's intention to kill. A few seconds before he had been making every effort to reach those vulnerable points but suddenly he is inhibited from actually doing so when they are clearly and deliberately presented to him.

So the savage and perhaps bloody fight suddenly comes to an end when the loser turns on his back and presents his throat with ears laid back and eyes reduced to slits. The victor stands over him, growling and fierce; there is his enemy's throat unprotected in front of him; a quick bite and it is the end of him. But however furious he may be, the victor is simply incapable of giving a real bite; his motional impulses are blocked; he just cannot do it.

The effect of this blockage is clearly reflected in the victor's expression. It does not show triumph but internal stress, as if he were the victim of conflict. The victor does not know what to do. He is powerless against this blockage and he wavers between aggression and a desire to make peace. If the vanquished makes a further move, the tendency to aggression comes uppermost; if he begins to whimper, the forehead and hackles become smooth. The victor wavers between these two attitudes until eventually his tendency to aggression has so far died away that the vanquished can venture to make off with his tail down.

The most variegated range of habits and attitudes designed to inhibit aggression is to be seen in a large grouping where an order of seniority is essential—an order decided and maintained by fighting. In other words the interplay of aggressive and submissive attitudes is a factor in holding a group together. This is the case with the northern wolf; during the cold season they form large packs, increased strength helping them to overcome the problems of winter feeding.

Dingoes living in pairs have no need of a mechanism to inhibit aggression and so behaviour in this respect is less fully developed. Possibly also the conditions under which they live are more conducive to a fight to the death. If all preserves in the area are occupied, mortal battle may take place about territory—where would the vanquished go anyway? Moreover it is better that the stronger dog should own the territory and ensure the continuance of the race. If untenanted areas exist, however, there is no need to fight. The stranger politely takes himself away.

If two dingoes are fighting and one can seize them by the scruff of the neck, separate them and hold them up in the air at arm's length, they will beam all over their faces. They are only too happy to be separated and show their gratitude quite clearly. Then, however, one must be careful to ensure that each has his own preserve. If one lets them go again at once, the battle will continue as savagely as before and the man who is imprudent enough to catch hold of one of them only, is lost; the other will tear him to pieces in one's arms. During that split second any affection which the captive dog may have had for the man concerned will vanish and can never be recaptured. Entirely by accident this happened to me with Luxl one day. He was fighting his grown-up son Motu. After I had separated them Motu escaped again while I was carrying Luxl, who had one or two minor bites, into the house; Motu sprang at me and again seized hold of his enemy, his father. In my stupidity I tried to protect Luxl, pressing him tightly against me, and this was contrary to all good dingo manners. Luxl now bit me! From that moment he was my enemy; he bit me again next day when I tried to feed him. Yet, as I carried him from the pen, he had pressed happily up against me and had made frantic efforts to lick my face—he was unadulterated gratitude itself. That split second of error on my part was enough to implant in him an enmity destined to last until he met his tragic death. I never dared enter his pen again; even a year later he would still growl at me with his hackles up if I so much as came near the fence. To the other members of the household he remained the affectionate obedient dog which at heart he always was.

We have drifted from habits of expression to a description of fighting techniques but so far have considered only the male dog. What about the bitches?

The reason for a fight between male dogs is usually some dispute about territory; with bitches, however, it generally has something to do with reproduction. The dog being a highly socialised animal living in a pack, the tendency is not so pronounced as with many other types of animal which live in herds but without definite social organisation. In the latter case males fight a ritualised battle during which many expressive habits are to be seen; the females, on the other hand, fight with no holds barred, in order to damage each other and without showing any particular habits of expression. This applies primarily to those animals among which care of the young is left solely or principally to the females.

In a canine society there is naturally an order of seniority among the females and this can only operate on the assumption that they do not bite each other to death forthwith. Obviously, therefore, bitches also adopt attitudes of menace or submission. The preliminary ceremonial designed to create an impression on the enemy, however, is not so elaborate with bitches as with dogs; they tend to pass straight from a threat to a fight. The more primitive forms of action, already mentioned, which are designed to inflict damage, persist in bitches to a greater degree than in dogs. This is principally to be seen when the dispute concerns choice of a mate or protection of the young. In the case of wolves the pack organisation has in any case been disbanded at this period—the warm season.

The Crislers, who have lived in the wastes of Alaska with tame though free-running wolves, once had a sad experience. They had with them a young she-wolf named 'Lady' and her husband 'Trigger'. About the mating period a wild she-wolf appeared and she became friendly with Trigger. He courted her and this naturally did not suit Lady. One night there was a battle between the two females and Lady was left dead on the field. In this case there was obviously no expressive ceremonial to prevent two of a kind killing each other as happens with rival dogs, stags, ibexes or other animals.

There are numerous stories of wolves being killed by members of their pack; in this case, however, there is no real fight; the entire pack falls upon the delinquent and tears him to pieces. In many cases this is the fate of over-age animals who can no longer fulfil their function in the community. The signal is the fact that the animal shows by his behaviour that his vitality is sinking. The community can only continue to exist if all its members can communicate clearly. If a member of the pack can no longer do this, he becomes a foreign body and so becomes subject to the savage law which alone keeps a wolf pack efficient.

I must now tell the tragic story of Luxl, my New Guinea dog, for it is highly indicative of the difference in fighting methods between a dog and a bitch. I had placed Luxl with his daughter Suki while she was still suckling her three puppies. The introduction gave rise to no difficulties; Luxl behaved like a tactful dog and subsequently played with the puppies as if they were his own. I merely noticed that he did not punish them as often as dingo fathers usually do. In this respect he was more diffident and retiring. Moreover he was soon so much under Suki's thumb that the spectacle was distressing. This was most clearly to be seen at feeding time—the bitch claimed everything for herself. Gradually

The Body as an Instrument of Expression

the puppies became self-supporting and so, for Luxl, the moment had come to rearrange matters and show who was master in the house. One day he gave Suki such a thrashing that she limped for two days. However she had not really been bitten since a dog will never bite a bitch seriously to hurt her—he merely nips and jostles her. Luxl, on the other hand, had some quite sizeable scars after this quarrel which had of course been a noisy one; Suki had really bitten him. This had not helped her, however, and she now trotted after her lord and master with an expression of extreme devotion. So it went on for four months and then the struggle for power began again. Suki became saucier and saucier and eventually she was once more 'wearing the trousers'. Her children were now six months old and the two dogs looked like becoming magnificent specimens. Late one evening we again heard the familiar noise of battle from their pen. Aha!, we thought, he is giving her another lesson—and it is high time. If you live with dingoes, you think in terms different from the owner of one of our nice domesticated dogs. One becomes used to their savage customs and one hears the noise of battle coming out of the darkness almost with pleasure. We were pleased that next morning Luxl would be able to get his food ration undisturbed and that Suki would once more be 'reasonable'.

When the noise of battle had subsided, we went down to the pen to see that all was well. By the light of a torch we could see, even from a distance, that Luxl was lying at the gate of the pen and, as we came nearer, we saw that he was covered in blood. We quickly opened the pen and the dog dragged himself painfully out for a couple of paces; he then collapsed and could hardly move as we carried him to the house. His whole body was covered in bites. Blood was streaming from a great wound in his stifle. We injected him with a pain-killer since he was obviously suffering terribly and then examined him in detail.

The result of our examination was a decision to put him to sleep, painful though that was. He had no hope; there were deep bites in his throat, the jugular vein had been torn, the breathing tubes damaged and blood had entered his lungs. Suki had literally torn him to pieces. For highly debatable reasons into which I will not enter since one cannot be sure, Suki no longer recognised him as her male—that much at least was certain. We examined her next day; she had one or two small scratches on her hind leg—that was all.

From the results of this battle it is easy to reconstruct what had happened. The dog had not really bitten seriously even when his life was at stake; possibly he had demonstrated his submission. The bitch, however, had taken no notice, contrary to what would have happened in a fight between male dogs.

In our domestic dogs the habits and attitudes described in this context may often not be fully developed. The outcome may therefore be the same as is produced by a communication failure—a fight in which the rules are not observed and which ends in the death of the weaker dog. In this case the absence of any inhibition to killing will be fatal to the dog which signifies submission.

One method of demonstrating submission is for the vanquished to turn on his back (or be thrown on to it); Schenkel has called this 'passive submission' in contrast to the active submission which we already know to be a group-forming posture. The gesture undoubtedly originates from puppyhood—a puppy lies on its back when the mother (or under certain circumstances the father) massages its stomach with his or her tongue to cause it to urinate or defecate. Puppies adopt this attitude of passive submission on every conceivable occasion and very often, particularly if the situation is somewhat fraught, they urinate at the same time. While they are still small they arouse maternal instincts in others of their kind by thus presenting the stomach. Later, when maternal instinct no longer applies, the posture serves to inhibit aggression. Passive submission also has its uses in relation to mankind; the dog learns, moreover, that in this way he can evoke reactions from his real friends which bear a strong similarity to the maternal caress—he is stroked. So the dog turns his passive submission into active submission. Of my dogs Binna is the one who quickly turns on her back if one fondles her—an invitation to have her stomach stroked.

We have already mentioned, as the counterpart to the threatening and domineering attitude, the posture indicating preparation for flight. We have not, however, looked at it in detail and this omission should be rectified. It is the contrasting attitude, not only of the mind but in outward expression. When threatening, a dog tries to make himself appear as large as possible; if he is ready

The Body as an Instrument of Expression

to run, or, as we should say, is afraid, he tries to appear as small as possible. The whole dog shrinks into itself; the tail is clamped between the hind legs and the eyes avoid those of its opponent. A dog will present this pitiable picture not only to another dog which has mastered him but also to a man and in face of situations which seem to him terrifying.

As with the dominating attitude, the position of the tail clearly plays a great part in the attitude, demonstrating readiness for flight. The dog which wishes to demonstrate his strength and superiority holds his tail stiffly erect; the dog which succumbs tucks his tail in, in other words clamps it between his hind legs. This is clearly a highly expressive attitude, an unmistakable visual signal. In origin it is also closely connected with the mechanism of olfactory expression. The position of the tail in fact indicates a desire either to parade or to conceal the dog's own scent. If the tail is tucked in, the glands of the anal region are firmly covered; the dog is concealing his own scent and so is saying: 'I'm not really there at all.' The dominating dog, however, holds his tail high, inviting everyone to take note of his presence with their nose.

It remains to deal with a very well-known method of expression in which the dog uses his tail—tail-wagging. This is an expression of pleasure and excitement and the rapidity of the movement indicates the degree of these feelings. When a dog approaches a strange dog, for instance, he does so with his tail wagging slowly; he is thus saying that he has nothing nasty in mind and would in principle be prepared for friendly negotiations about a future relationship. If, as he gets nearer, he sees that he is dealing with an attractive bitch, the tail will wag quicker, and even more quickly still if he realises that she is in season. The position of the tail as it wags if also of importance. If the dog is not quite sure what will happen, the tail will be slightly below the horizontal; this means that he cannot tell whether he may not have to tuck it in in the end. If he is entirely confident, the tail will be slanting upwards as it wags. Tail-wagging is therefore a morale barometer. Scent also plays a part once more; the dog which is happy is prepared to dispense scent in all directions; he is among good friends and so can disclose himself without further ado.

While on this subject, I recently heard of an oddity. A friend whose bitch was in season met a basset-hound on the street and noticed to his astonishment that this long-eared English breed wagged the tail not only laterally but with a circular propeller-like motion. The owner told my friend that all bassets do this. I know of no other dog which can perform this masterpiece—one lives and learns!

Undoubtedly much more could be said about this or that expressive attitude. As with facial expressions, attitudes can overlap. When issuing a threat, a dog often seems to hump his back; as a result his hinder ends are depressed and the tail seems to indicate uncertainty or may even be tucked in. This merely means that the dog is showing attitudes of aggression and fear both at the same time. 'He is threatening in front and running away behind,' Lorenz would say. Depending on the opponent's attitude, one or other frame of mind will eventually prevail and this will be shown by the dog's general behaviour.

ACOUSTIC EXPRESSION

We have looked at the dog's facial and physical expressions and have learnt something in passing about the sounds that he can make. So far we have dealt with the ears only as a method of optical expression. I now propose to examine their true function.

But first a word in all seriousness to every dog-lover. A silent bitter battle has been raging for years with a single objective—leave the dog's ears as they are. I am a whole-hearted supporter of the animal-lovers who object to the senseless and unnatural habit of cropping the ears (or docking the tail). They are perfectly right and none of the specious arguments that puppies do not feel pain, and so forth, carry any weight. It may be that man has a right to rule over the creatures of the earth, but he has never the right to mutilate them. I am entirely prepared to accept the breeding of bandy-legged or snub-nosed dogs; nature has provided the possibility of changing hereditary conformation and we are merely exploiting that possibility. I will not say that I am particularly happy about the existence of such distorted creatures. I know, however, that hand in hand with these physical changes go changes in character and requirements in life; so all this is acceptable. A dog of any breed, however, has a definite natural conformation and anyone who crops his ears or docks his tail is guilty of doing him grievous bodily harm,

Acoustic Expression

even though in the eyes of the law a dog is only a 'thing'. I trust that the Animal Protection Association and the government will ultimately find some legal method of preventing this medieval custom of ear-cropping and tail-docking. Britain and other countries have largely done so already.

Every veterinary surgeon knows that cropping the ears or docking the tail causes pain and a period of suffering while the wound is healing. In our enlightened days there can be no reason to inflict such mental and physical suffering upon a dog other than the rigidity of the rules concerning breeding standards; the result is a trauma from which the dog never recovers, a terrifying experience of his youth—an adequate body of opinion and evidence from experts exists to prove this. Fortunately many sensible people are now beginning to disregard the rules made by the defenders of the 'traditional' standards and an increasing number of dog-owners are refusing to do these stupid things. In recent years I have seen many boxers, bulldogs, terriers and schnauzers with their ears uncropped; comparing them with others of their breed, it is difficult to see what pleasure dog-lovers can find in these mutilations.

In the canine and similar races, as with all animals, the shape of the ears serves a vital purpose in preserving the species; biologically, therefore, it is functional. The purpose of the auricle is to intercept sound and locate both the direction and distance of its source. These 'sound-interceptors' must therefore be adequately mobile. A complex 'computer mechanism' in the brain then 'calculates' angle and time differential of the arrival of sound in the two ears and produces the necessary information about source. In this the dog is adept—far superior to us. In the first place he has outstandingly efficient sound-interceptors; secondly he has the capacity to hear sound frequencies of well over 20,000 vibrations a second. This is the limit of human ability to hear high-pitched sounds and so we can call our dog with an ultra-high-pitched whistle inaudible to the human ear.

It is not surprising that an animal with so delicate a capacity for sound-perception should be particularly sensitive to noise. I am not thinking of those dogs which howl at the top notes of some musical instrument which we can barely hear, but of the unhappy city-dwelling dogs. It has been proved in many instances that in dogs exposed to the intolerable noise of a city acuteness of hearing is considerably reduced. Sound-waves, as they arrive, produce a certain pressure or strain on the ear-drums; if this strain is above an acceptable level it will lead in course of time to a reduction of hearing capacity and actual physical pain when the dog is subjected to too great a volume of sound. The 'noise level' already constitutes a danger to human health and so it must indeed do so in the case of our dogs which are far more sensitive to noise.

Animals which can hear generally possess a voice which they use in communication between themselves. The purpose of the ears is not solely to locate the animal's prey or give warning of some danger; they also intercept the acoustic expressions of other dogs. In the dog these are very varied, as would be expected with a mammal living a socialised existence which has to communicate over considerable distances.

Every dog, therefore, has his own individual voice and the sounds he makes serve as recognition signals. Everyone knows how different are the barks of different dogs—some smart operators have even assembled small orchestras of dogs which can bark out little tunes. By the word 'bark' I mean in this case solely the sharp baying sounds which a dog emits in rapid succession (in technical books it is frequently termed 'baying' or 'giving tongue'); it is basically an expression of submission or inferiority caused either by joy or fear. As we have already seen, such methods of expression can be directed at a man with a very definite purpose such as an invitation to a game. Many dogs wishing to induce their master to play with them adopt the typical attitude which dogs use between themselves: they crouch down in front, rear ends in the air with wagging tail, head and eyes directed on the object of their challenge; it is an unmistakable posture of invitation. Since master is often busy with other matters and does not notice (or does not want to notice), our dog now has recourse to his voice—he uses his yelp, which signifies submission, in order to attract our attention.

I can well imagine that in this way the yelp can be turned into a signal between dog and man, although it is seldom used for communication between dogs. The sportsman whose dog is on a scent through a wood will soon lose sight of him, and he wishes to

Acoustic Expression

know the direction in which the chase is going; it is of importance to him, therefore, that the dog should 'give tongue'. This may well have led to dogs being bred specially for their cry. It has been proved that readiness to give tongue is an hereditary attribute. If the dog is intended as a watchdog, readiness to bark is a desirable quality. The spitz, which is not a hunting dog, is well known as a barker but no doubt the lake-dwellers of the middle stone age appreciated this since presumably they did not wish strangers to approach their huts unobserved any more than we wish the burglar to climb the garden fence; though our dog's barking can sometimes be tiresome, at other times it may be a blessing.

Before buying a dog those living in a built-up area should consider whether the neighbours will be pleased if he is a barker. I strongly recommend that the whole question be discussed with the immediate neighbours. The peace and quiet of our fellow-men is guaranteed by law. There is no need, however, to be intimidated if the neighbours are unfriendly and either dislike dogs or think they have some reason to dislike us; if they threaten to take us to court merely because our watchdog barks two or three times a day when someone comes through the garden, this can be taken quite calmly; no magistrate would be on the side of the prosecution in such a case. A whole series of precedents are available and the offices of the main breeding associations are well briefed on the subject; in case of doubt assistance can be obtained from that quarter.

There are enough good and handsome breeds of dog which do not tend to bark and, if one does not want to annoy the neighbourhood, one of these should be chosen. Just as dogs were once bred to bark or give tongue, non-barking dogs were also bred for other purposes. Some dogs are definitely mute—the greyhound, for instance. Greyhounds were bred as coursing dogs, to hunt in wide open spaces using their eyes—which are particularly sharp—and not their nose. They were generally bred in conspicuous colours and with a long flowing coat so that they could easily be seen from a horse. Giving tongue uses considerable lung-power and this would affect both the speed and endurance of the long-legged coursing dog. Therefore, as the saying is, they 'run mute'; in this they have handsome companions in the great borzoi and silky-haired Afghan hound. The dingo must also originally have run mute, since he does not bark. He is capable of making a few short sharp barking noises but he does so only when he wishes to give warning of major danger; in my pens this happens only if strangers go close to the fence and it is primarily the animals which have been born here who give tongue. Frequently I have the impression that they are emulating my elkhound cross-breeds who bark loudly. Otherwise this barking noise is only to be heard when puppies are being nursed in the kennel and something is seen which looks dangerous.

A Dane named Alwin Pedersen has made a detailed study of the Greenland husky and he says that dogs from eastern Greenland, in contrast to their western cousins, do not bark—'I never heard from them a sound even remotely resembling a bark. In situations when other dogs barked they made an inarticulate sort of cry which quickly turned into a howl. Howling was the normal and most frequent method of expression used by these dogs.' My dingoes do exactly the same; the barking noise—which I believe to be copied—generally turns into a howl. Pedersen also says, however, that east Greenland dogs could learn to bark if they had been brought up among west Greenland huskies as puppies. This is not the case with dingoes.

This shows that the sounds made by the domestic dog can be altered by means of breeding, upbringing or training. On this subject there is one astonishing example, as unique as the circular motion of the basset's tail. The hunting dog used in the Jura (it is reckoned as a Swiss breed) is a comparatively lightly built black and red dog which goes by the name 'hurleur', meaning howler. Friess, a forestry official, describes as follows how these dogs give tongue: 'It is a real deep long-drawn-out howl; in our experience it replaces and interrupts the normal deep hunting cry when on a scent; it seems to signify particularly "found" or "lost". When they howl the dogs stand quite still or even sit; in any case they cease all motion on the spot. They search round the area of the lair or "find" until they discover that the animal has turned, jumped or doubled back on its tracks and they howl with noses in the air. Then they hunt on with their normal cry, more or less frequently interspersed with howling.'

This is undoubtedly an ancient practice of the wolf, transmitted over thousands of years and appearing in specialised form in Swiss

Acoustic Expression

alpine hunting in that it is coupled with the normal hunting cry. Howling is used by wolves, jackals, coyotes and dingoes to indicate their location when separated from their fellows. It is audible over a great distance, far further than a bark or the higher-pitched form of bark generally known as yelping. My dingoes' howl can be heard more than a mile away. A dog can undoubtedly hear it at an even greater distance.

If no one is to be seen around the house for some time, my dingoes invariably start to howl. One begins and at once all the others follow suit so that the entire pack is 'singing' in chorus. At a distance it sounds like the fire alarm and, while I was living in the village, frequently got my neighbours out of bed. It is enough to open a window; the dingoes realise that one is still there and stop howling at once. They start howling straight away if we get into the car and drive off or if we take dogs on a lead and go out.

A friend of mine who had lived some years in Australia once insisted on adopting one of my dingoes. He had a large flat in a block in Munich and was able completely to clear one room. I had advised him to do this since I knew from experience that, if left alone, dingoes inevitably destroy the furniture. My friend worked in an office and five days a week had to leave his dingo alone for eight hours. Dingoes, however, are very gregarious animals, even more so than many of our domestic dogs, and are very unhappy if left alone. They will howl continuously for hours to summon their partner to them. The partner did not of course come but instead came a letter from the management which was both explicit and irrefutable. Heinz brought my dingo back and got married instead.

Howling is infectious. Erik Zimen can start his wolves howling since he can imitate a howl excellently. He can also howl like a dingo and tried to mislead my dingoes into howling by doing so from a window. But they did not fall for it. They knew very well that we were there—so why howl? There seems to be a definite difference here. Wolves in fact assemble and howl when the pack is complete. This is no doubt aimed at the neighbouring pack and means: 'Here we are; this is our territory.'

I have known occasions when dingoes were deceived by distant church bells and began to howl, but this only happened when they were not sure whether there was anyone at home. Otherwise they ignored it. I have already mentioned that many dogs will react to music by howling. An alsatian belonging to one of my friends would howl at the scream of a jet fighter. This reaction to sounds of a frequency obviously similar to that of howling or to certain sections of the howling spectrum, is understandable—one must answer the call of one's kind.

In the majority of our dogs the howl has lost much of its meaning; some can hardly howl at all or at least not intelligibly. The first generation of my elkhound cross-breeds can bark as well as they can howl. Later generations with more of the elkhound in their blood or with an elkhound re-cross do not howl but join the dingo chorus with barks—the result is not very pretty. Both howling and barking are therefore clearly hereditary. The good Strixi tried for a long time to imitate the dingo howl. He never succeeded; all he could achieve was a pitiable squawk. Since my pens contain both howlers and barkers, he reverted to his normal method of expression. Interestingly, Binna, the elkhound bitch who only came in contact with dingoes when full-grown, has acquired a perfectly serviceable, though not very convincing, howl—but it took her nearly three years to learn it. This again illustrates how careful one must be before describing the presence or absence of certain canine capabilities as hereditary or instinctive. Dogs have a great gift of learning. I think it entirely possible that many of our dogs' habits are not hereditary but have been learnt from other dogs.

A sound unpleasant to hear from our dog is the growl. All dogs without exception can growl. Between dogs only the senior one growls. Any dog will growl at a man, however, which perhaps indicates how little store he sets by man's superiority. One proviso must be made here and again it is connected with the important question of retardation in our dogs. If one happens to approach a kennel containing puppies more than three weeks old which have had little contact with human beings, they can clearly be heard growling. Puppies have a privileged status in a pack; they are permitted to growl even though they are anything but senior. Possibly, therefore, puppy habits, which are frequently retained when in contact with human beings, are the deciding factor, overriding man's superiority.

A sound often to be heard emanating from our dog is the 'wuff'. Eisfeld, to whom I often refer when in search of clear terminology, calls it 'a suppressed bark with mouth closed; it is well described by the word "wuff". It is used in case of danger to the young or other vexatious occurrence.' In nature it is a warning to other dogs that danger is in the offing but it is not loud enough to alert a potential enemy and so give away the dog's own position. If our dog is lying quiet and hears footsteps approaching the house, he will raise his head, prick his ears to locate the direction of the sound and issue his warning 'wuff'; then he will jump up and, being now sure of his facts, will start to bark. If he recognises the steps as those of a neighbour he does not like because stones have been thrown at him, the 'wuff' will be followed by a growl and the hackles will rise. Now we know who is passing by outside without even looking out of the window.

What one hopes never to hear from the full-grown dog is the loud shriek indicating great physical pain. If one hears a squeal from puppies at play, this generally means nothing, particularly if their parents are in charge. The cry of pain is in fact a method of expression designed to inhibit aggression. The small puppy soon observes that his brother or his father lets go of him at once if he lets out a squeal. Soon, therefore, he will squeal to high heaven if he even suspects that he might get a good shaking or be 'thrashed' in some other way. The young rascal is frequently to be seen giving his father a hefty tweak on the nose and immediately throwing himself on to his back squealing. The sly naughty boy knows that his impudence will then go unpunished.

Finally we must look at the last audible method of expression—the well-known whine. In my view this must derive from the sounds heard from a puppy on the very day of its birth. At least by the end of the third week it is distinguishable and its meaning plain. A whining dog wants something. The sounds varies considerably both in object, pitch, intensity and frequency. It is used by puppies crying for food but also by the old dogs when feeding their young, in which case it is an invitation. We hear it when a dog is lying at our feet, head between his paws, gazing up at us. Generally this means: 'Do come on; it's such lovely weather outside'; alternatively it can mean: 'Come on, Master, be nice to me; I won't do it again.' Used between dogs it indicates friendliness together with an invitation to closer contact, whether a game or marriage. In normal usage the word whine has an unhappy connotation; in fact the most apt summary of its various meanings is a well-intentioned 'Please'.

The foregoing paragraphs by no means give an exhaustive description of the dog's vocal methods of expression. Every dog has its own personal repertoire of noises indicating contentment, discontent or other emotions; sometimes they sound like a grumble or grunt; even heavy breathing and wheezing may be used. Here I believe that sympathetic contact is the best medium to bring about understanding of the dog's 'language'. Mere description of the methods of expression is inadequate in the case of an animal which can react with such sensitivity and to such fine shades of feeling. Description can be no more than a starting point leading to closer contact. The final stage of this road must be travelled by each individual by himself in the company of his dog; objective scientific methods cannot now and will not in future give us access to the more delicate reactions of the canine mind. I am equally convinced that much springs from a harmonious relationship between man and dog. All his life our dog remains a learner—always provided that the man to whom he is allotted remains a learner himself and does not try to force either himself or his dog into some preconceived pattern.

I have already referred on several occasions to the significance of nose to the dog and to the dog's world of scents. Any description of methods of expression would be incomplete if we did not look at the possibilities of 'olfactory expression' and everything connected with it. I propose to postpone this to a later chapter, however, primarily because this whole subject is of far greater importance in the case of the full-grown dog than of the puppy.

For the moment let us continue to deal with the puppy's seniority-classification phase. This is a real teenage period, producing numerous problems; the little dog, now a member of our household, shows a marked tendency to go off on his own—as he would do normally in the company of his brothers and sisters. Many puppies develop this tendency somewhat earlier—like Frau von Keiser's pugs. The puppy is now extremely interested in anything that moves and looks to the outward eye like some manageable victim. He stalks pigeons and sparrows—without the slightest success of course—and he scrapes away enthusiastically if he discovers a mouse-hole. Provided he has adequate oppor-

Acoustic Expression

tunity for practice, he will soon be complete master of the technique of mouse-catching. This is undoubtedly an innate habit present in all breeds of dog. He will soon be seen making the typical dog's 'mouse-jump': the dog springs straight up in the air, coming down with all his weight on his forepaws and crushing the surprised mouse into the ground. Among the family mice which they catch themselves form a most valuable addition to the puppies' diet.

It is now time to begin 'co-operative games' in order to develop the puppy's desire to learn. The attitudes and habits adopted during play should be carefully observed since they will indicate where his principal capabilities lie. This is the start of training and, by congratulating him and showing signs of pleasure, we should indicate to the puppy that we require something of him. He has now reached the stage where he will grasp this quickly provided we do not make the error of scolding him if he does not at once act precisely as we imagine. One of the main purposes of play at this age is to ensure the cohesion of a group; we must not be impatient, therefore, or try to counteract this natural tendency.

We can now begin to introduce simple obedience or discipline exercises. It is advisable to choose a definite time and continue for a defined period; a quarter of an hour is enough. 'Sit', for instance, is an easy command to teach; when the word is given, press the hinder ends of the puppy down with one hand and rub or stroke his chest with the other; this will prevent him lying down at once and also show him that Master is in a good mood and has no intention of hurting him. If he sits he is congratulated—then stop. Do not repeat the exercise that day or training will become much more difficult. The dog will realise that he has done right and that one is pleased and that we now go on to something else which he will regard as a reward. Continuous repetition makes the dog unsure of himself since it seems as if he were always doing something wrong. The exercise may be repeated casually outside the training period or on the next day. Equally we can now start to teach the other useful commands such as 'Heel,' 'Basket,' and the rest. These indications should suffice; this is not the place to give a complete description of a dog's training.

One fact can aptly be mentioned here, however, since once again it reveals something of the parent–child relationship: willing obedience on the part of the canine parents will be transmitted automatically to their children. I propose to quote an example.

Sascha is an exceptionally obedient dog; from him I have learnt what 'willing obedience' really is. If you tell him quietly to go to his box, he moves off with assured dignity. There is no trace of the subservient obedience so often shown by alsatians that Konrad Lorenz has labelled them obsequious descendants of the jackal. Sascha is precisely the opposite; on occasions he considers the order to go to his box to be unfitting—if, for instance, he has just found a splendid throwing-stick and wishes to hand it to us. He then looks questioningly at his mistress, making it quite plain by his attitude that he is of course ready to comply if needs must, but perhaps a little thought might first be given as to the absolute necessity. If the order is repeated, he saunters off and lies down, sighing at so much folly. If his mistress is in a bad mood and scolds him because he does not obey at once, he makes it abundantly clear what he thinks. He is an experienced old man and knows that at moments like this it is wiser to give way—but his expression speaks volumes!

I have already said that Sascha was given a completely free hand in the training of his daughter Rana from the time she was eight weeks old. From him she learnt to be a faithful obedient dog; in this respect she is totally dependent on him and there is nothing to be done with her if Sascha is not at home; she waits at the door for him as any other dog waits for its master; when he eventually returns the joy is tumultuous. At the age we are now considering she imitated Sascha assiduously in everything he did when given an order. If one said 'Sascha, go to your box,' she ran into it after him and lay down close beside him; if one said 'Sit', she sat down beside him; in this way she came to understand all the words of command such as 'Come,' 'Sit,' 'Go to your box' and 'Down'; she herself required no training. She obeys exactly as he does, though with slightly more trace of humility and submission; this seems to be primarily due to her age, however; the older she grows, the more self-assured she will become in doing what she is told.

THE PACK-FORMATION PHASE

In contrast to our domestic dogs the wild dog is restricted to certain definite reproduction periods; the puppy's development

The Pack-formation Phase

is therefore so arranged that his real period of childhood is at an end just as autumn announces the approach of winter. By October at the latest northern wolves are five months old; in areas inhabited by jackals the rains begin when the cubs have reached this same age. The great herds of herbivores now migrate. They are followed in the north by the wolves and in the south by the great felines. In the area inhabited by the yellow jackal, the felines have now been exterminated and this has forced on the jackal a far-reaching readjustment of his habits of life; previously he followed in the wake of the North African or Middle Eastern lion to the winter pastures of the animals on which the lions fed and of which he took his share; the remnants of the lions' meal he then shared with the vultures in the same way as he now feeds on the leavings of mankind. In Australia too the puppies are five months old when winter sets in. So now the happy life of childhood is over; the parents no longer provide food. Now the young wolf must go off hunting with his parents; the young jackal must ward off kites or other jackal families; the young dingo must chase after the flying kangaroo. The serious business of life has begun.

In the case of wolves the previous year's youngsters now arrive and join up with the family to form a pack. When they themselves were five months old they had registered their allegiance to their father. This sense of allegiance brings them back to their parents again; in some cases they may have been in more or less close or occasional contact throughout the summer. Possibly also even older offspring of the pair may arrive if they have failed to find a mate and form a pack of their own.

We know far too little about this forgathering of the wolf-clans in the wild state to be dogmatic about the sources from which wolves come to form a pack at the beginning of winter. This phenomenon of allegiance, however, may indicate that packs are formed as I have described. In the wild state this allegiance naturally ceases when a wolf is full-grown, has reared his own cubs through a winter and so himself has become a pack-leader; even so I would think it entirely possible that such a wolf, with his entire family, might join up with his parents again and so a wolf pack might consist of three generations.

I shall be dealing with these seasonal adjustments in more detail in the next chapter and so I will not pursue the subject now.

Instead let us look at the implications of the serious business of life during the pack-formation phase. It can be compared to the training of the craftsman; the period of primary schooling and subsequent introduction to the craft by means of games is now over; the puppy is now an apprentice, permitted to work with the Master—the pack-leader—in order to learn the final niceties. Having learnt his trade for three months, like any smart apprentice, he goes out into the world for a time and we shall later accompany him on his wanderings.

During the preceding seniority-classification phase the puppy has played pack games with his brothers and sisters; the father has directed these games himself and has organised them with considerable cunning so that the youngsters will later be able to cope with every subterfuge on the part of their quarry. Now, however, working as a pack is no longer a game. Now for the first time they are really pursuing a large animal. The hunt is no simple matter. Louis Crisler's accounts show that the two wolves, 'Trigger' and 'Lady', who had grown up with men and had had no parental instruction, attempted to hunt large animals in concert; they only did so, however, after reaching the age of eight or nine months when they had been in contact with other wolves and had undoubtedly hunted with them. I am convinced that five- or six-month-old wolves do not venture to attack large animals and probably they would not do so even later unless they had learnt from their parents or other experienced wolves. The same can happen with our own dogs. A perfectly well-behaved dog will be taken out poaching one day by another dog—and that is the end of it. He may never have ventured to poach until that day, but from then on he will do so.

I have already raised the question of the extent to which the art of hunting has to be learnt. Undoubtedly pursuit of the smaller animals does not have to be learnt from parents, as I shall show. In the case of larger animals, however, the method of hunting must be a more recent form, developed over the years and suited to the breed, of that employed by the wolf to obtain his food; as we know, the wolf's closest and most immediate relations are the coyote and the jackal and they do not hunt large animals; both in physical conformation and in behaviour they have remained more primitive. No instinctive methods of hunting the large animal have therefore

The Pack-formation Phase

developed and so expert leadership given by experienced parents is required.

I realise, of course, that someone will now ask: who were the first parents who taught their children and where did they obtain their knowledge? This is no mere fractious question; at some stage the 'discovery' must have been made that, with co-operation, large animals could be hunted. There is little point, however, in speculating whether this happened because some young animal separated from its herd was brought down or as the result of an attack by starving wolves on some old wounded beast. In this context the interesting fact is that observation in the case of many animals confirms that genuine traditions have developed and that these are handed down from generation to generation. This is enough for our purpose at this point.

The traditions associated with hunting large animals can only be passed on if the prior conditions already described obtain: absolute discipline, close co-operation and acceptance of the leader's experience, in other words the loyalty of the disciple. Clearly it is more practical that these principles should be passed on than that methods of hunting the larger animals should become innate habits of behaviour; otherwise some instinct would have had to tell the wolf or dog how to hunt each different type of prey. In the areas inhabited by wolves there were once wild horses and wild boars in addition to the elks, reindeer, red deer and Asiatic steppe antelopes still present today. The problem would have been highly complex since instinct would have to differentiate between the various types of animal; sight of a wild horse, for instance, would have to activate the instinctive behaviour suitable to the pursuit of wild horses. If, however, in certain areas wolves specialised in hunting wild horses only, and if the horses disappeared, they would starve.

The mere size of the large animal, together with the fact that it lived in a herd and was prepared to defend itself, made it a difficult problem, so a flexible and adaptable method of hunting was necessary; this could best be achieved by association and the transmission of knowledge gained by experience. The adaptability of this method constitutes the guarantee for the survival of the race through the hardships of the northern winter. This mere fact, however, spelt the doom of the wolf when he came in contact with man. His adaptability to his environment caused him quickly to realise that man's great herds constituted an easy prey and so he earned the illwill of mankind; he was even labelled a dangerous man-killer, which in fact he is not—a wolf will run from men; so today all the most modern technical methods are employed to exterminate the wolf. Such is the fate of the wolf, as it is of the sheep-killing dingo.

MAN AS PACK-LEADER

Pack seniority means that, under the guidance of the pack-leader, the young wolves learn what to do during a hunt, how to drive their quarry and the part each must play in a totally disciplined manner. Pack seniority means that knowledge is acquired through co-operation.

With this as his background the young dog now enters upon a new stage of his education. At this age action in concert under the stern but accepted leadership of some authority is a disposition of nature and for him, therefore, a requirement. He expects something from the man who has become his leader, although that man is, in addition, more or less a father-figure—this last because the man still brings him his food and the parent-child relationship therefore still persists. The dog now expects to act in concert with his man and will do so with pleasure, always provided that his previous upbringing has established a firm relationship of confidence. If, therefore, we do not provide him with anything of the sort, if we more or less leave him to himself, then we are preventing him from developing into a sociable personality; we are inhibiting his development into a genuine social partner of mankind.

We must now differentiate sharply between playing and working, although we must always remember that what we call work is to him a game—but a game the purpose of which is to learn. What I mean is as follows: we play with him, quite simply, without aim or purpose, without hindrance or constraint; it is playtime such as every dog requires. As something entirely separate, however, we should now seek to replace instruction in pack-hunting by exercises of a different nature. Naturally this depends upon the ultimate destination of the dog. If he is to be a sporting dog or a guard-dog, there will be a training plan. If, however, he is not a working dog but 'merely' an attractive little poodle or merry fox-terrier, then we must think out some method of exploiting his inclinations and his talents, which meanwhile we shall have discovered.

This reminds me of a small poodle which I always remember because he was living proof of the depths to which a sympathetic dog-lover can penetrate into a dog's mind. I had the privilege of making the acquaintance, on Austrian television, both of the dog and its master; Rolf Kutschera, a Vienna theatre manager, and his poodle came to help me in my television programme on dogs. They were a model illustration of the relationship between man and dog and for a highly encouraging reason described by Kutschera somewhat as follows: 'I start from the premise that the dog is a learner by nature and that he will become dull and mentally atrophied if no account is taken of his requirement to learn. From his very early days, therefore, I gradually taught my poodle all sorts of tricks while playing with him. But I went even further: I had previously owned an alsatian and so knew all about training them. I said to myself: a poodle should be able to learn all that an alsatian can do. In fact, without difficulty, he learnt everything that a regular police dog can do—and he took great pleasure in doing so.' This was what Rolf Kutschera said in an interview and his poodle licked my face to confirm. The little dog was completely at ease; he was not in the least shy of arc-lamps or cameras or coy about producing all his tricks, sometimes—and this is worth noting—without being asked. He simply thought it fun!

Anyone who can do this is giving his dog a full life in that he is providing the dog with the possibility of developing his brain to the maximum; such development, however, necessarily implies much more than the ability to do certain tricks; that is not the real point. The decisive factor is that the learning of these tricks or the training as a working dog really activate the brain. Although a dog's brain has by no means the capacity of a man's, it is nevertheless capable of quite remarkable achievements. This basic capability is of no use, however, if there is no training; this is the essential prerequisite if the dog is to act, not merely on impulse but with intelligence.

A further factor is that, as a result, the dog will become particularly attached to his man. He will say to himself: anyone so superb that he can teach one so much is deserving of very special respect; he is a really great pack-leader.

This somewhat liberal interpretation of the workings of a dog's mind is no exaggeration. Mental rather than physical superiority, whether in another of his kind or in man, is far more impressive to a dog. Between dogs which know each other well physical strength is always being measured, whereas authority remains unquestioned. Sascha and Rana sometimes tussle with such violence that to an outsider it looks like deadly earnest. Rana likes to challenge the dog's physical superiority; his role as leader, however, is to her a matter of course and, if he calls, she is on the spot at once.

Quite a tale attaches to this call. It sometimes happens that Rana is so occupied in flirting with the dingoes through the fence of one of the pens that she does not notice Sascha waiting for her in front of the house. He goes a few steps towards her and by his attitude— an ostentatious turn in the desired direction—gives her to understand that he wishes to take her away. If this does not succeed, he then barks fiercely at an imaginary enemy. This subterfuge brings Rana along at once, since she would never leave her friend alone in such a situation; she barks with equal fury and dashes aimlessly about the place in an attempt to discover where the enemy is actually hiding.

Solidarity in the event of danger is also inculcated during the pack-formation phase; at the same time the self-defence reaction may become very marked. At this period a she-wolf, which I brought up some years ago, was very apt to bite strangers or even people whom she knew slightly. I can well imagine that the fury with which a dog will defend its master originates during this period; unless, at this time, the young dog learns to love and respect man as the mentally superior leader, he will not subsequently give of his best if he has to fight for his master.

The young dog will now be subjecting his master to detailed scrutiny; he will register with equal exactitude his master's mental superiority or his uncertainty and inconsistency. He will also register if his master tries to demonstrate his superiority solely by physical force. He will take good note of that and draw his conclusions from it at some suitable opportunity. The dog requires to see in his master the sublime 'model' of the intelligent, far-sighted, self-assured leader; if, instead of this 'model', he

Man as Pack-leader

finds a master who is unfeeling and insistent on asserting his authority by brute force, it is possible that, when the dog is full-grown, he will feel that his existence can only be assured if he can assert himself as pack-leader. It will be remembered that puppies are enabled to fend for themselves if the protection and care of their parents is removed. Now the position is similar. Naturally, faced with such a master, fear will predominate, since the dog will realise his physical inferiority; one day, however, a moment may come when he will forget his fear and fight for recognition with his teeth.

The same thing happens, though without biting, when dogs are brought up by dear old ladies whose only wish is to do the best by their darling and who therefore get it wrong all the time. Even the smallest lapdog or miniature definitely looks for Big Brother—more in fact than many larger dogs do; by human standards he may be treated with every care and affection but the little dog finds nothing in all this to look up to. Inevitably these 'dear little creatures' turn into complete tyrants, inexorably seizing the role of leader.

But we have digressed a long way from the wolves hunting in concert. Our starting point was the differentiation between what is innate and what must be learnt and this we must deal with in more detail. As far as learning is concerned, enough has been said about the wolf pack's methods of hunting the larger animals. I would only mention that there is no such thing as a deadly snap of the jaws and this seems to me significant as a pointer to the fact that the capacity to hunt the larger animal was only discovered at a comparatively late stage. By our standards the wolf's methods of bringing down an animal are extraordinarily cruel; as they pursue the animal in its flight wolves take no form of risk and never attack from in front; they jump at its flanks and stomach, tearing the stomach open until the animal eventually collapses exhausted. Possibly they also go for the throat but only when there is no danger from antlers, horns or hoofs.

With small animals it is a different matter. I have already mentioned that jumping on a mouse is an innate habit. The smaller animal is killed ably and efficiently.

One day I was standing at my window, thinking no evil and looking at my neighbour's hens pecking and scratching around in a large field. Suddenly something flashed yellow in the sunshine, streaked across the grass and made a beeline for a hen. The hen made not a sound, though the others rushed flapping away, squawking agitatedly. As quickly as he came the yellow thief tore back, the white hen held high in his jaws. All was over in a second —rush in—snap of the jaws—rush away. It was a fascinating 'turn' which delighted me because it was so well done. Such an accomplished performance could only be the result of much practice.

In fact there had been no 'practice'. The thief was Abo, the six-months-old dingo dog, and this was the first hen he had ever killed—it was the prelude to many others! Abo had been brought up in the house with his sister Suki and had in fact been under control day and night. I know for sure that, apart from a few mice, he had never before caught a living animal. Naturally he had often seen these hens quite close but he had never learnt how to kill a hen; he had never even been given a dead hen to eat. How then was this young chicken-stealer so good at his job? 'Instinct'?

If the whole sequence of actions involved in killing a hen stemmed solely from hereditary reflexes, then the dog must possess some instinct which tells him how to catch all the various types of small animal, as I have already pointed out in the case of the larger animals—each type, after all, must be hunted and killed in a different way. A hare cannot be caught in the same way as a hen or a mouse. A stereotyped method of capture can only be adopted by the highly specialised form of predator who lives only on one particular sort of animal. The jump on to the mouse's back furnishes an almost complete example of a chain of hereditary reflexes; there are a few—but comparatively few—gaps between the links in the chain which have to be filled by acquired reflexes, in other words by learning. Owing to the dog's marked predilection for learning there is no difficulty here. This is therefore an indication that the forbears of the canine race were small and lived on mice. In the case of somewhat larger animals such as hens or hares, certain hereditary reflexes may play an important part, but there are vital gaps between them and these must be filled by experience; only by experience can a dog adapt his methods to the type of prey being pursued and to the situation.

This still does not answer the question how Abo could have

learnt to catch a hen with such perfect efficiency and success. The answer is: by playing with other dogs. Fox, the American student of behaviour, once made a highly revealing experiment. He first hand-reared six puppies separately. During their first five weeks none of the puppies had any contact with other dogs. When they were first shown a picture of a dog, they were nonplussed; it meant nothing to them. Then Fox allowed each of the puppies to play for half an hour with others which had been brought up normally. When he next showed them the picture of a dog they tried to seize its head or neck in their teeth.

Though reared in isolation, therefore, during this short period these puppies had learnt that in a fighting game the head and neck are targets. Here, therefore, was quite clearly a case of learning based on a hereditary tendency. The capacity to learn, however, for which certain 'positions' are available in the switchboard of the brain, is very 'basic'. What I mean by this is that only a simple pattern makes an imprint—the part in front of the neck and containing eyes is the head; if you can get a hold immediately behind it, you have got a grip on the animal and are then 'overcome' by a desire to shake it (a pleasurable hereditary reflex). We should also remember that the dog will equally recognise a man's head for what it is; even as a tiny puppy, barely able to see, he will realise where our eyes and mouth are, the latter being to him identical with the lips of another dog. If, therefore, the dog sees a hen, if only for a few seconds, this is enough for him to grasp its anatomy. He aims for the right place, therefore, because he has learnt to do so when playing with other puppies, as he has also learnt to carry away what he has caught without stumbling over it. Every puppy has a marked tendency to carry off large objects—our trousers, a book or a tablecloth; then there is an opportunity for splendid practice in tearing things to pieces!

This escapade also taught Abo something else. It had been a resounding success; no more was required than to take a firm hold, give a quick shake and then the dead hen could be carried away. So, because it had all been so successful, on his latest excursions into the village Abo has invariably killed five hens in a row (release of hereditary reflexes, particularly if they have been pent up for some time, is invariably accompanied by pleasurable sensations).

While on this subject a word about the sequel to such looting expeditions. In the first place it is highly significant that the capture is brought home. This is the normal procedure. Anyone who, at this point, belabours his dog over the head with the hen is merely teaching him to be cleverer next time and eat it in some hide-out somewhere. Having already read in a book by Konrad Lorenz that it was completely hopeless to try and stop a dingo hunting, I did nothing of the sort; I congratulated Abo, took the hen from him and gave it back to him later. I thus ensured that at least I was kept informed of the number of hens killed by my

Aboriginal as a young dog instinctively plucking his first pigeon

dingoes since they always handed them over. This also allowed me to check whether they were in fact all first-class laying hens, as the owners invariably maintained.

This brings us to another hereditary reflex—plucking. No one had taught Abo this and yet he could do it from the outset. A dog starts by systematically plucking the feathers from the stomach. Faced with his first dead bird the dog begins by searching for the stomach—or at least so it seems to me; he sniffs and pokes around with his nose for some time, turns the animal over and tries every angle. Finally it is clear where the stomach is and its contents are the first to be eaten. Tastes differ; for a dog well-filled intestines are a special delicacy!

To summarise: a dog's capabilities are developed by puppy

Man as Pack-leader

games and, if he is living wild, these will be put to the test in his fifth or sixth month. His pronounced readiness to learn ensures that the young dog's capabilities for hunting, fighting or avoidance of an enemy are further developed and improved under the guidance of an experienced older dog. In addition he learns the advantages and possibilities of action in concert, the niceties of co-operation and the purpose of action in support of others. He adjusts his attitude to conform to the moral superiority of the pack-leader; he finds satisfaction in acceptance of the leader's authority and his loyalty develops.

In general, therefore, this is an important stage in the life of the maturing dog and account must be taken of it if the dog is living in the company of man. Man must be the self-assured experienced teacher who brings the dog's capabilities to their highest point of development. He will thus ensure that his four-legged friend is at peace with his environment.

7 Puberty and Maturity

The Menzels, a couple who have carried out much research into canine behaviour, once suggested the term 'puberty phase' and this has now become current terminology. It begins from the end of the sixth month and lasts until the dog becomes capable of reproduction. In the case of many of our dogs the latter occurs as early as seven months, the puberty phase therefore being very short. Suki, one of my dingoes, first came properly in season—'on heat' in other words—when she was just eleven months old and I have known dogs able to cover a bitch at the same age.

There are many breeds which mature later and only become capable of reproduction at eleven or twelve months. People say that a bitch should not be covered before the fourteenth month; there is no harm in leaving it a little later and allowing her to reach 20–24 months before introducing her to a dog, particularly in the case of the more heavily built breeds which should have time to 'mature'.

I shall be reverting later to breeding and shall then be dealing with the differing lengths of the puberty phase. As far as behaviour is concerned it produces nothing new. If one thinks once more of the wolf pack—the young wolves hunt in combination with their parents with whom they remain until January or February. During this time their experience acquired during the pack-formation phase is widened and deepened but that is all.

Accordingly, during this period our attitude to the dog undergoes no change. We should continue to play games with him and these will meanwhile have been expanded into obedience exercises. If it is intended that the dog (and its handler!) be really highly trained, now is the time to look for a training area. An experienced handler will tell us when to begin. Some dogs mature earlier but many should be given a little more time. The expert will be able to advise what can be done with the dog by way of preparation and what is best postponed. At this age there can be too much training and instruction. Many dogs have been totally ruined by their

SCENT CONTROLS

The time is now approaching when our dog will demonstrate that he is growing up by lifting his leg and the bitch will soon come in season for the first time. I must therefore now broach a subject which has much to do with these matters—the dog's method of expression, using his own scent. Naturally in a dog these 'expressive

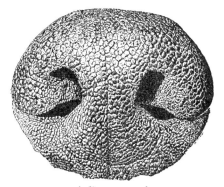

A dingo muzzle

olfactory structures' play an overriding part and they are closely associated with those methods of expression already described as optical.

The organ of transmission is the nose, the efficiency of which I have already described. I am including here a sketch of the dog's so-called muzzle intended to show how complex a structure is that black wet tip of the nose which serves as its outer protection and also as a conspicuous optical signal.

When two strange dogs meet each other, they approach with outstretched neck and muzzles forward, trying to catch the scent of the other from a distance. They move forward until the muzzles are almost touching. This is the nasal inspection, the nose-to-nose sniffing, seldom to be seen with dogs which know each other well since in their case more intimate checks are permitted. The whole posture makes it impossible for one dog to jump straight at the other. This is the dog's protection against surprise attack; he thus has time to discover the reaction and the attitude of the other dog. If, for instance, the other dog —perhaps an older male— makes a hostile face, perhaps with his hackles rising, it is possible to withdraw quickly if it is not desired to issue a challenge. If, on the other hand, the other dog is friendly and makes it clear (by wagging his tail, for instance) that he has no evil intent, then this nasal contact is the prelude to the ceremony of greeting, during which much use is made of the 'expressive olfactory structures'.

This nasal contact is also to be seen during the preliminaries to mating when the bitch is slowly beginning to come into season. Similarly dogs which know each other often use the frontal approach until the muzzles meet; in both these cases, however, there is no tense posture as is normally to be seen between strange dogs. Instead a friendly wag of the tail is given at once; the attitude and motions are uninhibited and relaxed. It is as if the dog were saying: 'Hello, chum; we know each other; I seem to know your nose.'

Although the human nose is, of course, very different from the canine nose, the dog still recognises it as such; if, therefore, our dog comes to meet us with his nose stretched out, we know what he means. If, when out for a walk, we meet a strange dog who shows no inclination to sniff our 'Rex' or 'Fifi' in the manner described, then something is wrong. He is almost certainly an uneducated boor, lacking instinct. The situation is naturally quite different if some stranger slips into the garden guarded by our dog. In this case there is no obligation to greet the intruder; he is given loudly to understand that he has no business to be where he is, a statement underlined, if necessary, by bared teeth; this is effective since no dog likes to fight on foreign territory. Urban dogs, who have had many meetings, some of them unpleasant, often demonstrate that experience has removed all interest in making the acquaintance of yet another dog. They look away and suddenly become extremely occupied with other matters. If our dog is polite, he will respect this attitude, retract his 'how-do-you-do' nose and pass on as if he had not seen the other dog. The situation must be considered as a whole if one wishes to draw conclusions about the instinctive behaviour of our dogs.

After this first nose-to-nose contact the dogs sniff along each other until the noses reach the opposite end of the body. This brings us to the 'expressive olfactory structures', with which we must now deal. We will not, however, start with the dog's rear end but first consider the other possibilities.

During his fourth week the puppy discovers these olfactory structures in his brothers and sisters but initially those of the head

Bente, the cross-bred bitch, rubbing the side of her neck

and neck play only a minor role. Possibly he discovers that they have some special property in his mother and somewhat later in his father during play. We have already seen that burrowing into the coat of the head and neck is a development of the burrowing motion typical of the puppy when still a suckling.

This habit is primarily to be seen during the preliminaries to mating, as described by Seitz and Eisfeld; both have emphasised the challenging nature of this burrowing motion. I have also seen half-grown puppies do this to their mother; on occasions it is an invitation to a game. All this is plain sailing were it not for the question: why particularly are the head, the sides of the neck and the shoulders targets for this nose-nudging? Why does the nose burrow into the coat and then sniff solely at these points? Why not equally along the back or on the flanks?

One may say that this is a purely academic question which need not concern the normal dog-owner. It brings us, however, to another habit which may very much concern us as dog-owners and which can occasionally be highly unpleasant. Sometimes it is really disgusting and can even put people off having a dog. Those with experience of dogs will know what I mean—the extraordinary canine habit of rubbing the head, neck and shoulders into some strong-smelling substance.

In this case 'strong-smelling substance' is a euphemism for the fresh droppings of cows, human beings, pigs and other animals, for the grass-green contents of a cow's stomach and on occasions even for paint (from a freshly painted garden fence, for instance). I once saw a bitch rubbing herself against a post against which many dogs had lifted their legs. I once saw it done by a puppy just over three months old when he was given a dog-biscuit—something quite new for him; he took it a little way from the others of his litter, placed it on the ground and rubbed his head and neck over it several times before starting to gnaw it. If one keeps as many dogs as I do, it often happens that a dog will be given a feeding bowl which does not belong to him; he will usually rub his head, neck and shoulders against it before starting to eat. I have even seen the same with a water-tin.

If I see my red and yellow dingoes all stained green in front, this is nothing unusual. I frequently give them the stomach of a cow unopened and they enjoy eating the contents; they are, after all, the most natural 'vegetables' which one can give a dog. But if our dog comes back from a walk with the side of his neck smeared with filth, this is really no joke. Unfortunately there is nothing to do but watch him and, as soon as you see what he is about, scold him sharply and drag him away if necessary. If he sniffs innocently at the corner of a house or fence and then rubs against it, this is comparatively tolerable—provided the paint is not fresh!; he is merely picking up the scent of another dog and it will generally

Scent Controls

not be perceptible to our nose. If, however, after sniffing something unattractive, he stops and sinks to his knees, turning his forequarters sideways, this is a major danger signal. Frequently, after rubbing his neck in something particularly evil-smelling even to our underdeveloped nose, our friend will roll in it in ecstasy.

Nose-nudging and coat-sniffing may therefore well mean: 'Where did you get that lovely scent?' *Why* our dogs like to scent themselves in this way, however, is a question I cannot answer nor can any of the books on the subject that I know. Sometimes I think that a splendid aroma raises a dog's status in the pack; more probably, however, the object is to overpower the dog's own scent —the scent of a predatory animal—to enable him to approach his prey unobserved. But this is supposition—no more.

The inexperienced dog-owner finds it hard to accustom himself to the fact that his pet's interest seems to be concentrated on the scent of those parts of the body of other dogs (and embarrassingly enough of his two-legged friend also) to which in general we do not like to refer. The majority of books on dogs eulogise the dog's wonderful nature, his faithfulness unto death and his overwhelming desire to be more intelligent than men; in short they emphasise the bright side. In this book I think it right also to deal with what might be called the seamy side. The expression is apt when applied to the thoughtless or unscrupulous exercise of the 'breeder's art' which turns natural healthy animals into poor pitiable creatures and so commits a crime against the dog; it is also apt if applied to the dog which has been turned by unintelligent upbringing and handling into a neurotic or an asthmatic mountain of fat. In my view, however, the natural habits evolved over millions of years and fulfilling some purpose in the slow development of the social aptitudes which have brought the dog so close to us, do not really belong to the seamy side, even when they are concerned with parts of the body which to us do not seem altogether fitting.

I have very often seen people, perfectly sensible otherwise, drag their good dog away with imprecations because it was proposing to smell the back ends of their neighbour's dog. Anyone who can be so uncomprehending about the canine world should be forbidden to keep a dog by law! I propose deliberately to inflict on the reader this highly important section affecting the dog's social life and dealing with the 'expressive olfactory structures'. To do

Puberty and Maturity

justice to the dog's nature, we must look at these matters with an unprejudiced eye, realise their vital importance and try to understand as best we 'non-smellers' are able.

Nature has so arranged that in the case of the dog there exist in the region of the rear ends certain glands producing olfactory substances. These are the glands of the anus, sphincter and anal sac. To us their products are imperceptible but to the dog's delicate nose they must have a significance similar to that of a passport to the customs official. Just as the official can thus identify the traveller, these particular scents tell the dog what sort of an individual another dog is.

My simile is an apt one in another respect. If someone asks for our passport or other papers, we first make certain that he has a right to make this request. He must therefore first legitimise himself unless this has already been done for him by his uniform. Police officers or immigration officials have this right of inspection; when on duty they have certain social prerogatives over us.

In canine society a check on the products of these glands is in a sense a social prerogative and it is that of the senior dog. He is allowed to inspect and he allows himself to be inspected without restriction; he ostentatiously presents his rear end. Just as the uniform vouches for the customs official, this attitude vouches for the dog. He presents his rear end, meaning thereby that he feels himself superior. If the other dog recognises this superiority he will express the fact by making every effort to present his own rear end as little as possible; if he does not recognise it, he will adopt the same attitude as his opposite number.

Here, therefore, optical methods of expression come into play; in fact they dictate the procedure since on them depends the question whether sniffing is permitted or not. We cannot tell whether the individual scent says anything more than 'Here I am' or whether it indicates the dog's seniority. Since such striking optical methods of demonstrating seniority are available, it may perhaps be concluded that these scents indicate no more than the dog's individuality.

In any case this rear-end inspection is an effective expression of a desire to make contact. We shall have frequent opportunity of confirming this when out for a walk. After the first nose-to-nose contact two strange dogs will stand alongside each other in order

Scent Controls

to make each other's acquaintance better and take the measure of the other's individual scent. They carefully sniff each other's rear ends and from then on a relationship is established—each knows the other.

To pursue the subject of these 'smell-pictures'—the faeces carry the scent from certain glands in this part of the body. When, therefore, our dog sniffs at the droppings of another dog, this will tell him whether he knows the producer of them or not. He can certainly also tell whether they are those of a dog or a bitch. Not only are dogs gregarious creatures but they also have their own territory. It is therefore important to them to know who has been in an area which they themselves are crossing and when. We know that dogs are able to estimate the time factor on the basis of scent. So the little sausage by the side of the road will tell our dog that the neighbour's little Suzy was taken for a walk by her master much earlier than in the last few days. To him this is a highly interesting discovery. Gregarious creatures like to discover such things; Mrs. Smith at the window opposite also notes that we are taking our dog out for its walk today at 2.0 p.m. instead of the usual 3.0 and constructs all sorts of theories since there must obviously be some interesting reason. We are only too ready to label Mrs Smith a 'tiresome busybody'. Possibly she is but the basic reason is a praiseworthy gregarious human attitude. In the days when mankind's present social structures were developing it was vital for the tribe to know who was doing what where and when. In this respect man is still a member of his primitive tribe; in exactly the same way our dog, obediently following on the lead, is a member of a pack in so far as his behaviour and mentality are concerned. The fact that in so many cases we are able to interpret his habits in human terms springs from the similarity between human and canine social structures.

Even with no sausage lying by the roadside, however, provided our dog knows the individual scent of another, he can tell that that dog recently went down the High Street. He can smell the sweat imprints of the other's paws.

This scent trail comes from the fact that a large number of sweat glands are contained in the pads of the feet and these give off a strong-smelling secretion. As every dog-lover knows, the sweat glands in a dog's skin have become atrophied and he can only sweat through his paws. This does not produce adequate heat adjustment, however, and the regulator is panting—deep breathing with mouth open and tongue hanging out. This is how the dog cools himself if too hot. As a dog runs, he leaves behind a scent trail perceptible to any dog with a good nose. Our dog sniffs along it and then he knows exactly: the neighbour's Suzy went along here an hour ago in the direction of Cathedral Square. This raises two questions: can a dog connect the individual scent of another dog's rear ends and the scent trail left by his pads? How does he know the direction in which the trail is leading?

The first question is answered by an experiment described by Otto Koehler, the great pioneer of behavioural research, during an address at the World Cynological Congress in Dortmund in 1956. This experiment was a test of the training in 'search by scent' developed by the Menzels who have also done much research into canine behaviour. Koehler described it as follows: 'Some ten people were present. Each was required to pick up a fir-cone, of which there were masses lying around, and hold it in his closed fist for one minute; he then placed some inconspicuous mark upon it and threw it away. The dog was now brought in and allowed to sniff at us under the armpit—we were allowed to specify which of us. His handler then let the dog loose with the command "Seek"; the dog searched round among the fir-cones until he suddenly seized one and brought it to his handler. In every case it was the fir-cone thrown by the man whom the dog had sniffed. A dog so trained can therefore recognise the similarity between the scent of a man's hand and his armpit, a remarkable sensory achievement of which no human being would be capable.'

We can therefore say without further ado that the individual scent of a dog's rear ends and that of his pads are recognisable as coming from the same dog. There is no need to emphasise the importance of this capability in the existence of a wolf pack.

Determination of the direction of a trail depends on a feat of deduction which is no less astounding. As we know, a scent disperses—in other words it spreads; the scent molecules move from the place at which they were deposited. The staler a scent is, the fewer of these volatile scent-carriers remain; finally they disappear altogether. Provided sufficient scent molecules remain, the dog, pursuing the trail for a little distance and checking care-

Scent Controls

fully with his nose, can tell from the rise or fall of the scent the direction in which his predecessor has gone. If he follows the trail in the wrong direction the scent will become weaker, if in the right direction it will become stronger.

This small digression into scenting rounds off what has already been said in the chapter on play. It also illustrates the importance of these 'expressive olfactory structures' for a gregarious animal like the dog which lives in a pack.

If a male dog discovers the scent of a bitch in season, this is for him, of course, a matter of great excitement. This scent must carry over considerable distances—anyone who possesses a bitch and lives in an area where there are many loose dogs will know that. Recently, for instance, I was called from a neighbouring village and asked whether any of my dogs were missing since a number of dogs which had not been seen before had suddenly appeared. I went cold for, if a dingo gets out, the poultry population in the area is liable to suffer badly and my dingoes apparently have a predilection for particularly good and prize-winning pedigree birds (at least that is what the bills say!). I hurriedly counted heads, therefore, and found to my relief that my family was all present. Eva, my kennel-maid, drove over to the village at once to see what was happening. In fact there was a considerable assemblage of dogs; some of them she knew personally and they came from villages miles away.

The function of this strong 'in-season' scent—which we of course cannot perceive—is clear. As always the purpose is the preservation of the race and here reproduction occupies a vital place. A bitch's period in season must not be allowed to pass, particularly seeing that she comes in season only twice a year at most and she is usually only capable of propagating the species for a few years. It is therefore essential that a broadcast announcement be made of the fact that the physiological process taking place in the bitch's reproductive system has reached the stage when fertilisation is possible. We shall be dealing later in this chapter with all the other things that happen in this connection.

While on this subject of 'sniffing' it should be added that, when strange dogs meet, the individual scent is inspected not only in the anal area but in that of the genitals also; after all it is of importance to know whether one is dealing with a dog or a bitch. Finally comes

Puberty and Maturity

the question whether this 'anal-genital inspection', as the whole process of sniffing the rear ends may be called, has any function in the communal life of the dog other than acquaintance of the individual scent. We have already mentioned the habit of presenting the rear ends; it demonstrates strength and power. The contrasting attitude, concealment of this region, is a sign of humility and submission, sometimes even of fear—a further illustration of the optical expression complementing the scent picture. Inspection of a well-known member of the pack is a demonstration of seniority, a symbolic action by which the pack-leader underlines his authority. Junior dogs in the pack never inspect—that is not allowed. Bitches, moreover, never, or only exceptionally, inspect except in the case of their own puppies. These are, of course, invariably and repeatedly subjected to the anal-genital inspection as long as they are in the nest; when they run around outside, their father does likewise, initially no doubt to be sure that he knows the new members of his family but later also to show the puppies who is in command. As we know, canine fathers are very strict and insist on discipline.

INDIVIDUAL SCENT AS A VISITING CARD

We have so far been dealing primarily with the dog's actions in relation to the scents of other dogs, starting from the puppy's transitional phase when he gives his first sign of life as a socialised creature by examining with his nose his brothers and sisters and his mother. Now we must look at the dog's actions in relation to his own scent.

The most practical starting point is his olfactory self-inspection, the sniffing of his own body and inspection of his own waste products. These will give the dog-owner many useful hints and indications.

Functionally self-inspection falls into the category of the maintenance of comfort. This is the expression used by the students of behaviour to cover all those actions associated with an animal's care of himself. We use the overall term hygiene.

A large book could be written about ways of keeping our dogs comfortable; there is at least as much to say as about our own hygiene. The dog-owner should be intimately concerned with his dog's hygiene—to his own profit and that of the dog. When our dogs' ancestors were living wild, all was quite simple; nature solved the problem in the best possible way. Then, however, man arrived and started breeding these creatures which were so well suited to and equipped for their world, and he did so with expert lack of discrimination. Man has reaped his reward: now he himself has to groom the modified creatures which he has produced; to give a single instance—man has bred the Scotch terrier with a coat reaching down to the ground but in his enthusiasm he has forgotten to breed into this attractive dog habits which will enable it to keep its own coat clean. The dog possesses at best his hereditary habits of grooming himself and these were designed for the wolf's pelt; the owner of the Scotch terrier, maltese, komondor or pekinese must do a lot of work to keep his dog's coat in condition. I am entirely prepared to admit, however, that this is a pleasing occupation which, if started in the right way, can form an additional bond between the dog and his master (or more likely his mistress). When one animal cleans another's coat this might be termed 'sociable grooming' and between animals it is one of the most effective methods of expressing affection. This is all to the good for the owner who has the time and likes his dog to have a clean well-groomed coat. It is unwise, however, to attack the little dog with brush and comb immediately on his arrival in his new home. The dog does not allow himself to be groomed by someone else unless he knows that someone else well and trusts him. It is essential to take one's time, to introduce grooming slowly and by stages and to give the dog the feeling that one is fully aware of its significance. Since dogs are usually acquired when still very young, not a great deal can be done anyway since the long coat will not develop for some time. With a full-grown dog of the long-haired breeds, however, this point should be remembered, particularly if in this respect he gives evidence of hereditary instinct. Only the wolf who is a friend would be allowed to clean the coat of another member of the pack!

The alsatian, the bulldog, the short-haired dachshund or the German boxer who accompanies the keeper on his daily rounds, however, need only be brushed on high days and holidays; the rest they will do for themselves. A dog with the right instincts will groom himself with attention and care, making full use of his nose. He sniffs around and notices at once if there is mud on his coat. The nose will also discover the flea whose life is usually a short one on the normal-coated dog. In a tangle of long unkempt hair, however, these little visitors can live like kings and multiply exceedingly; the only remedy in this case are the powders sold by any pet shop.

The nose also comes into action if the dog has damaged himself; the place is inspected in detail and then the all-healing tongue comes into action. There is no need to take the normal dog to the vet because of a small puncture in the skin; he will deal with the matter himself and cure it with his tongue. The vet need only be consulted if the wound is large and deep and must be sewn up. This is not to say, however, that it is not better to visit the vet too often rather than too seldom.

During self-inspection with the nose the anal and genital areas are those most frequently examined. For the puppy knowledge of his own specific scent has a definite significance and this we shall be dealing with later. Our dog will also sniff at his rear ends, however, when something is not right. If his digestion is upset he will do this with unusual frequency, also if he has worms; in the latter case the itching sensation may cause him to skate around on the floor in a sitting posture with his hind legs raised. If this only happens occasionally, it is merely an attempt to clean the part of the body concerned; naturally the best Persian carpet is chosen for the purpose.

Our dog will also be interested in his own genital area and this will be the object of frequent self-inspection. He will never understand why he is rebuked for doing so; he thinks it his duty to ensure that everything here is clean. He is merely being a normal dog.

Dogs combine what is pleasant with what is useful. The products of their metabolism form an integral part of their information system, following the principle of economy or killing two birds with one stone. Their waste products, therefore, are of vital significance in the life of the dog and these are something to which more attention is paid than we like. Unfortunately, in our civilised world, we cannot invariably make allowances for the dog and must do much that is contrary to his nature.

Individual Scent as a Visiting Card

I must mention at the outset that in many of our present-day breeds all that I am about to say will only be seen in attenuated form; dogs even exist which have totally lost these instincts. The Council of a certain Swiss town seems to be fully alive to this fact since they have just issued a regulation under which only fully 'humanised' dogs (the term used in the newspaper announcement) may be kept—dogs which do not lift a leg or leave 'uncleannesses'

Schlapp, the alsatian dog, giving a demonstration of leg-lifting

behind them. The breeder's art can produce anything, even dogs which are no longer dogs. I would no doubt make myself popular with all animal lovers if I now launched into a tirade against such 'aberrations'. But I have become circumspect and I ask myself which dog is really worse off: the dog which is continually being shouted at because he wishes to obey his fully developed instincts —must do so in fact; or the dog which no longer possesses these instincts and therefore does not come into conflict with the requirements of human civilisation.

I do not propose to embark on a discussion of these alternatives; mere expression of opinion is not enough; the subject is too important for that. There is no point in my saying that personally I prefer a normal dog with normal instincts; that would not do justice to the matter. An answer might perhaps be found if experts on behaviour and veterinary surgeons with experience as 'canine psychiatrists' could combine not only for discussion but also in considered experiment. Unless such experiments prove the contrary, the possibility cannot be excluded that the dog out of which all instinct has been bred may really constitute the solution to the problem of the 'city-dwelling dog'.

To return to the subject of the dog with normal instincts and the trouble which he sometimes creates for us—we must try to understand the meaning and purpose of the 'urine and droppings ceremonial'.

The purpose of leg-lifting, as any dog-lover knows, is to inform other dogs that claim has been laid to a certain area of territory. Since this is equivalent to a public notice, some conspicuous territorial feature must be selected. Such features are the corner of a house, a tree in the avenue or the corner of a garden fence. An imprint must be left on these landmarks to ensure that no passing dog can overlook—or rather 'oversmell'—them. How could such landmarks be designated, however, if one merely squatted like a puppy or bitch? There is no alternative but to lift the leg in order to hit the right place.

We have bred both large and small dogs. According to ancient custom they all lift their legs. I do not think, however, that a large-size dog is greater in the eyes—or rather nose—of another dog because he can lift his leg higher. It sounds good and seems logical that the dog should seek to make an impression by the height at which he leaves his mark. But we should take a look back to the wolf pack. Erik Zimen, who is practically a pack-leader himself, told me that the more junior wolves do not lift their leg at all. This is the prerogative of the strong, of the Great White Chief. A wolf pack's territory, therefore, is marked by the leader in person. The leader in the neighbouring territory equally leaves his mark and he is undoubtedly as large and strong as his neighbour. If a pack-leader comes across a landmark which has been stamped by another leader, he will simply overprint it; in other words, in order

Individual Scent as a Visiting Card

to extinguish the scent-mark of the other dog, he places his own mark over it.

This, in fact, is the ultimate purpose of the whole affair. One has only to watch a dog who enters a territory previously occupied and marked by another dog. The new arrival takes possession, reconnoitring in detail to see where his predecessor has left his mark and staking his claim with his scent-mark precisely at these points. A small dog is not in the least impressed if his predecessor was a large one but he has difficulty in lifting his little leg high enough to hit the exact spot. I repeat, this is an age-old inherited habit from the time when large and small dogs did not exist. Size makes no difference to the method of marking; the object is solely to overprint the mark left by the preceding dog. For this reason the St Bernard only lifts his leg casually if the previous visiting card has been left by a dachshund. If the dachshund comes by next day, he observes that his scent-mark has been obliterated by that of another dog and so he renews it. If, a couple of hours later, the St Bernard comes by again, he too notices the same thing and aims at the precise spot, not five or six inches higher.

For the dog there exist only other dogs; he has no ideas about larger or smaller dogs and does not realise what changes man has introduced by breeding. The St Bernard is simply another male, just like the miniature dachshund. Anyone lifting a leg is a dog staking a claim to territory and leadership, no more and no less. Any dog which does not live in a pack where there is no question who is in command, will stake these claims for himself. In this respect, therefore, all our domestic dogs behave like pack-leaders, for all the dogs of the neighbourhood are pack leaders, each in his own right. In villages, however, where the dogs are running loose day and night, a seniority classification is to be seen; there the claim to leadership can be decided by battle and the dogs in fact form an exclusive pack.

In this respect there is a yawning gap in the man–dog relationship. We like very much playing the part of pack-leader with power of command; *vis-à-vis* our dog we claim the position of leader. When it comes to laying claim to territory, however, in our dog's eyes we are a lamentable failure; we are pack-leaders who leave no mark. We pass the landmarks by heedlessly; we do not even recognise them—is this the way for the strong pack-leader to behave? Our dog adjusts matters and feels it his duty, at least in this respect, to appear as pack-leader. How indulgent a dog has to be if he is to come to terms with these extraordinary two-legged creatures!

Our dog lifts his leg on our neighbour's freshly painted garden fence. Not wanting a scene, we drag him away at the last moment and forbid him to do what he feels to be his duty owing to our obvious failure. Naturally, as pack-leader, we have the right to forbid him to do this—but, for crying out loud, how is a proper pack to exist if no one does it? What on earth is the matter with a leader who insists on his claim to be the sole leg-lifter and then never leaves his mark? We should be kind to our dogs because there are many other such absurdities which we insist upon. I am continually astounded at their capacity for adaptation and at the equanimity with which they tolerate behaviour contrary to all good canine custom.

Dingoes have a somewhat limited repertoire of facial expressions but I am invariably fascinated when one of them shows what he thinks of me. Dingo dogs are very self-assured and do not relish being forbidden to do something, though generally one can gain one's point. They are not in fact averse to accepting man in the role of leader. If a dingo dog proposes to leave his mark on the table-leg in the best room and is called to order by me, he will generally let it ride. But he then turns round slowly and calmly, looks me straight in the eye and sums me up in a way which can only mean: 'The fellow is obviously crazy; there's something wrong with him.' Indeed—how can one forbid something which simply must be done because it cannot be done any other way? With our patient domestic dogs our failure in respect of the decent canine customs clearly constitutes no reason to become really savage; they have resigned themselves. In the case of dingo dogs, however, repeated and serious failures by Master in respect of things which the dog considers proper may lead one day to a breach, to a final and irreparable severance of all friendly relations.

The dog's leg-lifting ceremony, therefore, can frequently cause us distress; our dog is undoubtedly equally distressed with us because in his eyes we are often so unaccountably unreasonable. It is comic that almost every dog-owner hails the day when his

Individual Scent as a Visiting Card

little dog lifts his leg for the first time, for now the dog is grown up. Many dogs are slow in this; Master then pulls a long face and is tortured by fear lest something is wrong with his dog; finally he breathes a sigh of relief when, at the age of nine months, his late developer first gives a performance of a real leg-lifting ceremonial. At last—it's happened! A week later the dog will be scolded because he has lifted his leg on a spot which does not suit us. Such is the illogicality of mankind.

Some bitches also lift their leg; they are mostly the more elderly aunts with a marked sense of territorial possession and of their own seniority. This is, however, exceptional and possibly has something to do with hormones ('masculine women'). The bitch does, however, practise a urine ceremonial with an aimed jet but this is primarily used when she is in season. As far as the position adopted is concerned, this differs little from the normal position when urinating. The dog, of course, observes at once and superimposes his own claim to possession on the spot concerned. A bitch can nevertheless stake her claim to territory at the necessary height without lifting her leg. She draws one hind leg forward and raises her rear ends high in the air as if she were going to do a handstand at any moment. Dogs and bitches frequently leave their visiting cards on a certain spot in turn as an indication that they have been there; in this case the function of the leg-lifting ceremony differs from that conducted between male dogs. At the appropriate time, in other words when the bitch has come in season, it may lead to mating. The dog and bitch may never have met face to face but, by leaving their marks, they have long since made each other's acquaintance and then, at the right time, find the way to each other. The dog is kept continuously informed of the physiological condition of his 'pen friend' and knows exactly when the right time has come to elope at an unguarded moment. On her side the bitch knows that the dog knows because the fact that she is in season causes him to leave his card more frequently. If our dog continuously lifts his leg and refuses to answer a call, we know that there is, or was, a bitch in season in the vicinity. There is nothing to be done but put him on the lead or he will run away.

This liquid scent-mark, therefore, serves a number of purposes: delineation of territory, acquaintanceship, mating and, in the case of the pack-leader, demonstration of his social pre-eminence.

When used for the latter purpose, as the scent-mark is deposited it is accompanied by an ostentatious leg-lift and so becomes an optical signal. This is the dog's method of demonstrating his superiority. On one occasion when Sascha's father came to visit us, Sascha was standing on the lawn. Schlapp, the father, took a few steps towards his son—whom he barely recognised—then stopped in the open and demonstratively lifted a leg, although there was nothing there which could possibly need marking; he simply watered the lawn. Only then did he execute a dignified approach to the younger dog and make nasal contact.

Of course there is no problem about keeping a male dog in the house. He was house-trained long before he had any thought in his head of leaving his visiting card. This has been his home from his youth and so he has no reason to leave his mark. The situation will change in a flash, however, if some acquaintance has the idea of paying us a visit accompanied by his own dog. As a precaution we shut our dog up, since—who knows?—they might perhaps fight. Now the visiting dog comes into the house, naturally sniffs around and makes the discovery: a dog has been here. His next reaction is to lift his leg. The acquaintance is a genial fellow and expatiates about his dog, the dog meanwhile lifting his leg against every table—and chair-leg and the sideboard, to ensure that our own dog will discover his cards later. When the genial visitor and his dog have finally departed, under no circumstances let your own dog in; he will feel under an obligation to put matters in order and superimpose his own mark on every spot. There is nothing to be done but give every chosen place a thorough washing with strong-smelling soap or vinegar. Although the etiquette book does not say so, it should be a rule, if you own a male dog, never to take him to visit someone who also has one. The same applies to a bitch in season; for the same reason she is better left at home.

So much for the social function of the liquid waste products. We must also deal with the solids which equally serve as an indication of a dog's own scent and have an auxiliary function as a visiting card. But first I would like to revert to this problem of house-training.

I would remind the reader of Stina, my problem bitch. She could never be house-trained and she still is not today; she never will be. Her inveterate timidity prevents it. There is no means of

Individual Scent as a Visiting Card 223

explaining to this dog that one does not deposit a sausage in the middle of the room. I have reached the stage when I watch her resignedly—if I were to say a word she would rush back in terror into her hiding place. And after all the poor dog must do it some time!

I once thought I knew how to get the better of Stina. If one opens the door and calls her out into the garden, she comes out at once. She will not come in again, however, when I want her to but when she wants to. One trick could be played on her, however: she does want to come in if Sascha and Rana are called into the house; she is very fond of the two larger dogs and runs gaily in behind them. On the face of it, therefore, it should have been comparatively simple to await the moment when Stina showed a desire to do her duties and let her out at the right time. I have at least achieved one thing—she does not now wait to do her duties until she is back in the house, but, if the moment is right, will also do them outside. This might have been the solution, had Stina been the only dog in the house. Anyone, however, who keeps forty dogs and, moreover, in contrast to the normal dog-owner, is not so much interested in incorporating the dog into the human world but is insistent on studying canine behaviour based on the untrained dog, must put up with these things; he must somehow adapt his life to that of the canine world. Moreover, how can one find the time and energy to house-train a dog—and such a small one at that—when great pains must be taken and subterfuge used?

The example of Stina, however, is instructive because it illustrates almost all the circumstances which make house-training impossible. I need not re-emphasise our own inconsistency. The case also proves that inadequate contact between man and dog makes matters harder. Stina's behaviour in those first few weeks, however, when I was proposing to turn her into a lapdog, was something often seen in dogs. These are the dogs which, like Stina, suffer from mental strain, dogs confronted with a situation to which they are not equal. Such situations involving mental stress are frequently the reason for lack of cleanliness in the house. It is the dog's way of registering a sort of protest.

Such matters would be difficult to understand, did we not know that these waste products are closely associated with the dog's own scent and fulfil a purpose in the social field. The dog which does not leave his individual scent, his visiting card, all over the territory available to him but on the contrary deposits it only in his home, this dog is withdrawing into himself, is creeping away into his own little world, has become shy. The burden of his unsolved problems has made him insecure; he no longer dares to mix with other dogs even by leaving his mark. He is a clear case for the psychiatrist.

In 1957 A. Zweig described an instance, by no means isolated, of this nature. A couple had a five-months-old cross-bred dog which was perfectly house-trained and had been with them three months. One day a friend brought them a large and exceedingly handsome doll; it amused them and they played with it a lot. The dog became very jealous and even went so far as to gnaw off one of the doll's shoes. He was, of course, punished at once for damaging human property. The dog was most downcast; he no longer displayed jealousy, but quietly deposited his businesses in the house. This, of course, produced scoldings and smackings with the nose held down near the dirt (in my view a highly unsuitable procedure anyway). When this did no good, the couple, now at their wits' end, tried kindness. Having deposited his sausage, the dog waited for the usual punishment, but it was silently removed, the dog was given a biscuit and treated more affectionately than usual. The effect was immediate; from that moment the dog was once more clean in the house.

It would be wrong to think that this dog was trying to take reprisals or draw attention to himself. A dog does not protest in this way; such methods are not available to him as they are to a human being, because he cannot think out beforehand the possible effect of such a protest. As we know, the dog can be highly intelligent but not as intelligent as that. For this dog the diversion of his master's love to some other object was a blow of fate before which he collapsed. He had done all he could to demonstrate his love for his master; he disliked the doll because it had taken this love away; he became aggressive in order to show how matters stood. This was the limit of his capacity for expression. When he was now punished for trying to destroy or remove the object which had come between him and his friends, for him this was the end of everything; he could no longer cope with the situation. It had become impossible for him to make himself understood to the

Individual Scent as a Visiting Card

society in which he lived; so he withdrew into himself behind the 'invisible wall' separating him from that society. Only here could he develop his 'ego', in other words construct his own scent-world. He was precisely like those unhappy people who withdraw into themselves and talk only to themselves or figments of their imagination. A dog's own scent is part of his means of communicating, part of his 'language'. There is no analogy, therefore, between uncleanness in the house and the well-established Bavarian custom of smearing the door-knob of an unpopular neighbour with filth.

To summarise—cleanliness in the house depends primarily on the man's intelligence and consistency. Anyone who punishes a dog because, against its true nature, it becomes unclean in the house, merely shows that these qualities have, at least temporarily, deserted him.

There are two further reasons for a dog to be unclean in the house; one is fear, the other is joy. Great fear may even cause a dog to wet the seat of a chair. We have all known a dog pass water in fear of punishment or something else. Anxiety neuroses are by no means unknown in dogs, particularly in the cities where the whole environment differs so fundamentally from the primitive natural habitat of the dog. The noise of traffic, the overcrowding (both human and canine), the flood of external stimuli—all this is frequently too much for the dog to absorb if he has been brought up in the peace of some country kennel. It all assails him too suddenly and can damage him mentally. I have already referred to Ferdinand Brunner, the veterinary surgeon who deals with such problems daily in Vienna; the stories of his practice which he can tell are shattering. Poor tortured creatures are brought to him— dogs which tremble when taken out on to the street, dogs which are terrified of anybody and everybody and pass water out of sheer fear. I will not distress the reader by further description of the variety of these mental disturbances. One thing only would I emphasise because it stands out from Brunner's accounts like a case for the prosecution put forward with an air of resignation: always and in every case the fault is that of man and it cannot be remedied by tea or pills. The vet can help—a great deal in fact— but veterinary science can do nothing if man does not take advice and continues to treat the dog as a plaything, a luxury article, a status symbol, in short as a 'thing' which in the eyes of the law he unfortunately still is.

I trust that I have succeeded in showing how sensitive is the mind of the dog and how easily a great deal, if not everything, can be destroyed if one fails to remember at all times that the dog is a highly socialised creature. The smallest disturbance or obstacle placed in the way of his effort to satisfy his innate requirement for social contact can destroy him mentally. In many respects he is far more highly developed than man and more discriminating; but above all his brain is not sufficiently developed to enable him to look over or through situations of social conflict. He can be wrecked by them far more easily than can man.

In many cases unwise inbreeding leads to a weakening of the nervous system frequently combined with general constitutional deterioration; this means that many pedigree dogs are over-soft and over-sensitive both physically and mentally. These are the dogs which tend to pass water out of fear or joy. Emotional excitement—when Master returns, for instance—then gets the better of them and, particularly in young dogs, can lead to this unpleasing phenomenon. Patience and sympathy are the answer here, perhaps combined with sedatives. This emotional bed-wetting generally disappears as the dog becomes older and more self-assured. If it is thought, however, that he can be cured of this 'nasty habit' by punishment, then he will be ruined for ever.

Enough of these less pleasing aspects; basically they tell us nothing except that the dog is not being permitted to lead a life worthy of a dog. We now return to the healthy dog with normal instincts. For him the 'big job' is by no means a matter to be dealt with casually and unobtrusively; for purposes of contact and communication it is taken very seriously.

Sometimes choice of the precise spot seems to set our dog a serious problem with which he wrestles for some time before proceeding to action. One's patience may be severely tried. This should cause no surprise, however, for we already know that deposition of the faeces has an important auxiliary function.

An interesting question is the significance of the violent

scratching with the hind feet to be seen in some dogs, primarily males. The object is certainly not to bury or conceal the droppings, as is frequently said. This would be in complete contradiction to everything we know about the importance of the dog's own scent. Moreover some dog or other—or perhaps a wolf, jackal or other wild dog—would have been seen covering up his droppings completely and successfully. This, however, has never yet been seen and it would be in complete contrast to the behaviour, for instance, of the fox who deliberately deposits his droppings on some tree stump to ensure that they are recognisable from a distance. This scratching is undoubtedly an additional method of marking the spot; possibly the scent of the clods of earth strewn around the spot serves to produce a stronger and more varied field of scent. Strixi, the black mongrel already referred to, who is a particularly self-assured dog, takes a great deal of trouble over this; he has proved to me that experience as well as instinct may enter into this habit. He does not invariably scratch with the same violence; sometimes he merely goes through the motions, scratching casually two or three times; alternatively it may be a violent prolonged process, a great deal of earth being scattered about; there may even be a careful examination of the spot followed by a repeat performance. All this is preceded by a thorough inspection of the locality, and if for some reason not comprehensible to the human mind the place is of special importance, careful inspection is made between the bouts of scratching and at the end before the dog finally decides that he can depart in peace.

These ostentatious procedural differences in the ceremony of depositing droppings are clearly connected with the situation at the time; in any case they show that the implications of the action are far wider than the mere satisfaction of the internal urges. Scratching with the hind legs may take place when something quite different is in view, for instance at the sight of a strange dog against whom a grudge is borne. It is then an optical demonstration, definitely of a challenging nature and similar to the leg-lifting to which we have already referred.

A dog's individual scent, therefore, plays a major part in a system of communication not always easy for us to understand; the dog with normal instincts uses it with great deliberation. It forms a highly significant part of his existence.

THE TIME OF MATURITY

In process of time the majority of dog-owners grow together with their dog, if one may use the term; they accommodate themselves more or less to the dog's tendencies and peculiarities. The same thing happens in reverse direction. An extremely satisfying and harmonious relationship can develop, for the dog's capacity for adaptation is often astoundingly great. This raises the question once more whether suppression of the instincts may not in fact be a blessing for the dog. He will, however, easily be disconcerted if confronted by dogs differing from himself.

At this point I would like to tell a story which illustrates very well the difficult decisions with which one may be faced when dealing with such dogs; it is also interesting in that it concerns two litter brothers so different in character that they had difficulties with each other. These two dissimilar brothers also prove that one breed can hardly be characterised as possessing a greater or smaller degree of instinct than another; differences can occur even within a single litter.

The story begins with a telephone call. The problem concerned two Leonbergers from the same litter who had grown up from puppies in a house with an enormous garden; the older they became, however, the less they could agree and their quarrels were becoming increasingly serious. Since, given the circumstances, two dogs with normal instincts ought to be able to live happily together, I suspected major differences of character and suggested that the dogs be tested. These tests may be of interest to the reader since he could easily submit his own dog to them.

The most diverse kinds of men have often been brought together by their dogs and I owe it to these two dissimilar Leonbergers that I made the personal acquaintance of Carl Orff, the great composer. My study smells strongly of dog; I sat Orff and his wife down in a corner opposite the door and the first of their dogs was let in. He was called Asko and he did exactly what one would expect of any grown-up dog in strange surroundings: he inspected with his nose every inch of floor from the door to the corner from which we were watching him. Only after this meticulous inspection did he turn to his master and mistress. He was taken out and Arras, his brother, appeared. He looked neither to right nor left but ran straight to his

The Time of Maturity

owners, showed them how pleased he was to find them and then sniffed around the room a little but without particular interest in spite of the numerous scents.

This first test alone spoke volumes. Oversimplifying somewhat, Asko was interested in other dogs, Arras only in men. I now wanted to pursue the problem of the marked difference in instinct between these two dogs. Asko was confronted with a puppy. He was very interested in it but, when he saw that the puppy was frightened, he drew back and did all he could to show that he was trying to be friendly. He lay down, wagged his tail and invited the puppy to play; all this was done in a way which made clear that he had no wish to frighten the little creature; he was extremely circumspect in all his movements. When we now brought Arras and the puppy together, the result was precisely the opposite. The dog behaved in a most tactless way towards the little thing: he rushed upon it, tried to pick it up in his teeth and seemed unable to understand the little one's screams of terror. We had to take the puppy away quickly to prevent this unedifying game going too far.

So here was a second proof that, in contrast to his brother Arras, Asko was a dog with perfectly normal instincts. We then carried out a further test at the Orffs' garden fence. Again the two brothers were tested separately. My kennel-maid led the alsatian Sascha, who as we know is extremely friendly, along the outside of the fence. Arras launched himself against the fence barking furiously and obviously threatening Sascha. Asko, on the other hand, behaved like any normal dog; he walked slowly up to the fence, his bearing indicating neither aggressive intent nor friendliness—a neutral wait-and-see attitude. When he realised that Sascha too had nothing nasty in mind, he gradually began to wag his tail, became increasingly amicable and would obviously have been prepared to make friends with the strange dog outside the fence.

The final test involved the young bitch Rana who was just beginning to show the first signs of coming in season. She was also led along the garden fence. Arras hurled himself against the fence just as savagely and furiously as he had with Sascha; he was just aggressive and uncouth; Rana was frightened and strained away against the lead but even this made no impression on Arras. Asko, on the other hand, clearly welcomed his 'visitor across the fence': he crouched down inviting her to play and would undoubtedly have been a suitor for her favours—another indication that he possessed the full range of natural instincts. No wonder, therefore, that Asko and Arras could not agree together. They were at the time just eleven months old and felt themselves old enough to establish a claim to precedence. Asko was stronger than Arras and he thought it obvious that he should be leader. Arras, however, as his owners themselves admitted, was a 'cunning devil' who knew how to worm his way into the good books of human beings and, under their protection, refused to acknowledge his brother's prerogatives. Here was another illustration of the phenomenon described by Konrad Lorenz: an animal weak in instinct has a greater capacity for learning; he compensates in this way for his lack of instinct and so may become superior to others of his kind. This Asko was naturally unable to understand and so there were continual quarrels which, with such powerful dogs, were of frightening proportions. I was once present during a fight between Asko and Arras and my knees were knocking together; I was all the more admiring of Frau Orff who, with complete disregard of danger, managed to tear the two great dogs apart.

Now, however, came the great question: what to do? I was in no doubt about my advice: get rid of Arras, whose instincts were at fault, and buy a little bitch puppy as company for Asko. I described to the Orffs with all the emphasis I could muster the charm of seeing Sascha bringing up his little daughter Rana, the beautiful happy pictures which it had produced and the pure joy of such experiences with dogs. Of course it was all very well for me to talk; Asko and Arras had not grown up in my house. No doubt it would have been sensible to give Arras away but can one say goodbye to a dog whose development one has watched from puppyhood? The Orffs have not done it and continue to quake when the two dissimilar brothers growl at each other. Arras, the 'cunning devil', has wormed his way too deep into his master's soul. This should be an example to us all, even though we can put forward commonsense arguments against it. For the genuine dog-lover the decision to obtain a small dog is one which should never be revoked except for reasons of *force majeure*. It is no case of *force majeure*, however, if a dog develops differently from what one expected. Perhaps, when these two brothers came into the Orffs' house at the age of eight weeks, some expert on puppies might have detected the

The Time of Maturity

differences in character and been able to advise accordingly. This would be a good subject for behavioural research.

For many a dog the attraction exercised by the childhood image of the sweet little puppy has spelt unhappiness. Someone has acted on the spur of the moment and, when the dog is full-grown, it is realised that it fits neither into the family nor the accommodation available. But then it is too late. This must continually be re-emphasised, for the modern tendency to downgrade the dog to an article of 'consumer goods' is intolerable.

Membership of an association is not everyone's cup of tea but I do believe that the breeders' associations for the various species of dog are necessary and valuable organisations; even those who dislike 'this association business' should not shut their eyes to their importance. To some degree they are a social service since one of their duties is to ensure not only that dogs get into the right hands but also that they are properly treated. If a dog-owner has problems, they offer him an opportunity to discuss them and ask advice of experienced handlers and breeders, thus avoiding distress both for himself and the dog.

To me, however, a point of special importance is that, with the help of these associations and with their expert advice, a dog-owner can visualise doing his own breeding. In the first place this is a matter of great happiness to the dog; it is simply part of his make-up; in addition, however, for the owner it is the most wonderful experience which life with his dog can provide.

The fact is that the life of a dog is unhappily very short. He is granted twelve years, perhaps fourteen, certainly no more. This is the saddest aspect of the whole man–dog relationship problem. Unfortunately it often results in people failing to spare their dog the misery of prolonged old age and debility. Blind egoism leads to stubborn rejection of the vet's advice; the adoring gaze and some occasional activity on the weary animal's part are taken as proof that all is in fact still well with him. But it is no good. The provisions of nature do not allow for the continued existence of a dog not in full possession of all his faculties. Ageing wolves are mercilessly torn to pieces by their pack. Thus they are spared the fate of the semi-invalid, unable to 'make the grade'. Modern veterinary methods are now so perfect that the old dog will unsuspectingly doze away into the hereafter.

The faithful friend, however, should not continue to live in our memory alone; for us he can continue to live through his progeny. When I look at my Paroo, I see Abo, his father, standing in front of me and I am less conscious of the pain I felt when I lost him. I have therefore deliberately placed the vital chapter on mating and whelping at the end of this book in the hope of leaving the reader with both the interest and the courage to do some breeding himself. Before broaching this subject, however, I must mention one further step in the grown-up dog's development of which I am reminded by the fate of Abo, my first dingo dog.

During the first few days after his bitch has whelped the dog is allowed to do little more than keep guard over the lair. I have already described Abo's behaviour when Suki, his wife, had her first litter. He was full of curiosity but even so his reactions were those of the guard-dog when strangers pass by. To us Abo was extremely friendly, as he was when Suki had her second litter; he made no difficulty when one took puppies out of the nest to weigh them. When Suki whelped for the third time, however, then it happened.

It was a fine Sunday; I was showing my dogs to some friends and telling them that dingoes have a marked inhibition about biting men, that if a stranger touches them, they will snap but it is always a well-aimed snap close to the hand; it is a really menacing sound. I also told the story of a small boy who once put his finger through the fence; Abo snapped at it but he never closed his jaws and the boy was able to withdraw the finger without the teeth ever touching it.

I had just told this story when Eva, my assistant, called out that Suki had had her puppies. She went unconcernedly into the great pen; Abo welcomed her at the entrance, wagging his tail, and jumped up to her as usual trying to lick her face. She played with him for a moment or two and then moved towards the kennel at the rear of the pen. She had hardly taken five steps before Abo sprang at her throat with hackles up, growling furiously. She managed to catch him by the ears and hold him. But the pen was bolted on the inside. After a few seconds' hesitation—the whole thing was so incredible—I climbed into the pen and shot back the bolt; Eva dragged Abo to the gate but he had meanwhile succeeded in sinking his teeth deep into her forearm just above the wrist and,

The Time of Maturity

as she shook him off, his four long eye-teeth left wide gashes in her arm. Eva had to be taken to hospital at once and carries great scars to this day as a reminder of Abo; from that moment he was so savage to her that for reasons of safety the only solution was a sad one. With me Abo was as trustworthy as ever and with a friendly wag of the tail he allowed me to give him the injection which produced a long deep sleep from which he never awoke.

The question now was: why on this particular occasion, after the third litter, the dog should show such a savage determination to defend his young. It would seem that hitherto his adolescent attachment to us had taken priority over his defensive reactions. Meanwhile he had reached the age of three years. We had noticed for some time that he seemed more self-assured, less communicative and generally more grown up; so presumably his defensive reaction now burst through the old barrier. Since then, before looking at a litter, we invariably take the older dingo dogs out of the pen on a lead (at which they are overjoyed!). Outside and on a lead even an old dingo is still a friendly animal—he has no reason to sever his old friendship. A false step on man's part, however, may evoke aggressive tendencies and not only in dingoes; even the best dogs can become savage.

The fact is that with the start of his third year the final change in the dog's personality takes place. He is now mature; his development is finished; to use our previous simile of the craftsman and apprentice, he is now a 'Master'.

This can best be explained by considering once more the development of the wolf. As we have seen, wolves do not start a family of their own until they are twenty-two months old; the pair are about two years old when they have their first cubs. They rear these cubs and, by all accounts, only exceptionally join up again with their parents in the autumn. In most cases the pair with their cubs form their own pack. By the time the cubs have reached the pack-formation phase the parents are two and a half years old; they must now play the part of the strong leader to their cubs; they must be superior to them in every way and be their model; in short they must be 'Masters'.

The fact that the personality has matured is not easily recognisable in all our dogs. The decisive factor is the strength of the inherited qualities or alternatively their disappearance or attenuation through changes due to domestication. Knowledge that our dog matures during his third year may be of importance for our relationship with him; we must play the parental role with somewhat more circumspection. How often have we heard youngsters protest that their parents refuse to realise that their children have gradually turned into grown-ups. There are certain parallels here and they are particularly obvious in the case of dogs which have no solid foundation of confidence with their master. If man merely acts the tyrant and does not appear as the model, socially superior, pack-leader, there is grave danger that one day the dog will rebel against continuous coercion. I once saw an outraged alsatian revolt and I came away with a lasting impression of such an animal's pugnacity. I dislike intensely the fact that dogs are sometimes trained to be 'savage watchdogs' which will bite on sight but in this case I could not help admiring an animal which could see no solution other than to defend his rights with his teeth.

In this book I have been at pains to emphasise that, although in theory a 'predatory animal', the dog's mental make-up is pacific and that his tendency is to form cohesive groups; I have attempted to show that in a canine society aggression plays only a minor part in the maintenance of order. Dogs with a normal adolescence behind them use all means in their power to form bonds of friendship and avoid fighting; they play at fighting with simulated violence and ferocity, thus downgrading its importance—I could write pages on the subject.

All these things are clear indications and they emphasise the fact that there must be very serious reasons before a normal dog is driven to real aggressive action. I am also sure that in the majority of cases, when a dog attacks other dogs or human beings, the cause is not the immediate visible occasion; the real explanation is that his development in his young days ran contrary to nature. As a result the 'threshold of stimulus' for aggression becomes so low that comparatively trivial incidents may spark it off.

What is to be seen in the dog during his third year, therefore, is the development of a sense of duty and property at the expense of that which has been inculcated into him during his youth. Admittedly hereditary changes also take place in the fields of social behaviour and tendency to aggression. Dogs have often enough been bred to be savage; any dog-lover shudders at the thought that civilised men in Europe once enjoyed the entertainment of watching dogs tear each other to pieces. Nowadays particularly aggressive dogs are not used for breeding so the risk of an inherited increase in aggressive tendencies is very small. I still think, however, that far too little is being done towards a detailed examination of the hereditary element of social behaviour. If the instinctive element in social behaviour is reduced, the dog will by no means be turned into a 'criminal' provided he has a sensible upbringing; it does mean, however, that the 'threshold of stimulus' for aggression will undoubtedly be lowered to a greater or lesser degree.

The conclusion which the dog-lover should draw from this is that the procurement, maintenance and breeding of dogs all entail great responsibility.

Anyone proposing to obtain a dog will do well to consider the matter at length; he should reflect on the suitability both of the dogs on his short list and—of himself. Bringing up a little dog and incorporating it into the family is a delightful game, but it is a game which will only have a happy ending if played with the necessary discernment, the necessary seriousness, much patience and even more sense of responsibility.

What this means is that for ten to fifteen years we are going to keep a creature which can only live a full life and so fulfil the purpose of keeping a dog at all if it is allowed to become a genuine member of the family—with all the obligations, but also with all the prerogatives that that implies. Anyone who regards a dog merely as a piece of property, with which he can do as he likes, should not keep a dog.

The final point—breeding—I can only recommend. I would say: anyone willing to take the responsibility, anyone who likes responsibility for living creatures, should undoubtedly breed. If his situation is such that he does not have to wonder whether he can earn good money by breeding, then indeed he should do it. He should also breed if, from a sense of responsibility, he can impose on himself a self-denying ordinance and allow only the best to survive. Finally I would say that if anyone is ready to learn the hard way and really find out what is best, it is in fact his duty to breed and so make his contribution to the continuance of the canine race.

Puberty and Maturity

The reader will, I hope, agree with me when I say that breeding should be in the hands only of responsible people and that everything must be done to prevent its becoming an arena for the smart operator or speculator, 'manufacturing' dogs in vast kennels like mass-produced articles. I am no prophet of gloom but we are already approaching that stage in Europe.

MATING AND PREGNANCY

We have already referred to the fact that a bitch normally has two annual periods during which she is ready for reproduction. I do not propose to go further into the physiological aspects of this six-monthly cycle leading to the production of fertilisable eggs. We are more interested in the visible indications of the oestrum and in particular those which have a bearing on behaviour.

Some time before the onset of the actual oestrum or 'season' anyone who watches his bitch closely will notice a marked increase in activity, a certain restlessness which tends to find its outlet in play. There can also be a degree of irritability and this may increase noticeably during the week preceding the actual 'heat'. Far more often, however, the main indication is playfulness and, if there are two bitches in the house, the games may be really grotesque. Quite often two bitches living together will come in season at the same time; probably this is the result of a form of sensation transference in which one bitch's glandular secretions activates the other's.

Immediately preceding the period of season there is a considerable increase in production of that scent, to the long-range effects of which I have already referred. Our daily walk is now productive of certain difficulties since we shall be persistently followed by all the loose dogs of the neighbourhood. The bitch will like this, but she will show them her teeth if they become too importunate. She will in turn entice and then repel the dogs, a procedure which students of behaviour, who are generally averse to transposing these matters into human terms, aptly call coquetry. Naturally this merely stimulates the dogs to further efforts, which is of course the object of the whole thing.

An interesting fact, indicative of the height at which the dog stands in the social scale, is that, contrary to popular ideas, the

Mating and Pregnancy

love-lorn dogs do not fight over the bitch. They entreat her in concert but in peace and leave it to her to decide on whom she will bestow her favours. I have frequently seen love-lorn dogs, unable to control their emotions, trying to mount each other.

During this period a dog and bitch living together will show those signs of affection, details of which we already know. Just like two lovers they become quite childish and moon about; there will be much nose-nudging and sniffing with, of course, frequent genital inspections.

After the preliminary week the real heat begins with the onset of bleeding. A bitch with normal instincts will herself observe the bright red drops and remove them with her tongue. In most of our bitches, unfortunately, this instinct has largely been lost and this leads to problems in the house. Occasionally a bitch will mate during this bleeding period but generally no fertilisation results. In most cases, however, the bitch will resist the dog's attempts to mount her and evade him by simply sitting down or standing with her rear ends against a wall.

The owner of a bitch will by this time long since have realised what is liable to happen next. The first question is: is the bitch suited to reproduce at all? In the case of a pedigree bitch the owner's decision is made for him by the regulations. If the answer is 'No', then he faces a number of difficult days, for a love-lorn bitch in the house is a misery to everyone involved. In addition one must be permanently on guard to prevent the beloved creature escaping. That leads to terrible complications!

I have already pointed out that dogs have no innate concept of the size of another dog. If our mastiff bitch falls in love with a small terrier, no harm is done unless the bitch is an experienced hussy and makes things easy for her little suitor by lying on the ground. But if a dachshund bitch happens to meet an alsatian, this is a crisis. Contrary to what many people think, it is no great catastrophe if a bitch is covered by a dog of another breed. The idea that she is then ruined for life is an old tale which one would think had long since died out, were not this one of the questions most frequently asked. If, however, the bitch is covered by a dog of a considerably larger breed, that is a different matter; it may lead to very serious complications during whelping which may render the bitch incapable of reproducing ever again. In such cases go to a reliable vet and as quickly as possible. There are ways and means of preventing the fertilised egg-cells developing.

If the bitch is covered by a dog of about her own size or smaller, however, I would not be agitated. I would allow the bitch to complete her pregnancy and take the puppies away from her as soon as they are born.

This is by no means as cruel as it sounds. Nature has made provision for such cases. The happy, free and glorious life in the wild exists only in our romantic imagination; in practice difficult living conditions may often lead to the death of the puppies. In the case of one of my bitches, Stasi, her milk production stopped because her puppies were unable to produce enough 'sucking pressure'. Similarly, therefore, if the puppies hardly even reach the teats, milk production and with it the nursing instinct will cease. For the bitch in this case delivery is merely the conclusion of her pregnancy; she will resume her normal life and six months later come in season again as if nothing had happened.

If new-born puppies are put to sleep by a vet, they will hardly know anything about it. Under no circumstances should one try to drown them or use some similar method to be rid of them. Nature has given them considerable tenacity and an astonishing power of resistance to outside influences. They are geared to exist for several hours without nourishment and we can profit from this fact if we do not wish to bother the vet in the middle of the night. All that is necessary is to lay the puppies on something soft in a shoe-box and place the box somewhere warm but sufficiently far from the bitch to ensure that she knows nothing about it; the puppies will sleep peacefully until the morning without suffering from hunger or any other pangs. Anyone who doubts this should think of new-born babies in a clinic; they are taken away from their mother and usually left without food for twenty hours.

Turning now to the case when the bitch is suitable for breeding —many people have doubts because they think that they have not the facilities to rear puppies. Usually they imagine that it is far more complicated than it is. These doubts are easy to dispel and I shall do my best. A word of warning at the outset, however: it is essential that some destination for the puppies is assured. Otherwise one day you will be in my position—I bear no one such a grudge that I would foist one of my wild beasts upon him!

Mating and Pregnancy

One must start from the assumption that any sensible dog-owner has adequate space for his dog. People who keep a St Bernard in a bed-sitter are not included; I am thinking more of a griffon, a miniature poodle, a maltese or some other miniature breed. Where, however, there is room enough for the bitch, there is room enough for her puppies, even if she is allowed to keep six. Until their eighth or ninth week this will be quite enough. As we have already seen, until that time the space requirements of the puppies are no greater than those of their mother. For those who are afraid of the actual process of delivery what I am about to say will be helpful. I would only say this as a prelude: the man who should really be afraid is the one owning an unwisely inbred bitch who will undoubtedly have difficulties; if he is a responsible person and dog-lover, he will not breed anyway.

Provided all these conditions are fulfilled, I can, with a clear conscience, promise the owner many hours of pure pleasure; the actual process of whelping and the subsequent mother-and-child relationship are among the most wonderful experiences which the dog-owner can have—and his life with his dog is rich in experience anyway. This presupposes, however, that the bitch has been brought together at the right time with the dog selected. The right moment is easy to determine; it is between the ninth and thirteenth day after the start of the blood-discharge which normally lasts a week. During this second week of her season the majority of the bitch's ova are ripe and therefore capable of fertilisation. Usually one mating is enough to ensure that an adequate number of ova are fertilised.

The ova do not all ripen at the same time; if the right moment has been chosen, even with only one act of mating ova ripening two or three days later will still be fertilised, since the sperm cells remain active for that length of time. If a bitch has been covered and then, two days later, is covered by another dog without the owner's knowledge, he may have a rude shock: in addition to his pedigree puppies the litter-box will contain obvious half-breeds. This has happened to many people who thought that nothing more could occur once their bitch had been covered. Admittedly after a successful mating the signs of oestrum usually disappear quickly but this does not exclude the possibility that some additional ova may have been fertilised by a second dog if some of them were not ripe when the bitch was first covered. Even when her season is on the wane many a bitch is not averse to taking another dog; my elkhound bitch Binna, for instance, contrived to seduce Strixi, my mongrel, on the eighteenth day after the start of her blood-discharge, in other words when there was hardly anything to indicate that she had been in season and I thought that I need no longer keep watch. Admittedly she did not produce any mongrel puppies but this shows that such a possibility cannot be excluded. Anyone who does not want his bitch to be covered would do well to be on his guard for the whole four weeks: one preliminary week, one week of blood-discharge, one mating week and one cooling-off week. It is better to be sure and with many bitches the onset of the blood-discharge is not immediately recognisable.

When one takes a bitch to a dog, hope need not be abandoned if she shows him her teeth when they first meet. Having sung the praises of the mental capabilities of the canine race, we can hardly expect her necessarily to accept our choice without question. As I have already said, under natural conditions it is the bitch who selects her suitor. Our bitch, however, knows nothing about pedigrees or champions; she merely possesses a sound sense for the qualities of a proper dog with whom she can fall in love. She may not, therefore, necessarily agree with our ideas on breeding and in extreme cases it may be that she will stubbornly refuse to accept the dog of our choice.

Generally no more than a little patience is necessary; the bitch must be allowed time to make friends with the dog. If he is a proper fellow, he will press his suit so adroitly that she will be captivated by so much charm and eventually give her consent. If, however, the dog does not understand the courting ceremonial, then he should be rejected, however good his pedigree. If the proper instinct is lacking in so far as reproduction is concerned, serious thought should be given to the possible consequences if a quick decision is not made. Attenuation of instinct in this field may lead to sterility in the next generation and it may eventually be necessary to have bitches artificially inseminated by a vet. Many people possibly do not object to this; the really bad side of this, however, is the fact that many bitches already exist unable to give birth because the breeders have followed this principle; they have to be delivered by caesarian. For this there can be no forgiveness. Such unnatural methods of breeding are tantamount to cruelty to animals.

It is sad that our dogs' love life has become so exiguous. Knowing how high in the social scale the dog stands, it will be realised that in this case the reproductive process cannot consist simply of the sex act alone. If dogs are allowed to live naturally, in other words in pairs, what can be seen in the pens is in no way inferior to the human conception of love. The difference lies in the symbolism of our speech which is a far more delicately shaded method of expression than anything available to the dog. The background to these methods of expression, however, the 'unspoken' feelings, I believe to be no less delicate than our own.

We should not be led astray if, about the eleventh day of our bitch's season, we see her simply position herself and allow the dog to mount her. The first reason for such expressionless conduct is attenuation of instinct; another reason, however, may be that, if the bitch has been kept in isolation for some time beforehand, she is simply no longer in control of her emotions. This, of course, makes matters easy for us and, with the incomprehension of which we are sometimes capable, we are very pleased with so 'good' a bitch. Many people also think that the dog who mounts the bitch without more ado is a 'good stud dog'. They understand no more about dogs than they can read in the pedigree. In fact this merely means that there is no opportunity to judge whether reduction of the initial reproductive instincts should be considered as an alarm signal indicating future biological weaknesses such as difficulty in conception, pregnancy or delivery, absence of maternal instinct and so forth. As a result the products of our breeding inevitably show signs of such degeneracy.

Naturally, in the case of a pedigree strain, much thought must be given to the choice of stud dog; it may be that he lives in some place over one hundred miles away. The owner can hardly be expected to take one or two weeks' holiday in order to allow the animals to play with each other for several hours a day. These are problems to which there is frequently no solution. There is nothing to do but go over there for a couple of days with the bitch and complete the business as quickly as possible. For this reason every opportunity should be taken to test the dog or bitch beforehand. If the test is negative, if it shows that the normal reproductive habits of conduct are seriously deranged, the owner should have sufficient sense of responsibility to refuse to use the animal for breeding and so avoid perpetuating these deficiencies.

I should add that negative indications in the reproductive field should not be regarded in isolation. An organism does not consist of separate individual parts; any derangement in one sphere influences the entire system. Reproduction is a primary functional sphere with its roots deep in the organism as a whole and closely associated with all other functional spheres. An old Chinese proverb says: if a leaf moves in the wind, the whole tree shivers.

Behaviour when a bitch is in season is similar to that already studied under the heading of games preliminary to mating. The dog now hardly leaves the bitch's side; the pair barely give themselves time to eat; they play, they wrestle, they sniff each other over. Finally the bitch gives it to be understood that she is ready. She no longer jumps away; she no longer defends herself during a fighting game; she stands still with her tail askew. Now the dog can mount her and insert his penis into the bitch's vulva; the bitch standing stiff and motionless, he clasps her round the flanks with his forelegs and bores his muzzle into her coat at the shoulder or presses his head against her shoulder or the base of her neck, corners of the mouth drawn back and eyes glazed.

This position is not maintained for long, generally no more than one minute. Then the dog lowers himself and the bitch turns towards him but the two animals remain united. There follows the phenomenon of 'tying' which is so often misunderstood and which lasts between ten and twenty minutes. This is to be seen in all canine-type animals and it results from certain anatomical and physiological peculiarities in the male organ of copulation. It contains a tumescent body which ensures that the animals remain united during the act and which only reduces in size very gradually. Dousing dogs that are 'tied' with cold water or other similar stupidities are unpardonable cruelties.

As soon as 'tying' is over, the dogs clean themselves. Usually the bitch shows great signs of pleasure combined with insistent invitations to play, jumping about with extraordinary contortions; the dog, on the other hand, shows little inclination to match his partner's exuberance.

Occasionally a dog may be seen mounting a bitch when she is

not in season; there is no erection or union, however. This will almost certainly happen when a dog and bitch are brought together and given an opportunity to make friends. This 'symbolic' mounting is a demonstration of the right of possession. A dog will also demonstrate his 'conjugal rights' in this way if faced with another dog. A dog will often mount another dog; this should be regarded as a demonstration of seniority.

With our dogs, as with wolves and jackals, pregnancy generally lasts 63 days with variations ranging from 59 to 65 days. With my dingoes the time has never been other than 59 or 60 days. Many of our domestic dogs also do not go longer than this.

During the first month of pregnancy nothing particular occurs. Towards the end of this period the bitch gradually begins to take precedence over the dog and in the second half of her pregnancy this becomes most obvious. The bitch is now wearing the trousers; the dog allows her to do anything she likes and respects her in every way. The bitch wears an expression of self-assurance and self-assertion.

The bitch's superiority is particularly obvious at feeding time. Hitherto the dog has insisted on his right to feed first and the bitch has had to make do with his leavings; now the positions are reversed. This is essential too since, from the fifth week onwards, the embryos are growing quickly and accordingly the mother's requirement for nourishment rises. There is a widespread misconception that our domesticated dogs have turned into feeders on vegetables and carbohydrates. At least during pregnancy a dog-owner must be sensible and use carbohydrates only in small quantities as makeweights; otherwise the bitch should be fed meat, as is natural to a dog. The meat or offal should be raw, not cooked; it will not 'make the dog savage', as people tend to say. The dog will not become savage but merely healthy if fed in this way. Only if a dog is fed on meat will it become active and really develop all its capabilities and powers. Dogs fed primarily on a diet lacking in protein become stupid, indifferent and sluggish; their whole attitude is one of debility. Only a dog which is properly fed will develop his innate habits of behaviour; for this reason I propose to discuss feeding at this point.

Naturally the smaller or miniature breeds of dog with snub noses and therefore badly placed teeth cannot tear great lumps of meat to pieces like a wolf. In their case meat should be tender or alternatively minced. The pregnant bitch must not become fat (as she will do if fed carbohydrates) since this not only affects the development of the puppies but also may lead to difficulties in delivery. The puppies now growing in the bitch's womb must form gristle and bone, muscles, nerves and all the other organs; none of these can be made from porridge; they need vitamins and protein; the menu must be arranged accordingly. Raw eggs are a useful addition; any gaps can be made good with cod-liver oil and vitamin pills. The bitch should now feed as frequently as she likes; if she feeds only once a day she will overfill her stomach. During the final three weeks she must have at least three meals a day.

During the second half of her pregnancy the bitch's requirement for rest increases. The daily walk need not be given up altogether but it can be left to the bitch to say when she wants to go home; she knows best how much exercise she needs. Her stomach now gradually begins to swell, but we should not be continually prodding it to see whether we can feel the puppies; it is easy to damage one of them and the results may be serious. If we are really uncertain whether the bitch is pregnant or not or for some other reason we wish to confirm the fact, the best solution is to visit the vet. Another indication of pregnancy is the fact that from the fifth or sixth week the teats grow larger and harder. The milk itself, however, does not appear until a few days before whelping.

During the final weeks the bitch may be nervous and irritable and this should be patiently accepted; usually this only happens during the first pregnancy; on subsequent occasions the bitch 'knows' what is happening and is more relaxed. There will be a colourless scentless discharge but when this takes on a greenish tinge, then there are generally only a few hours to go. Those who take the temperature regularly will now observe that it has fallen by one or two degrees. During the last twenty-four hours the bitch will usually be disinclined to eat—another indication that the great moment is approaching.

PUPPIES ARE BORN

I now propose to describe the process of a normal delivery. My account will be based on my dingo bitches since in their case I have been able on several occasions to watch and photograph every detail. All these deliveries followed precisely the same pattern and I could use my notes on any one of them as typical of them all. In such importance matters nature has so arranged that everything passes off in the most painless and the best possible manner. Only the wild animal can provide the criterion of normality; nature cannot afford anomalies. Under man's loving care these anomalies

A spasm of scratching before childbirth

may be acceptable in some degree, but if they are such as to give the bitch a difficult time in delivering her puppies, then we are quite simply being cruel to animals.

Some hours before her time a dingo bitch will become extremely occupied with her whelping box; she sniffs it all round, scratches at it and, if necessary, scrapes out any remnants of straw or other material. The floor of the box must be smooth and clean. Now begins the 'opening-up phase' lasting a maximum of one hour, during which the puerperal passages are made ready in a series of spasms. This is the only period during which a dingo bitch shows that she is in pain. She humps her back and draws herself together; her muscles contract and her face is set. Each spasm lasts barely a minute and there will be two or three at a time. Between spasms the bitch will lick her vulva carefully, clean all those parts of herself and in between whiles rest a little. She does not remain still for long, however, but jumps up again and busies herself once more with her nest. Apparently purposeless convulsive scratching against the smooth wood of the whelping box is another clear illustration of the hereditary reflexes; each bout of scratching is followed by a careful sniff round, as if the bitch were on the bare earth. That this instinct to scratch is involuntary is shown by the animal's tense attitude, set face—the corners of the mouth are drawn right back and the bitch's mind is clearly elsewhere—and by the fact that she does not react to the voice at all.

Between the labour pains and bouts of scratching all my dingo bitches have been extremely affectionate; they are clearly pleased that a human being is present and lay their heads on one's knee when a spasm of labour pain begins.

Once this phase is over the bitch curls up in her box and rests for about a quarter of an hour, sleeping lightly. Every now and again she wakes, raises a hind leg and inspects her passages. Now one must keep close watch if one wishes to see something of the extrusion phase. Sometimes the hind leg will remain raised and, instead of inspecting herself, the bitch will be found to be licking the amniotic membrane of an emerging puppy. Usually the bitch has completely consumed the membrane by the time the puppy is on the floor near her—a dingo bitch is so quick and self-assured even with the first puppy of her first litter. I have only succeeded in taking one flashlight photograph of the first extrusion; it takes seven seconds to reload and by that time the bitch has already consumed the afterbirth and severed the puppy's umbilical cord $1-1\frac{1}{2}$ inches from the stomach. By the time I am ready to flash again the bitch is already licking the soaking wet puppy and he is opening his little mouth, stretching out his tongue and taking his first deep breaths.

The bitch now has ten to twenty minutes during which she can busy herself with her puppy and take a little rest. The puppy struggles round to her belly and clamps himself to a teat. Then

Puppies are Born

comes another spasm of contraction followed by a second and in rare cases by a third; the next extrusion takes place. The entire process of delivery of five or six puppies takes no more than two hours.

Such is the course of what I might call the ideal delivery. I have read of bitches which complete the process more quickly but there is something here which I do not altogether like: the bitch has too little time to rest, to deal with each puppy as it arrives and meanwhile to recover somewhat. At least five minutes is required to lick

Binna is always busy with her puppies. Her body, forelegs and hind legs form a rectangle enclosing the puppies

a puppy dry; it takes some time to lick up the discharge of blood and also to clean the passages. Such rapid delivery, therefore, hardly seems to me desirable.

On each occasion Binna, my elkhound bitch, has taken four hours from the emergence of the first puppy to that of the seventh, in other words twice as long as in the case of a dingo bitch. Binna does not release the puppy from its membrane until it has emerged completely and is lying beside her. One can follow her action in detail as she gnaws at the umbilical cord and takes out the afterbirth; I have been able to take two photographs before the puppy is licked dry and so to record two phases of the process. Compared to a wild dog, therefore, everything goes more slowly. Binna is admittedly a domestic dog but only to a certain and somewhat insignificant degree. During the preliminary phase of labour, moreover, Binna shows no great signs of pain; in fact my impression is that at this stage she is more relaxed than a dingo bitch.

Eugen Seiferle, one of the most experienced veterinary experts, says: 'In the case of large litters the process of delivery generally takes eight to twelve hours in all'; he adds: 'the entire process should be completed within a maximum of twenty-four hours.' So this is the stage already reached by our dogs. So slow a process is, in my view, a clear indication of a considerable reduction in vitality in our domestic dogs.

Seiferle, however, refers to 'large litters'. A simple calculation is enough: if my dingo bitches can produce six puppies in two hours, they would produce twelve puppies in four hours; adding another hour for abnormalities, this still only gives five hours, certainly not eight to twelve.

This brings us to the question of the number of puppies. In all types of wild dog more or less closely related to our domestic dogs, four to six is the normal size of litter. With us, however, it is quite a sensation if a bitch has twelve puppies; we are very proud and think that we have a particularly good bitch. Man's passion for records stops at nothing, not even violation of the laws of nature. What is the good of such record litters anyway? A bitch has ten teats, of which the first pair are usually small, the large litters of the early days having disappeared in canine-type animals. Eight fully operative teats are adequate for a normal number of puppies but obviously not for more than eight. Any responsible breeder with a bitch who produces more than eight puppies will not use her or her offspring for further breeding. We have no need of mass propagation; we require the normal healthy increase. Equally a bitch should not be used for further breeding if, in her second litter, she produces only one, two or three puppies; there is something wrong with her too.

This statement is no figment of my imagination. I have deliberately carried out experiments, the outcome of which was bound to be bad, because I wanted to know how such biological defects arise so that they could be avoided in the future. By extreme inbreeding therefore, I have 'succeeded' in producing a dingo strain in which the bitches never have more than two puppies. This is not the end of the story, however: during the initial phase of labour these bitches writhe in pain and they often take over two hours to produce their two puppies. In one of them instinct is so defective that sometimes, when severing the umbilical cord, she gnaws away part of the puppy's stomach—another illustration of the interconnection of all these matters. This 'success' has been quite enough for me and I have stopped this experiment. I would add this, however: these bitches are particularly affectionate and, were a 'standard' laid down for dingoes, they would undoubtedly earn good, if not very good, marks. Their praises would be sung and they would be allowed to perpetuate their defective strain—their papers would carry no word about what goes on in the semi-darkness of the whelping box or their shrieks of pain during labour.

Enough of this subject; we can now turn to certain other matters connected with whelping and the first is the whelping box. This should be prepared at least ten days beforehand so that the bitch is accustomed to it.

The bitch is very insistent that the box be kept scrupulously clean. Her main concern is that it should be completely dry, for nothing is worse for puppies than damp. One of my bitches once took it into her head that she would not have her puppies or rear them in the kennel provided; she clearly thought it more proper to revert to the customs of her ancestors and so she dug a hole underneath the kennel. This was in the middle of winter with twenty degrees of frost at night! I was not entirely happy about this; admittedly I like to sermonise about rearing under natural conditions, the stern law of selectivity and preservation of the natural instincts; but when it is so cold that there are icicles in my beard, I tend to throw all my sound principles overboard.

I decided that I would fill in the nest prepared by my bitch and force her to accept the kennel. While standing in the pen, however, and ruminating how I was to arrange this, I became so cold that the thought of spending an hour in the snow wrestling with frozen ground, ice-covered boards and other joys of winter assumed horrifying proportions. I decided to stick to my principles and allow matters to run their course. I hurried back to my warm room.

So the bitch was allowed to have her way, bring her puppies into the world and rear them in this hole. To start with the end of the story: everything went perfectly splendidly. For two whole days the bitch lay with her puppies like a hen sitting on her chicks. The little things could be heard squeaking, but neither more loudly nor softly than in the most comfortable whelping box conceivable. On the third day I took up a board of the kennel floor since this was my only access to the nest and I wanted to see what the bitch had produced for us. There were six puppies and they could not have been in better shape. Thereafter they were weighed regularly and seemed to prefer their ice-cold hole to the warm weighing-room.

The mother had 'thought out' everything for the best. The hole in the frozen ground was obviously colder than the whelping box prepared for her in the kennel; the puppies' coats were full of sand; but the hole was dry, beautifully dry, and in addition the following overriding reason probably governed the bitch's choice of location: the kennel was simply too large for her; she wanted a small, well-covered hide-out, neither too large nor too small but precisely the right size for her and her puppies. There she felt secure and well hidden; she and her puppies could huddle against each other all round and the puppies could be kept close together.

Bitches have their own ideas on choice of a nest. On one occasion I brought a dingo bitch in to whelp in an unheated room where the ground temperature was minus one or two degrees. A stout whelping box of the right size was available which had stood the test several times before. Beside it was a shallow wooden box of sawdust. A dingo knows at once what that is for. My bitch, however, scraped out the sawdust industriously and only used it for the purpose intended when she had removed it from the box. The box she considered to be exactly right for sleeping and having babies and she was not to be dissuaded when I put everything to rights and placed her back in the whelping box. She went to work again at once and cleared the sawdust box again. I now wanted to find out what the idea was and so I took the box away. She simply curled up in the corner where it had stood, ignoring all my remonstrances and signals indicating the suitability of the whelping box with the obstinacy of which only a dingo is capable.

I gave way. The bitch got her box back and there she had her

Binna dragging a puppy into the whelping box. She seizes it by the first part of the body within reach

puppies and was content. I made one further attempt to gain my point: after weighing the puppies I placed them back in the fine whelping box. The bitch, now accustomed to all this fuss, patiently and resignedly took the puppies one after another back to her own box. Then she lay down and shut her eyes. She wanted to be left in peace at last and stop this interminable argument with me about her choice of place.

Anyone dealing with a nursing bitch has undoubtedly had similar experiences. However well intentioned one may be, the bitch will insist on what she thinks right and sensible. One can place the puppies one hundred times over in the box prepared for them but every time she will carry them back to the place which she thinks right.

We should not be fussier than the bitch who will be guided by her instinct. Our super-hygienic and in many respects exaggerated paediatrics have given us so many over-sophisticated ideas that we always think we know better than the bitch. But she knows what puppies need and she is not too finicky about it. Her innate knowledge of puppies' requirements has been so arranged by nature that it produces neither too much nor too little mother-care. In addition to this inherited knowledge experience plays a part. The canine brain does not merely react to spontaneous occurrences or instinct; it can also process additional knowledge acquired by experience of the squeaking wriggling mass in the whelping box. With their first litter almost all bitches are agitated, anxious and frequently almost over-zealous. With subsequent litters they seem more relaxed; they radiate self-confidence and they do their job with practised ability. This in itself shows that the canine brain can do somewhat more than react to unconscious instinct. The bitch at least learns one thing: for her this unique occurrence is no reason for agitation; everything seems to happen automatically; tensions disappear and the final sensation is one of well-being.

Action of the hormones before, during and after whelping releases a whole range of instincts essential to the rearing of puppies. As we have already seen, these instincts are aroused by stimuli to the central nervous system and they clamour for release. A bitch whelping for the first time knows nothing of this; she does not know that these puppies form the channel into which these pent-up urges are diverted and so relieved. Satisfaction of an urge, however, is linked with a sense of pleasure. The experienced bitch knows the sense of pleasure produced by fulfilment of her maternal duties.

As applied to the nursing bitch, the words 'mother love' have a special significance; they should lead us, not simply to stand gazing sentimentally into the whelping box but to understand how wonderfully the behaviour and attitudes of mother and puppy complement each other. The harmony between two behavioural complexes so closely geared to each other is a sufficiently marvellous sight anyway, but we should look for the miracles where they really exist. For me the great miracle is this 'biological entity', each part perfectly adapted to the others in every detail—the practical shape of the nest, the innate knowledge of nursing, the puppy's habits; as research reveals all this to its more profound depths, one can only stand in greater awe.

The sight of a bitch with her puppies is so appealing that even non-animal-lovers feel their hearts touched. For the bitch this is the crowning point of her life and for us, under whose protection she has placed herself, it is a great and moving experience. The animal is never so close to us as during these weeks. Then comes the further miracle of puppyhood and the process of development which I have already described. I trust that I shall have encouraged some of the readers of this book to experience all these things for themselves.

BJÖRN'S FAMILY

Neither this chapter on child-bearing nor this book would be complete without a small but highly indicative story about my cross-bred dog Björn and his family. It will be remembered that Björn and his sister Bente were the offspring of a marriage between the elkhound bitch Binna and the dingo dog Aboriginal. With them lived Baas and Baara, born in the same pen, who had meanwhile reached the age of one year. Björn had educated his children properly and so there was no quarrelling when he covered his wife Bente; the son stood by unconcerned. Barely two months later Baara came in season and, as head of the family, Björn took her as his second wife; again Baas took no notice.

I was somewhat worried however. The four dogs lived together in a spacious kennel; there had already been some tension between Bente who was pregnant and Baara who was in season (both a bitch in season and a pregnant bitch have certain prerogatives). How would it go when Bente had her puppies?

Puberty and Maturity

When I arrived with the food one day Bente was not to be seen. So here it was! I threw as much food as possible into the pen as quickly as I could in order to avoid any quarrelling. But nothing happened. Björn, Baas and Baara stood quietly waiting at the back of the pen; this time they did not rush up to the outer fence as usual. Bente's head then suddenly appeared. She had had her puppies—I could now clearly hear them squeaking—not in the kennel but in a hole by the side-wall, half underneath the kennel. Bente came slowly forwards, stalked from one chunk of meat to the next, smelling each with relish, and then chose the piece she thought best. She carried it back to her nest and only then did the other dogs move to get their food.

For me this was an incomparable lesson in social behaviour within a family. But this was not the only lesson. First, the nursing mother was treated with similar consideration at each feeding time. Two days later it began to rain and Bente carried her puppies into the kennel, but she allowed Björn, Baas and Baara to use it as well.

Three weeks later, according to schedule, the puppies first waddled out into the open. I was astounded to see nine puppies—a litter of most unusual size; like all cross-breeds Bente had so far always had six or seven. Björn rushed round excitedly and drove his offspring back into the kennel. Though the lie of the land was difficult—the pen is on a steep slope—all the puppies succeeded in reaching the shelter of the kennel quickly: they had passed the 'efficiency test' with good marks. Soon they were coming out of the kennel at feeding time and from now on Björn kept close watch to ensure that the puppies could reach the food; with an unmistakable glare and sometimes bared teeth he kept Baas and Baara at the back of the pen to ensure that they did not disturb the little ones during their first efforts at eating. Baas and Baara were only allowed near the food when the puppies had had enough. But their father himself had eaten nothing either.

So the first few weeks went by and now Baara's belly was becoming more swollen. What would happen when she too had her puppies? Sometimes I was on the point of taking her out of the pen but I kept to my purpose: I wanted really to know whether there would be serious fighting or even infanticide within a family living under natural conditions. Moreover so far all had gone far better than I had expected.

Björn's Family

I did not enter the pen again and left everything to the dogs. When Baara was a fortnight away from whelping, the order of precedence changed. Again it was Björn who made the arrangement. Now Baara, as a bitch nearing the end of her pregnancy, was allowed first pick at the food, roughly on a level with the puppies; Bente had lost her predominant position; she now treated Baara most amicably.

Baara had her puppies in the kennel; they lay alongside Bente's practically in the same nest. No one even ruffled the coats of the new arrivals; they were clearly growing well since Baara still had pride of place at feeding time; the good Björn kept a close watch on this, helped by his son Baas. Baara's puppies also appeared in the open twenty-one days after birth.

Now, however, something did go wrong, but it was no fault of the dogs. Nature has clearly not provided for bitches of the same family to whelp at an interval of only two months. It will be recalled that at this period all wild dogs are still living in pairs. Naturally, therefore, puppies have no inhibitions about playing with younger and less agile brothers and sisters. Bente's puppies played the games suitable to their age and they included Baara's puppies in them. This was too much for the younger element. In addition it had begun to snow and so day by day I found a puppy lying dead somewhere. Of Baara's five puppies only one bitch survived—obviously either lucky or particularly tough. As a rule a father-and-daughter marriage does not produce very strong puppies (and in this case the daughter was the offspring of a brother-and-sister mating); this may have contributed to the fact that only one puppy survived these rather severe tests. In any case this mortality among the puppies was in no way connected with the dogs' social behaviour—it would probably not have happened had Baara whelped a month earlier.

Today all the members of this family are still living happily together. Bente's puppies are meanwhile nearly eight months old and Baara's little daughter six months; so far all has proceeded in a wonderfully orderly manner. Björn, assisted by Baas, has brought up the children as disciplined members of the pack; he lies on the roof of the kennel looking down on his clan with pride and composure. Only Bente is allowed up there with him—it is a position of privilege. When occasionally two of the youngsters squabble too violently about something, he casually descends, separates them and re-establishes order. Any aggressive tendencies are worked off in small doses, generally by means of a somewhat over-violent game. So, in a space of sixty square yards, fourteen dogs are living in perfect harmony and I would venture to prophesy that Bente's next litter (she has meanwhile been covered again by Björn) will not affect this idyllic situation.

This story is no exception; I see my other dogs behaving similarly every day. Wherever natural canine families have been allowed to grow up the dominant feature has been considerate communal behaviour including many group-forming aspects. Anyone wishing to study aggressive tendencies would have to exercise a great deal of patience; even then he would see only preliminary posturing or declarations of intent; he would hardly ever see what might be called serious quarrelling. The family pack owes its peaceful existence to that which is in the true nature of the dog: an innate requirement for friendly contact with others. That is what our dog can offer us too.

Bibliography

BRUNNER, F.: 'Die Anwendung von Ergebnissen der vergleichenden Verhaltensforschung in der Kleintierpraxis', *Zeitschrift für Tierpsychologie*, Vol. 26 1969.
CRISLER, L.: *Arctic Wild*, Harper Bros, New York 1958, Secker & Warburg, London 1959.
EIBL-EIBESFELDT, I.: *Grundriss der vergleichenden Verhaltensforschung*, Piper Verlag, Munich 1967.
EIBL-EIBESFELDT, I.: *Liebe und Hass. Zur Naturgeschichte elementarer Verhaltensweisen*, Piper Verlag, Munich 1970.
EISFELD, D.: 'Verhaltensbeobachtungen an einigen Wildcaniden', *Zeitschrift für wissenschaftliche Zoologie*, Vol. 174 1966.
FOX, M. W.: 'Behavioural effects of rearing dogs with cats during the "critical period of socialisation" ', *Behaviour*, Vol. 35 1969.
HOLST, E. VON: *Zur Verhaltensphysiologie bei Tieren und Menschen*, Piper Verlag, Munich 1969.
KOEHLER, O.: 'Psychologie des Hundes', World Cynological Congress, Dortmund 1956.
LEVY, D. M.: 'Finger-sucking and accessory movements in early infancy', *American Journal of Psychiatry*, Vol. 7 1928.
LORENZ, K.: *So kam der Mensch auf den Hund*, Borotha-Schoeler, Vienna 1952;
Man meets Dog, translated Marjorie Kerr Wilson, Methuen, London 1954.
LORENZ, K.: *Über tierisches und menschliches Verhalten. Gesammelte Abhandlugen*, two vols, Piper Verlag, Munich 1965.
Studies in Animal and Human Behaviour, translated R. Martin, 2 vols., Methuen, London 1970–71. Harvard University Press, Cambridge, 1970–71.
LUDWIG, H.: 'Beobachtungen über das Spiel bei Boxern', *Zeitschrift für Tierpsychologie*, Vol. 22 1965.
MARTINEK, Z., LAT, J.: 'Long-term Stability of individual differences in exploratory behaviour and rate of habituation in dogs', *Physiologia Bohemoslovaca*, Vol. 18 1969.

OGNEV, S. I.: *Säugetiere und ihre Welt*, Academie Verlag, Berlin 1959.
PFAFFENBERGER, C. J.: *The new Knowledge of Dog Behaviour*, Howell, New York 1964.
SCHENKEL, R.: 'Ausdrucks-Studien an Wölfen', *Behaviour*, Vol. 1 1947.
SCHENKEL, R.: 'Submission. Its Features and Function in the Wolf and Dog', *American Zoologist*, Vol. 7 1967.
SCHMIDT, H. D.: 'Zur Sozialpsychologie des Haushundes', *Zeitschrift für Psychologie*, Vol. 161 1957.
SCOTT, J. P.: 'The social behavior of dogs and wolves. An illustration of sociobiological systematics', *Annals of the New York Academy of Sciences*, Vol. 51 1950.
SEITZ, A.: 'Beobachtungen an handaufgezogenen Goldschakalen', *Zeitschrift für Tierpsychologie*, Vol. 16 1959.
ZIMEN, E.: *Wölfe und Königspudel. Vergeleichende Verhaltensbeobachtungen*, Piper Verlag, Munich 1971.
ZWEIG, A.: 'Über die psychischen Leistungen eines Hundes und deren mögliche Beziehungen zur Human-Psychologie', *Schweizerische Zeitschrift für Psychologie*, Vol. 16 1957.

Index

Aboriginal (Abo), 27, 28, 35, 46, 158, 200–2, 232–3, 253
aborigines, 27, 51, 113
affection, 144–7
age, 231
aggression, 152, 157–8, 168, 171–82, 232–3, 234–5
albinos, 47–52
Ali, 33
Alsatians, colour and behaviour, 49
 head-stroking, 104
 transfer of loyalty, 98–9
anxiety neuroses, 225–6
Arras, 228–30
Arta, 43, 45
Asko, 228–30
Australia, 27–30, 51
authority, parental, 116

Baara, 253–6
Baas, 253–6
barking, 87, 184–7
Bäsche, Heinz, 128–9
Ben, 33
Bente, 35–6, 158, 253–6
Binna, 21, 24, 27, 35, 36–7, 68, 104, 105, 107–8, 145, 180, 188, 240, 247–8, 253
biotonus, 64
Birkmann, 47
birth, 46, 54, 58–64, 244–53
birth weight, 60, 64–70

Björn, 35–6, 68, 71, 158, 253–6
black coloration, 49–50
bottle feeding, 78
boxers, play, 123–5
breeders' associations, 231
breeding, 34–40, 235–44
Brunner, Ferdinand, 52, 225
Buna, 41–2, 59–60, 137
buying a puppy, 99–100

Canis aureus, 32
Canis hallstromi, 28–9
Canis lupus pallipes, 32
childhood image, 111–16
children, and dogs, 111
circus, training, 133
colouring, 29–30, 42, 43, 44, 47–52, 167
command, dogs' understanding of, 147–9
 and obedience exercises, 191–2
copulation, 242–3
Crisler, Louis, 88, 178, 194
cropping of ears, 182–3
Cuon, 51
curiosity, and play, 121
 as a stimulus for learning, 86

danger, puppies learn about, 91
 signals, 91, 189
 solidarity in the event of, 198
Darwin, Charles, 109

Dingo, 42
dingoes, domesticated features, 29–30, 51
  origins of, 27
  relationship to domestic dogs, 30
discipline, 138–53, 192–2
  see also training
docking of tails, 182–3
domestic dog, origins, 30–4, 41, 43–4
domestication, albinos and, 48–49
  features, 29–30, 50–1
Dove, 44–5

ears, hearing, 82–3, 183–4
  cropping of, 182–3
Eibl-Eibesfeldt, Irenäus, 92, 103, 117, 120, 121
Eisfeld, D., 91, 102, 188, 207
elkhounds, elk hunting, 26–7
  origins, 24–5
Ewald, G., 64
exercise, during pregnancy, 244
expression, acoustic, 182–92
  body as instrument of, 171–82
  of flight, 180–1
  gestural and facial, 165–71
  of pleasure, 87, 181–2
  tail-wagging, 87, 181–2, 206
  threatening, 171–80
eyes, opening in puppies, 82, 87
  visual expression, 167–9

face-licking, 144–7
facial expression, 165–71
feeding, and the developing puppy, 87–9
  during pregnancy, 243–4
  food-procurement games, 126–36
  new-born puppies, 77–80, 81, 100, 103
  overfeeding, 129
  puppies' reflexes, 59, 60, 61–4
  starving, 128–9
Fella, 35–6
fetching games, 134–6
fighting, 173–80
  as a game, 123–4, 126
  see also aggression
flight, expression of, 180–1
food, *see* feeding
Fox, M. W., 201
Frankfurt, 30
Freud, Sigmund, 78
Friess, 186

games, 118–19, 120–38
genital areas, sniffing, 213–14, 216, 237
gestation periods, 56–7, 243
gestural expressions, 165–71
Gina, 46
Goethe, Johann Wolfgang, 49
greyhounds, 185
grooming, 214–16
group formation 117–19
growling, 87, 188
  in play, 123
guard-dogs, 104, 129–30, 136, 196
guide-dogs, 155

half-breeds, 34–40
Hallstrom, 28

Hamilton Station, 155, 160
handling puppies, 65–6
head-stroking, 104
hearing, 183–4
  in puppies, 82–3
heat, bitches on, 213, 236–43
Heck, Lutz and Heinz, 37
hereditary reflexes, 61–4, 85–9
hereditary retardation, 114–15
Holst, Erich von, 63
house training, 22–3, 222–5
Hovawart, 110
howling, 186–8
hunting, 194–6
hunting games, 126–36, 137–8
huskies, 186
hybrids, 34–40

imprint phase, 93–9
inbreeding, 41–7
individuality, 52–3
injuries, healing of, 173, 216
inquisitiveness, *see* curiosity

jackal, and origins of domestic dog, 32–4
R. B. Jackson Memorial Laboratory, 96
jumping, 132
juvenile qualities, retardation and inducement, 52

Kala, 36
Karlsruhe Zoo, 47
Keiser, Frau I. von, 162–4
Kiel University, 29
Kira, 96–7
Knud, 36, 37

Koehler, Otto, 147–8, 212
König, Kurt F., 110
Kor, 96–7
Kutschera, Rolf, 197

Lady, 178, 194
leader, man as, 196–203, 219–20
learning, hereditary reflexes and, 85–9
  and hereditary retardation, 115
  and play, 121
leg-lifting, 217, 218–22
Levy, D. M., 78
litter, games, 137–8
  size of, 56, 65
locomotion, development of, 85–6
  in the new-born, 54–5, 57–8, 71–3, 79
Lorenz, Konrad, 7, 18, 33, 63, 93–5, 112, 115, 160, 165, 170, 175, 192, 202, 230
Ludwig, Hanns, 123, 136, 137
Luxl, 29, 46, 47, 177, 178–80

man, as pack-leader, 196–203, 219–20
  relationship with dog, 95–9, 115, 117–20
markings, 29–30, 44
  see also colouring
Martinek, Zdenko, 50
mating, 236–43
maturity, 228–36
Menzel, 204, 212
Mertens, Robert, 30
mimicry, 165–92
Motu, 42, 46, 177

mounting games, 136–7
see also copulation
movement, development of, 85–6
  in the new-born, 54–5, 57–8, 71–3, 79

nasal contact, 205–7
New Guinea, 27–9, 51
noise, effect on dog's hearing, 183–4
nose, *see* smell, sense of
nose-nudging, 103–6, 144–7
Nyctereutes, 38

obedience, 138–53, 191–2, 204
  see also training
oestrum, *see* season
Ognev, S. I., 57
Orff, Carl, 228–30
orphans, 161–2
overfeeding, 129

pack-formative phase, 192–6
pack games, 137–8, 194
pack-leader, man as, 196–203, 219–20
pads, joined, 34, 42, 43, 48
panting, 212
'Papua dogs', 27–8
Paroo, 46–7, 51, 158, 232
paw-giving, 100–3, 147
Pedersen, Alwin, 186
Pfaffenberger, Clarence J., 155
play, 118–19, 120–38
pleasure, expression of, 87, 181–2
Ploog, Detlev, 78

plucking birds, 202
poaching, 127–8, 131–2, 200–2
poodles, 197
pregnancy, 57, 243–4
protection, 113
pugs, 113–14, 115, 162–4
punishment, 140, 143, 146, 224, 225, 226
puppies, birth, 46, 54, 58–64, 244–53
  buying, 99–100
  curiosity in, 86
  and father-dogs, 71
  feeding, 81, 87–9, 100, 103
  feeding reflexes, 59, 60, 61–4, 77–80
  first excursions, 90
  first weeks, 54–89
  handling, 65–6
  hearing, 82–3
  hereditary reflexes, 61–4, 85–89
  and human contact, 95–9
  learning about danger, 91
  locomotion, 54–5, 57–8, 71–3, 79, 85–6
  nose-nudging, 103–6
  number of, 59, 248
  opening of eyes, 82, 87
  putting to sleep, 238
  reaction to each other, 80–1
  senses, 73–7, 81–5
  sight, 82, 87
  sleep, 80, 106–11
  sucking, 62, 75–6, 77–80
  warmth requirements, 81, 250
  weight, 60, 64–9, 70
  see also breeding, pregnancy

Index

Rana, 100, 104, 105, 106–7, 117–18, 119, 125–7, 137–138, 142, 192, 198, 223, 229, 230
red dogs, 51–2
reflexes, hereditary, 61–4, 85–9
regurgitation of food, 87–9
retardation, hereditary, 114–15
retrieving games, 134–6

San Diego Zoo, 29
Sascha, 96, 97, 106–7, 117–18, 119, 126–7, 133, 137–8, 142, 175, 192, 198, 222, 223, 229, 230
scent, controls, 205–14
  following a, 128–31, 211–13
  individuality of, 211–12, 214–27
  see also smell, sense of
Schenkel, Rudolf, 105, 141, 144, 165, 170
Schlapp, 222
Schmidt, H. D., 109
Schultze-Westrum, Thomas, 28
Scott, J. P., 82
scratching the earth, 226–7
season, bitches in, 213, 236–43
Sieferle, Eugen, 248
Seitz, Alfred, 17, 27, 42, 81, 105, 207
Senckenberg Marsh, 30
seniority-classification phase, 156–92
'sense of feel', 149–51
senses, in puppies, 62, 73–7
  see also individual senses

Severzov, 56
sex, differentiation in puppies, 66, 67
sexual games, 136–7
shyness, 44–5
sight, 82, 87
  see also eyes
size, 37–8
  and inbreeding, 37–8, 41, 43, 44, 46–7
  and leg-lifting, 218–19
  and mating, 237
sleeping, 106–11
  puppies, 80
smell, sense of, 75–6, 81, 83–5, 95, 128–31, 211–13, 205–214
sociable grooming, 215
socialisation, 116–20
spitz, 24, 185
stalking, 132, 211–13
starving dogs, 128–9
Stasi, 238
Stina, 20–3, 37–8, 44, 45, 222–3
Strixi, 38, 40, 188, 277, 240
stroking, 103, 104
stud dogs, 240–2
  180
submission in fights, 175–6
subordination, 138–9, 142
Suki, 27, 46, 158, 161, 178–9, 200, 204, 232
superiority, 141
Sven, 44, 45, 175
sweat glands, 211–12
Sydney, 46
Sydney Zoo, 28, 29
Sylvia, 136

taboos, 140–2
tails, curved, 29
    docking of, 182–3
    wagging, 87, 181–2, 206
Tanila, 42, 43, 46, 60, 92
taste, sense of, 76–7
teaching, *see* training
territorial fights, 176, 177
territorial ownership, 218–19
thinking, in dogs, 147–8
threatening expressions, 171–180
tracking, 132, 211–13
training, 116, 117–18, 120–53, 154–6, 204–6
Trigger, 178, 194
Troshinin, 75–6
Troughton, 28
tug-of-war games, 136
tying, 242

upbringing, psychological disturbances and, 52–3

vets, and anxiety neuroses, 225–6
    and dog injuries, 216
visual expressions, 165–71
vocal expressions, 182–92

warning signals, 91, 189
weight, birth, 60, 64–70
whelping, 46, 54, 58–64, 244–53
whining, 189–90
Whipsnade Zoo, 141
white markings, 29–30, 50–1,
    see also albinos
wolf-pack games, dogs and, 137–8

wolves, affection, 144–5
    behaviour, 32
    differences between individuals, 52
    fighting, 178
    gestation period, 56–7
    howling, 187
    hunting, 26–7, 195–6, 199
    lairs, 57
    leadership, 116, 141, 157, 193, 196
    as man-killers, 196
    nose-nudging, 105
    and origin of domestic dogs, 30–2, 41, 43–4
    pack formation, 193, 233
    seniority classification, 116, 141, 157, 196
    'sense of feel', 149–50
    stalking, 127
    territorial marking, 218–19
    visual expressions, 166–7, 170
words of command, dogs' understanding of, 147–9
    and obedience exercises, 191–2
working dogs, training, 196
    see also guard-dogs, guide-dogs
wounds, healing of, 173, 216
wuff, 188–9

Xanthi, 58

Zimen, Erik, 32, 88, 112, 187, 218
Zweig, A., 224